Rowan
University

The

Domosh Collection

A Gift

FOR COURAGEOUS FIGHTING
AND CONFIDENT DYING

FOR COURAGEOUS FIGHTING AND CONFIDENT DYING

Union Chaplains in the Civil War

WARREN B. ARMSTRONG

UNIVERSITY PRESS OF KANSAS

Published by the University Press of Kansas (Lawrence, Kansas 66049), which was organized by the Kansas Board of Regents and is operated and funded by Emporia State University, Fort Hays State University, Kansas State University, Pittsburg State University, the University of Kansas, and Wichita State University

Library of Congress Cataloging-in-Publication Data

Armstrong, Warren B. (Warren Bruce), 1933–
For courageous fighting and confident dying : Union chaplains in
the Civil War / Warren B. Armstrong.
p.   cm. — (Modern war studies)
Includes bibliographical references and index.
ISBN 0-7006-0912-1 (cloth : alk. paper)
1. United States—History—Civil War, 1861–1865—Chaplains.
2. United States. Army—Chaplains—History—19th century.
I. Title. II. Series.
E635.A75   1998
973.7'78—dc21   98-21026

British Library Cataloguing in Publication Data is available.

Printed in the United States of America

10 9 8 7 6 5 4 3 2 1

The paper used in this publication meets the minimum requirements of the American National Standard for Permanence of Paper for Printed Library Materials Z39.48-1984.

For Joan
and
in memory of my great-grandfather,
James Luther Griffin,
140th Pennsylvania Volunteer Infantry

CONTENTS

PREFACE

The military chaplaincy was not a new institution at the time of the American Civil War. Armies have been accompanied by representatives of deity throughout the ages of recorded history. The armies of the ancient Egyptians had in their midst the priests of Ammon-Re, whose blessing they invoked upon their military exploits. The Bible records the presence of the priests of Jehovah with the armies of Israel under their commander Joshua (Joshua 6), and the ancient Greeks and Romans were known to seek the intervention of their deities on behalf of their armies in the field.

In modern history the concept of the chaplaincy has been substantially altered. To the mere seeking of divine blessing upon military activities was added the idea of service to the soldier. The military chaplain, in addition to being a servant of God, thus became a servant of the soldier as well, and spiritual counsel to the men of the army became his primary duty.

In colonial America pastors accompanied the militia units in the numerous conflicts with Native Americans and with the French. During the Revolution the Continental armies were served by chaplains, some of whom were paid by the states, others by the Continental Congress. Chaplains served with American forces again in the War of 1812 and the Mexican War. Between the Mexican War and the Civil War, however, the chaplaincy was subjected to controversy and much opposition. Some of this opposition was based on the belief that the chaplaincy violated the constitutional principle of the separation of church and state. Others opposed the continuation of the chaplaincy because of the blatant manner in which some clergymen lobbied to obtain appointment at one of the few military posts in the country at which chaplains were employed. The constitutionality of using public funds to pay chaplains was again a subject of discussion in the United States Congress as the statutes that formed the chaplaincy for the Civil War armies of the Union were debated. The issue was resolved in favor of the chaplaincy, however, by substantial margins in both houses. President Lincoln, too, supported the chaplaincy, because it assured that the men who served their country at risk of life and limb would find readily available to them religious counsel at times of great stress and mortal danger.

In a very real sense, then, the Civil War rescued the chaplaincy from possible extinction as an American military tradition, for the services rendered to the nation by the men who served as chaplains from 1861 to 1865 did much to commend the retention of this office in the army since that time. In a nation deeply committed to the principle of the separation of church and state, the chaplaincy has become, nonetheless, a national public policy that recognizes the breadth and depth of religious belief among the American people. In a word, the chaplaincy is the embodiment of what is now our American motto, "In God we Trust."

This study proposes to explain what the government of the United States did to address the religious concerns of its soldiers through the chaplaincy during the division of our nation between 1861 and 1865; to explain the duties of the chaplains; to reveal, where possible, the character of the men who served in this capacity; to examine their attitudes toward the conflict in which the nation was then engaged; and, finally, to assess the value of the service these men rendered to their nation in those years of social, political, and moral crisis. Throughout, I have chosen wherever possible and practical to give the chaplains a direct voice, to let them narrate both thoughts and actions in that great epoch of American history we call the Civil War.

The research that led to this volume was begun more than thirty-five years ago when I was a graduate student at the University of Michigan. My career as a historian was interrupted for nearly twenty-five years of academic administration (as a dean of liberal arts and university president), and when I retired from administration and returned to full-time faculty status in 1994, I was able to renew and update the research that completed this study of Union chaplains.

I am indebted to many people for their assistance in writing this book. They include the late Sara Jackson of the National Archives; Milton Chamberlain, also of the National Archives; the late Father Thomas McAvoy, Curator of the Archives at the University of Notre Dame; Howard Peckham, Professor of History and Curator of the Clements Research Library at the University of Michigan; the late Professors Dwight Dumond and William Leslie of the University of Michigan under whose direction I completed the dissertation that is the heart of this volume; and the late Professor David Overy of Saint Cloud State University and Professor William Unrau of Wichita State University, both of whom read and critiqued the manuscript for me at different stages of the project.

I am also indebted to Professor Willard Klunder of Wichita State University for suggestions concerning the bibliography; to Professor James Duram, also of Wichita State University, and to Eleanor Duram for lending me the diary of Chaplain Andrew Hartsock, which the edited; Mike Kelly of Ablah Library's Special Collections at Wichita State University, and Jim Meyer of Photography Services, Media Resources, also at Wichita State University, for assistance with the illustrations; to a former student assistant at Olivet College, Ann Kleimola, now Professor of History at the University of Nebraska, for able research assistance at the very inception of this enterprise; and to Deborah Taylor, my current graduate research assistant at Wichita State University, for invaluable assistance in the final preparation of the text.

Olivet College provided me with generous research grants that enabled me to spend the better part of two summers at the National Archives and the Library of Congress, and Wichita State University provided the support system that has made it possible for me to complete this work.

My thanks, also, are extended to my publisher, Fred Woodward, Director of the University Press of Kansas, for his many practical suggestions that make the text more readable, and to his able assistant, Sara Henderson White, for her courteous support. Special thanks are extended to the two scholars who critiqued the manuscript for the University Press of Kansas, Professor Steven Woodworth of Texas Christian University and Professor Herman Hattaway of the University of Missouri at Kansas City. Both men made many helpful suggestions both as to form and substance.

I also drew both encouragement and inspiration from my parents, Mead Armstrong and Mary Griffin Armstrong, both deceased, who told me often during my boyhood about the service of my maternal great-grandfather, James Luther Griffin, in the Union army during the Civil War. It was a privilege for me, while conducting research in the National Archives, to read Great-Grandfather Griffin's service record. He volunteered on August 15, 1862, and was mustered into the 140th Pennsylvania Volunteer Infantry as a private in Company B on September 4, 1862. Wounded twice, at Gettysburg on July 2, 1863, and at Spotsylvania on May 12, 1864, he rose to the rank of first sergeant and was mustered out on May 31, 1865, after nearly three years of honorable service. His regiment was in the Third Brigade, First Division of the II Corps, and, though a devout Presbyterian, he received absolution along with the entire First Division, General John Caldwell commanding, from Father William Corby, chaplain of the Eighty-eighth New York, before going into battle at Gettysburg on July 2, 1863, the date of his first wound. I have always been thankful that he survived his wounds, for he had not yet married and, had he died, obviously I would never have been born.

Finally, the most important person in my life for these many years, my wife, Joan, has been most instrumental in helping me to complete this volume. She has read and reread every chapter numerous times, and her suggestions and insights have helped greatly to improve the text. In addition she has enriched my life immeasurably.

1

DEFINING THE CHARGE

"In *your* hands, my dissatisfied fellow countrymen, and not in *mine*, is the momentous issue of civil war. The government will not assail *you*. You can have no conflict, without being yourselves the aggressors."[1] So spoke Abraham Lincoln in his Inaugural Address on March 4, 1861, to those in the process of attempting to establish Confederate independence and threatening to seize federal properties located in Southern states, through force if necessary. On April 12, 1861, the first hostile action of the civil discord that would disrupt the Union for four long years began in Charleston Harbor as Confederate batteries commenced the bombardment of Fort Sumter, a barrage that would last some thirty-four hours and end with the surrender of the fort to Confederate authorities.

On April 15, 1861, the day after Fort Sumter fell to Confederate forces in South Carolina, President Lincoln issued a presidential proclamation to the nation declaring the existence of organized resistance in seven states of the Deep South to the government and laws of the United States, "by combinations too powerful to be suppressed" through ordinary judicial proceedings or by federal marshals. Because of this situation the president exercised his constitutional powers as chief executive of the United States to "call forth, the militia of the several States of the Union, to the aggregate number of seventy-five thousand, in order to suppress said combinations, and cause the laws to be duly executed." He promised also to submit the details of his call for volunteers to state authorities via the War Department. The president closed with an appeal to all loyal citizens for support in the effort to maintain the honor, integrity, and existence of the national union, "and the perpetuity of popular government."[2]

At the moment of this proclamation, the entire strength of the United States Army was approximately seventeen thousand officers and men.[3] Serving this tiny army were thirty post chaplains, all that were authorized by current federal law.[4] Obviously this number would prove insufficient to serve a tremendously expanded national force should the services of chaplains be deemed essential.

The chaplaincy was not new to the American military tradition at the time of the Civil War. From the earliest days of the British colonies, clergymen had accompanied military actions against both hostile Native Americans and the French. And when the colonies/states united to declare independence from Great Britain, chaplains served the Continental armies throughout the Revolution. The tiny standing army created by Congress in 1783 in response to the recommendations of President Washington was served by chaplains, one per regiment. This military tradition remained intact throughout the decades that followed, although from time to time questions were raised about the propriety of expending public funds for "religious purposes." This was particularly true of the interval between the war with Mexico, which many Americans regarded as an unjust war—a war to wrest territory from Mexico into which slavery could be extended—and the Civil War. Such issues never resulted in a change in the basic public policy of providing religious counsel for the men enlisted in the American military, however, and the chaplaincy as a feature of the military tradition remained in place, both North and South, at the outbreak of the Civil War.[5]

The standing militia units forwarded by state governors to answer the president's call had been organized under state rather than federal authority. In most instances each regiment was served by a chaplain, usually a clergyman in the community in which the regiment had been raised, who accompanied the troops when military exercises (drill, as the citizen soldiers called it) were held from time to time. In such circumstances the chaplain was well known to the men he served.

On May 3, 1861, another presidential proclamation called for 42,034 additional volunteers, to serve three years; it also increased the size of the regular army to 22,714 officers and men.[6] The next day the War Department issued General Orders Numbers 15 and 16. General Order Number 15 provided for the organization of the volunteer regiments, including the appointment of a chaplain chosen by the vote of the field officers and company commanders. General Order Number 16 made similar provision for the new units of the regular army. The chaplains appointed by this authority were to be regularly ordained ministers of a Christian denomination.[7]

The rapid expansion of the Union military contingent ordered by these presidential proclamations and War Department general orders clearly meant that newly raised regiments being obtained by state governments to meet their federal quotas would be raised from as many as three or four counties (sometimes even on a statewide basis). In such circumstances it was much less likely that chaplains appointed to these new regiments would be known to more than a few of the men they served.

In the proclamation of May 3, Lincoln stated his intent to submit to Congress for its approval his call for volunteers, the increase in the regular army, and the plan of organization for the volunteer and regular forces.[8] Until Congress could be convened in special session, set by Lincoln for July 4, 1861, the volunteer forces acted under the general orders of the War Department. Because there was no specific legislative authority for these orders, some army paymasters refused to pay the chaplains of the three-months regiments, resulting in a situation that required a specific order from the secretary of war to pay these chaplains in the same manner as those in the regular army.[9]

The special congressional session of July 1861 considered the status of the entire military establishment, including the chaplains, and on July 22 a bill was passed that gave legislative authority to the provisions of the general orders of the War Department of May 4. Section 9 of the bill, entitled "An Act to authorize the employment of volunteers to aid in endorsing the laws and protective public property," stated the requirements for appointment to the chaplaincy. To be eligible for appointment as a chaplain, it was necessary only to be a regularly ordained Christian minister.[10] This legislation assured that volunteer chaplains would be paid as were their counterparts in the regular army.

On August 3, 1861, Congress enacted a similar bill to provide for regimental chaplains in the regular army. This bill, entitled "An Act providing for the better organization of the military establishment," stated that each regiment would be allowed one chaplain, selected and appointed according to the direction of the president, providing that only regularly ordained ministers of "some Christian denomination" were eligible.[11] Apparently the appointment of chaplains to serve in regular army units followed the pattern set by General Order Number 16 of the War Department. There is no record of any direct executive order concerning such appointments.

None of this legislation had provided for chaplains to serve in the army hospitals, an omission readily apparent after the first battle of Bull Run.

As the number of sick and wounded mounted, it seemed wise to have chaplains in military hospitals to minister to the spiritual and temporal needs of these men. Although President Lincoln believed that he had no constitutional authority to appoint hospital chaplains in the absence of a statute, he did request the voluntary services of seven clergymen by use of a form letter stating the necessity for hospital chaplains. He acknowledged the absence of a law providing for their appointment but affirmed his desire that these men should volunteer their services. In his presidential message to Congress in December 1861, the president submitted this matter for congressional consideration, as he had promised he would when he sought volunteers for this work.[12] The president explained what had been done, noted the work accomplished by the volunteer chaplains without compensation, recommended that they be paid, and suggested that legislative provision henceforth be made for hospital chaplains.[13]

Congress responded to this recommendation by enacting a statute approving the appointments of the president and providing for the appointment of a chaplain for each "permanent" army hospital by the president, by and with the advice and consent of the Senate. Compensation was to be at the same rate as that of regimental chaplains.[14] Although President Lincoln did express frustration that some chaplains seemed interested only in the prestige of military rank and the emoluments of office, he was vitally concerned that Union soldiers be afforded the religious sustenance that good chaplains could render.[15]

In all of the legislation concerning the chaplaincy before July 17, 1862, appointment was restricted to ministers of Christian denominations, a requirement many considered to be discriminatory. In fact when the bill for the organization of the volunteer forces was being debated in July 1861, an amendment to substitute the words "religious society" for "Christian denomination" had been proposed by Representative Clement L. Vallandigham of Ohio, who pointed out that a large number of Jews were serving in the army. These men, he argued, had the right to chaplains of their own faith. The amendment was defeated, however, and for the first year of the war Jewish rabbis were ineligible for the chaplaincy.[16]

Because this provision excluded rabbis from the chaplaincy, the then newly organized Board of Delegates of American Israelites presented to the president and to Congress a memorial requesting that laws providing for chaplains be amended to eliminate apparent discrimination against those of the Jewish faith. Rabbi Arnold Fischel was given a personal interview with President Lincoln concerning the problem early in December of 1861 and was assured that the matter would be corrected.[17] In a letter dated December 14, 1861, Rabbi Fischel was so informed by the president: "I find that there are several particulars in which the present law in regard to Chaplains is supposed to be deficient, all of which I now design presenting to the appropriate Committee of Congress." In addition Lincoln promised him: "I shall try to have a new law broad enough to cover what is desired by you in behalf of the Israelites."[18]

Subsequently, on July 17, 1862, Congress passed an act that amended the earlier legislation defining the restrictive religious qualifications for chaplains. The new law substituted the words "religious denominations" for "Christian denomination," thereby removing the discriminatory provision. It also required substantial verification of the appointee's credentials as an ordained clergyman.[19] It is true, however, that most of those appointed to the Union chaplaincy during the Civil War were Christian, a reflection of the religious profile of the general population.

On September 6, 1862, the War Department, through the Office of the Adjutant General, issued General Order Number 126, requiring that any chaplain appointed under the act of July 17, 1862, be mustered into service by an officer of the regular army. Section 2 of this order stated: "Mustering officers before mustering chaplains into service will require from them a copy of the proceedings on which the appointment is based." This copy, if it was found to conform to the requirements of the law, was to be "indorsed by the mustering officer, and by him forwarded to the Adjutant-General's Office for file with the muster-in roll."[20]

Nowhere in the legislation affecting the chaplaincy were minimum educational qualifications to be found. As long as the various denominational authorities were satisfied with the fitness of the prospective appointee, or if five fellow clergymen of the same faith would recommend him, the army would not question his appointment. The result of this policy was that men of widely varied educational backgrounds served in this capacity. Nor, apparently, was age a major factor in the appointment of chaplains. Chaplain Charles McCabe of the 122nd Ohio Volunteers referred to his associate while a prisoner in Libby Prison, Chaplain or "Father" Brown, as he was fondly called by the men, as being nearly eighty years of age.[21]

The process of selecting and assigning chaplains was defined in General Order Number 15, May 4, 1861, which stated: "One chaplain shall be allowed to each regiment of the army . . . and the wishes and wants of the soldiers of the regiment shall be allowed their *full* and *due* weight in making the selection."[22] This general order and the legislation that confirmed it established a dual principle in regard to the chaplaincy. The first both permitted and required that the wishes of the men be considered in the selection of their chaplain. The second set the ratio of one chaplain to one regiment, a ratio that remained constant throughout the war.

Usually the regimental chaplain represented the denominational choice of the regimental majority. In some instances the regimental officers and the president were willing to go further than the War Department would permit to accommodate the men. One such instance involved the unanimous election, subsequently confirmed by the colonel, of Ella E. Gibson as chaplain of the First Wisconsin Heavy Artillery. Reverend Gibson was an ordained minister of the Religio-Philosophical Society of Saint Charles, Illinois, and when President Lincoln received the regiment's request for approval of her appointment, he forwarded it to Secretary of War Stanton with this notation: "This lady would be appointed Chaplain of the First Wisconsin Heavy Artillery, only that she is a woman. The President has not legally anything to do with such a question, but has no objection to her appointment." This transferred a perplexing situation to Secretary Stanton, who, not wishing to set a precedent, declined to recognize the appointment and mustering of Gibson because of her sex.[23]

Another and somewhat unusual example of an attempt to meet the specific needs of the men of a regiment concerns the appointment of Reverend Ferdinand Sarner to the chaplaincy of the Fifty-fourth New York Infantry in April of 1863. An immigrant from Prussia, Sarner was a highly educated man and a Jewish rabbi. The board of chaplains which certified him as eligible for the chaplaincy, however, stated that he was a regularly ordained Lutheran minister. The regiment was not predominately Jewish but was largely composed of recent German immigrants, and Sarner was probably chosen because of his fluency in the language. The reason for his certification as a Lutheran clergyman is unclear. The requirement that chaplains be of a Christian denomination had been amended in July of the previous year to permit non-Christian faiths to be represented. Possibly the credentials of Rabbi Sarner, which indicated that he had received his theological training at the Royal University of Berlin, created some confusion in the minds of those chaplains who certified him for the chaplaincy.[24]

The concept of the regimental chaplaincy, although it remained constant throughout the war, was not unchallenged. When the first bill for the organization of the volunteer forces was being debated in Congress during July of 1861, this provision was given the force of law with very little change even in the wording. The act stated: "That there shall be allowed to each regiment one chaplain, who shall be appointed by the regimental commander on the vote of the field officers and company commanders on duty with the regiment at the time the appointment shall be made."[25] A year later, however, during the debate on the bill of July 17, 1862, an attempt was made in the Senate to reduce the number of chaplains by assigning them one per brigade, a move apparently based on a desire for economy.[26] The proposal failed, and no further attempt to change the ratio of one chaplain for each regiment is recorded. The concept of the regimental chaplain was extended to the regular army as well as to the volunteer forces. The act of August 3, 1861, to organize the enlarged regular army stated "that one chaplain shall be allowed to each regiment of the army."[27]

As previously noted, assignment to duty as a hospital chaplain was at first a voluntary act in response to a specific request of the president. The act that made these appointments official in May of 1862 assigned one chaplain to each permanent army hospital.[28] The term "permanent" was later extended to cover divisional field hospitals, the mobile hospitals set up a short distance behind the lines to give immediate aid to those wounded in battle. Technically the chaplains who served these field hospitals were not hospital chaplains but regimental chaplains on detached service of specified duration.[29] The policy of appointing only one chaplain per division hospital was opposed by some chaplains for a time on the ground that this would require chaplains to serve too great a number of men. A petition to this effect was submitted to President Lincoln on July 3, 1863, and was forwarded by him the same day to Surgeon General William A. Hammond. Hammond responded four days later, pointing out that the number of men in any divisional hospital seldom exceeded six hundred; hence the burden was no greater than service to a regiment.[30] This rationale was apparently satisfactory, as no further protest is recorded.

The system of schoolmaster-chaplains for army posts throughout the country was continued during the war. The number of posts for which these chaplains were authorized had been established by law on March 2, 1849, at thirty and was not increased during the war.[31] Army regulations stated that "Chaplains, not to exceed thirty in number, are also allowed to posts . . . to officiate as Chaplain and perform the duties of schoolmaster."[32] The posts were permanent military garrisons, located throughout the country, many of them in the far west or in Indian country. There was a stability to assignment as chaplain on a post, lacking in either hospital or regimental assignment; chaplains thus assigned were considered as regular army personnel and were required by law to live at the post.[33] These chaplains in most instances were remote from the theater of war and hence did not play the role of combat chaplain as did their colleagues in regimental or hospital service.

Chaplains appointed under the general orders of the War Department in May and June of 1861 were to receive the pay and allowances of a captain of cavalry. During the debate in Congress on the bill passed on July 22, 1861, it was noted that post chaplains were then receiving compensation valued at $1,100 per year, including all allowances. Because the pay and allowances of a captain of cavalry amounted to $1,746 per year, some question was raised as to the propriety of granting this higher rate to volunteer chaplains. The higher rate was allowed after extended debate and reconsideration, however, when it was pointed out that the chaplains of the regular army enjoyed the security of permanent status while volunteers were interrupting private life for an uncertain duty, many at heavy cost to themselves. Another consideration in granting the higher rate was the fact that chaplains would usually find it necessary to maintain a horse, hence the allowances of a cavalry officer seemed reasonable and proper.[34] As passed on July 22, 1861, the bill stated, "The chaplains so appointed . . . shall receive the pay and allowances of a captain of cavalry."[35]

In December of 1861, when the president asked Congress to provide for hospital chaplains by paying them at the same rate as regimental chaplains, his request prompted a somewhat lengthy debate in the Senate. Some senators argued that Lincoln had kept his promise by simply recommending payment for these men and that Congress was not obligated to act. Most believed, however, that these chaplains should be paid, although many thought that the lower rate of pay of the post chaplain would be sufficient. Senator James Harlan of Iowa advanced a plan designed to utilize clergymen in the vicinity of a given hospital for part-time duty on a rotating basis—a move for economy. This suggestion was opposed by Senator Lafayette Foster of Connecticut, who stated that he did not favor engaging chaplains who would occasionally walk through the hospitals offering prayers at random. In his view, devoted, full-time men should be selected for this service. He supported his arguments by pointing out that the work of the hospital chaplain was actually more, rather than less, rigorous than that of a regimental chaplain. Frequently, he argued, a chaplain who had been on duty all day would be called for emergencies at night. The hospital chaplain was constantly exposed to infectious disease and was burdened with the cares of men who were suffering from sickness and wounds. Senator Foster insisted that a good hospital chaplain rendered services ten times more valuable than those of a regimental chaplain. A majority of the Senate was apparently convinced by Foster's arguments; the bill passed on May 20, 1862, providing hospital chaplains with compensation the same as that of volunteer regimental chaplains.[36]

During this debate, the justice of the pay of the regimental chaplains was seriously questioned. A few senators felt that regular and volunteer chaplains should receive the same compensation. Senator William Fessenden of Maine argued that regimental chaplains had little to do and that the present level of pay was needlessly high. He proposed a reduction to $1,200 per year, a cut of some $546, in the interest of economy. This reduction was passed but later amended to allow two rations per day while on duty.[37] This provision as included in the act of July 17, 1862, stated: "That hereafter, the compensation of all chaplains in the regular or volunteer service, or army hospitals, shall be one hundred dollars per month and two rations a day when on duty." Section 2 of the same act also provided forage in kind for one horse.[38]

Basic compensation, as authorized by the statute of July 17, 1862, remained unchanged throughout the war. A minor defect in form, however, the omission of a single comma, permitted an interpretation of the act that Congress had never intended. The section of the law open to this misinterpretation was the phrase in Section 9 which stated that "the compensation of all chaplains . . . shall be one hundred dollars per month and two rations per day while on duty."[39] Army paymasters interpreted the phrase "while on duty" as applying to both the rations and the monthly pay. Consequently pay was withheld not only from chaplains on regular leave, but also from chaplains who were sick, wounded, absent on special duty, or who had been captured. This unfortunate situation was brought to the attention of the Senate early in 1864 while amendments to the act of July 17, 1862, were being debated. Senator Foster demonstrated the injustice of this interpretation of the law by citing the case of Chaplain Lorenzo Barber of the Second United States Sharpshooters. The senator said that when the chaplain was absent from duty on account of wounds received in battle, his pay was stopped. He had been wounded in one of the skirmishes during the advance of the army, while endeavoring to assist to the rear some of the wounded men from his regiment. He was, at the time of the debate, confined to a sickbed in the city of Washington at a boardinghouse kept by the widow of a chaplain killed in combat a short time before. The widow was left by law wholly unprovided for, and Chaplain Barber, who was then suffering under these circumstances, could not draw pay or allowances until he regained his health and returned to duty.[40]

The result of the senator's speech and his answers to his colleagues' questions on the matter was the passage of an act early in 1864 specifying that chaplains absent from duty be treated in the same manner as any other officer in similar circumstances, a provision that was made retroactive. The same law entitled chaplains or their dependents to a pension of $20 per month in case of death or disability incurred after March 4, 1861, the date of President Lincoln's first inauguration.[41]

A matter involving allowances to chaplains, rather than actual compensation, arose from the provision in the act of July 17, 1862, allowing chaplains forage in kind for one horse. Paymaster General Benjamin F. Larned reported that some chaplains, rather unethically he thought, seemed to regard this as an emolument and sought to draw commutation for more than one horse.[42] In the debate of the Senate before the passage of the pay bill of June 20, 1864, it was stated that chaplains needed a second horse while in the field, as they were not permitted to use army transport wagons to carry their personal baggage.[43] The act was then amended to provide forage for two horses.[44]

Another matter pertaining to allowances rather than pay involved

Chaplains of the Ninth Army Corps, October 1864.

numerous requests from chaplains for an allowance for fuel and quarters. These requests prompted Quartermaster General Montgomery C. Meigs to write the Office of the Adjutant General, asking that the provisions of the laws relating to this subject be published as a general order.[45] Accordingly the War Department issued General Order Number 158 on April 13, 1864, providing that quarters and fuel were authorized for chaplains assigned to posts, hospitals, or forts, based on an act of Congress of April 9, 1863.[46] Regimental chaplains used the conventional army shelter tents for protection from the elements and burned fence rails, as did the men in the ranks, for fuel.

The appointment of black ministers to serve as chaplains of black regiments raised a legal question as to their proper rate of pay. The act of July 17, 1862, had, as one of its provisions, authorized the employment of black labor on fortifications, roadbeds, and other such projects, at a rate of $10 per month.[47] This provision was interpreted by army paymasters as requiring the payment of all blacks at that rate. A black chaplain of the Fifty-fourth Massachusetts Infantry, Samuel Harrison, who had been regularly appointed and commissioned by Governor John A. Andrew of Massachusetts, refused to accept payment at that rate and appealed to Governor Andrew to intercede with the War Department for him. The governor forwarded the appeal to the president, who in turn forwarded it to Attorney General Edward Bates, asking for a legal opinion. The opinion of the attorney general was that Chaplain Harrison should have been paid $100 per month and two rations per day inasmuch as his appointment to the chaplaincy was a regular appointment, not one based on the provision of the law of July 17, 1862, which related to the employment of "colored persons," and consequently that it was the duty of the president to direct the War Department to notify all army paymasters of this legal opinion.[48] Because the Senate had been considering legislation to define the status of black troops, the president transmitted the opinion of the attorney general to that body, where it was read by Senator Charles Sumner of Massachusetts.[49] This ruling with reference to chaplains apparently satisfied the majority of the Senate, and Senator Henry Wilson of Massachusetts withdrew his motion to amend the pay bill then under consideration, an amendment explicitly stating that black chaplains were to be paid at the same rate as any other chaplain.[50]

Questions about the appropriate rank and uniform for chaplains were commonplace throughout the war. Army regulations in 1861 requiring a uniform for chaplains became the subject of a continuing controversy: "The uniform of chaplains of the army will be plain black frock coat with standing collar, and one row of nine black buttons; plain black pantaloons; black felt hat or army forage cap, without adornment. On occasions of ceremony, a plain *chapeau de bras* may be worn."[51] Chaplain William Young Brown of the Douglas Hospital in Washington, D.C., in his handbook on the chaplaincy, commented on the dissatisfaction of many chaplains with the prescribed uniform, which was considered unmilitary.[52] Many discarded this style of uniform and wore instead the uniform of a captain, including insignia and side arms. To regularize this situation, the War Department issued General Order Number 247 on August 25, 1864: "The uniform of Chaplains in the Army, prescribed in General Orders, No. 102, of November 25, 1861, is hereby republished with modifications, as follows: Plain black frock-coat, with standing collar, one row of nine black buttons on the breast, with 'herring-bone' of black braid around the buttons and button holes. Plain black pantaloons. Black felt hat, or army forage cap, with a gold embroidered wreath in front, on black velvet ground, encircling the letters U. S. in silver, old English characters. On occasions of ceremony, a plain *chapeau de bras* may be worn."[53]

The herringbone braid on the coat and the insignia for the front of the hat or cap were the only modifications this order allowed. Evidently this modification did not satisfy everyone concerned, for in October of 1864, the Chaplains Council[54] of the Department of the Mississippi met in Atlanta, Georgia, to hear Chaplain N. B. Critchfield read a petition addressed to the adjutant general urging the adoption of an insignia for use on shoulder straps. This petition was forwarded to the Office of the Adjutant General on October 25, 1864, by Chaplain Isaac E. Springer, acting as secretary for the council. The petition further stated that the adoption of such an insignia would enhance the chaplain's usefulness by increasing respect for his position and by making him readily recognizable.[55] There is no record of any further revision of the War Department policy relating to the chaplain's uniform. It is probable that no style would have been universally satisfactory to the chaplains. Chaplain Ezra Sprague, a member of the same council that had forwarded Chaplain Critchfield's petition, wrote the adjutant general three days after the petition had been forwarded to inform him that of the fifteen chaplains present at the council meeting, nine had voted for the petition and six against it. "Lest the department should be misled," said Chaplain Sprague, "it is believed that you should be informed of the number present and the majority."[56] Apparently the desire for a uniform more military in appearance was not unanimous.

Rank was another matter of controversy and concern to many chaplains. The general assumption early in the war was that the chaplain enjoyed a rank equal to that of a captain. This belief was based on the act of July 22, 1861, which stated that the chaplain "shall receive the pay and allowances of a captain of cavalry."[57] The act of May 20, 1862, which had provided for the appointment of chaplains for the army hospitals, stated that the hospital chaplains would be paid at the same rate as the regimental chaplains.[58] This led to the belief that the hospital chaplains also carried a captain's rank because they received a captain's pay. In his handbook on the chaplaincy, Chaplain Brown stated that "originally having the pay of captain of cavalry, he is generally considered as having the assimilated rank of a staff captain."[59]

The chaplains' concern was not due solely to a desire for prestige based on rank; there were more practical considerations. In discussing the irregularity in methods of commissioning chaplains from the various states, Chaplain Brown mentioned the possible consequences: "If the regimental chaplain in the volunteer force is a commissioned officer, all should be commissioned; if he is not, none should be commissioned. Very grave questions may grow of this diversity, in the case of the chaplain being disabled, or dying in the service, as to the rights of himself or heirs. If he is a commissioned officer, he or his heirs will be entitled to a pension of twenty dollars per month, according to his assimulated [*sic*] rank; if a noncommissioned officer, he will only be entitled to the pension of a private soldier."[60] Thus it seems that the chaplains of the volunteer service had good reason for desiring a clarification of their status regarding rank.

The law of April 9, 1864, previously mentioned in connection with pay and allowances, referred to the "rank of chaplain without command," a designation that did little to clarify the position of the chaplain.[61] At least one chaplain commented on the uniqueness of being unranked and without command. Chaplain Henry Clay Trumbull of the Tenth Connecticut believed it to be a great advantage because it opened the way for communication with men of all ranks. "In this a chaplain had a position utterly unlike any other person in the army; and it was his own fault if he did not avail himself of it, and improve its advantages."[62]

Apparently there was more displeasure than satisfaction with such an anomalous position, however, and in October of 1864, a report from the Adjutant General's Office to the secretary of war contained the following analysis of the situation with a proposal to remedy it: "There seems to be some slight amendment necessary in the legislation con-

cerning chaplains, by which the basis of their rank shall be better defined. The act of April 9, 1864, section 1, gives them 'rank without
command' and provides that they 'shall be borne on the field and staff
rolls next after the surgeons.' From this the inference is drawn, though,
it is believed, erroneously, that chaplains are to hold a new intermedi-
ate grade below that of major, which is a full surgeon's rank, and above
that of captain." The report continues: "It was probably the intention
of the act that chaplains should be rescued from the anomalous position they before occupied, being neither commissioned officers nor
enlisted men, and should take a position on the official records among
the non-combatant commissioned staff; that their place was to be next
after the medical officers, the term surgeon in the act being used simply in a general sense, and not being intended to attach to it the specific rank of 'major.'" The remedy: "The amendment suggested, then,
is that the chaplains' rank shall be, as it formerly was in reference to
pay and allowances, assimilated to that of captain, and that their names
shall appear on the rolls and returns next after those of the medical
officers."[63] There is no record of any legislative action on the subject
before the conclusion of the war, and uncertainty about the chaplain's
actual rank remained a problem for the duration of the war.

These statutes, executive orders, and general orders from the War Department defined the charge of the chaplains, and despite the technical
ambiguities relating to rank and uniform it is clear that chaplains performed a wide variety of tasks that served both the temporal and spiritual or religious needs of the men in their regiments and the military
hospitals they served. They wrote letters for those confined to the hospital or otherwise incapacitated and acted as "regimental postmaster";
they maintained libraries of both religious and secular literature; they
taught illiterate soldiers elementary reading and writing; they performed
the painful task of informing loved ones of a soldier's death; they aided
the former slaves who flooded army camps during Union advances into
Confederate territory, often teaching them to read, write, and cipher.
Chaplains frequently carried both men and equipment on horseback
while on the march; they dug rifle pits while the men were entrench-
ing for battle and dug wells at encampments; they foraged for fresh
vegetables (and for an occasional chicken or pig) to add variety to the
diets of their men. During battle they assisted the wounded to medical

attention and aided the surgeons who treated them. Often they aided the wounded of the enemy as well in an effort to diminish the horrors of war for all its participants.

In a word, chaplains attempted to befriend those in desperate need, to intervene in times of both physical and spiritual crisis, to offer both sustenance and solace.

2

WHAT TO DO AND HOW TO DO IT

In explaining the purpose for writing his handbook on the army chaplain, the Reverend William Young Brown indicated that the duties of the chaplain in the army were "very imperfectly defined." A handbook, if kept within the scope of army regulations, he explained, would aid in promoting the efficiency of the chaplain and thus indirectly serve the country.[1]

In his introduction to the handbook, Chaplain Brown outlined what he considered to be essential qualities for successful performance as an army chaplain. As the highest qualification, without which he regarded all other qualifications as valueless, was the need for "ardent piety." To attempt the functions of the ministry as they pertained to the chaplain without true piety was to Chaplain Brown utter folly, as it would not only result in failure but would also discredit the office.[2]

Proficiency as a teacher was another quality Brown considered to be vital to a chaplain's success. Teaching the men was "the highest duty of his office"; hence without real ability for such a task a chaplain would fail in one of his major responsibilities, because the circumstances in which a chaplain was forced to function were often less than favorable. Even the most gifted at teaching frequently found the task nearly impossible in the army. In Brown's opinion, then, a minister who was not a proficient teacher should not attempt to serve as a chaplain.[3]

A suitable personality—one exhibiting kindness, patience, generosity, cheerfulness, and courtesy—was also deemed essential; and because numerous difficulties faced the chaplain in the performance of his duties, Chaplain Brown considered resolution and energy as other necessary qualities of the successful chaplain. Good health was also rated as extremely important. Chaplains serving in hospitals lived in constant exposure to contagious diseases; those serving regiments were constantly exposed to the extremes of weather, to epidemic, and to irregular living, all being detrimental to even the strongest constitution.[4]

Finally courage, or self-possession, and self-control were required of the good chaplain: "There are sometimes scenes of suffering so terrible, scenes of excitement so intense, and scenes of carnage so awful, with which the chaplain comes in contact, as to completely unnerve many men, but which demand the most prompt attention and the most vigorous treatment; and sadly deficient is that chaplain, who cannot command himself at such a time, and under such circumstances. He must be a man of general self-control."[5] Brown's handbook, though not an official governmental publication, was well received and widely used by chaplains throughout the war as a compendium of their duties, codified by a seasoned colleague. It was, in effect, a "what to do and how to do it" guidebook for clergy in uniform.

Chaplain James H. Bradford of the Twelfth Connecticut Infantry expressed sentiments similar to those of Chaplain Brown as he reminisced some thirty years after his service. To be a good chaplain, in Bradford's opinion, it was absolutely necessary to be broad-minded. To be narrow-minded, theologically or in regard to conduct, drastically limited the chaplain's usefulness. It was also difficult but essential for the chaplain to retain cordial relations with both officers and men. Because there was only one chaplain per regiment and replacement was difficult if not impossible, the chaplain had to remain healthy. While others became discouraged, he had to sustain morale by his personal example. He also had to face the reality that despite the promotion of others there would be none for himself. Others might succumb to temptations, but the chaplain could not: "An officer or a private, when angry might swear— once and a while men did that in the army! The chaplain must not swear." Above all the chaplain had to be an example of obedience, for that principle was the bedrock of all he taught and believed. He needed a strong constitution and nerves that could bear the severest pressures. Yet despite all these difficulties, Bradford was convinced that no other officers were in a position to do more for the welfare of the men in the regiments. The chaplain was unique.[6]

The duties and responsibilities of the men who served their country as chaplains in the Union armies fell into four general categories. Some duties were official, prescribed by law or the War Department, while others were unofficial or assumed responsibilities, not definitely required but frequently undertaken as a service to the men. Some duties were religious, or spiritual, and others were secular, or temporal. It is readily apparent that these categories overlapped in many instances: that is, some religious duties were officially required, others were of necessity done on a voluntary basis. For example, conducting weekly worship services was a required religious duty while baptizing converts was voluntary. A required secular function was the forwarding of written monthly reports; a voluntary secular function was the transmission of funds to the families of the men. The difficulty of precise delineation among these categories is such that discussion of a chaplain's duties is more clearly understood if based on assignment—to a regiment, hospital, or post.[7]

Every post should have a chapel, Brown urged, in which public services should be held at fixed hours, similar to the practice of regular churches. He also thought that there should be prayer services, Bible lectures, and regular evening vespers of a devotional nature. Since the chaplain was required to reside at the post, Brown believed that this provided an opportunity for the organization of regular classes in Bible doctrine or book studies for those who were interested.[8]

Chaplain Brown also suggested that a library of "a miscellaneous type" should be available, under the supervision of the chaplain. Tracts and other religious literature (from the various boards of publications) were available for distribution to the men and officers and should be utilized. Chaplains were also required to serve as schoolmasters to the children of the officers living at the post. At times they were assisted in this task by "intelligent and educated" soldiers; at some posts the presence of schools nearby made it unnecessary for the chaplain to perform this duty, thus making more time available for visitation, counseling, and religious duties.[9] It is reasonable to conclude that the duties of the post chaplain differed from those of the regimental and hospital chaplains mainly with regard to the setting in which they were performed.

Most of the clergy who volunteered in the Union armies served as regimental chaplains. Altogether some 2,300 ministers, priests, and rabbis rendered service to the volunteer regiments that made up the Union armies.[10] General Order Number 15, issued by the War Department on May 4, 1861, required regimental chaplains of the volunteer forces to submit quarterly reports to the officer commanding the regiment to which they had been assigned.[11] The act of July 22, 1861, gave this the force of law.[12] The officers who received these reports were not obligated to transmit them to the adjutant general's office nor to act on the suggestions contained therein, however, and some chaplains regretted that the commanding officer was granted such latitude in handling their reports. Chaplain Brown stated: "It is to be regretted that it is not made the duty of the colonel commanding the regiment to forward the quarterly reports of the chaplains to the Adjutant-General's office, to be filed among the department papers. Were they to be filed, they would perhaps, be more carefully prepared, and they might be of great interest to the future historian, if not of present advantage to the Department."[13] This policy was finally changed in April of 1864, when Congress passed a bill requiring regimental chaplains to submit monthly reports directly to the adjutant general.[14]

The reports of these chaplains were usually quite similar in form, although the length and subject matter varied greatly. A typical report began with a statement concerning the chaplain's assignment, his location, and the date, followed by a brief account of the duty performed by his regiment since the previous report. Next were detailed the number and type of religious services conducted with comments on the attendance (or lack of it). After this came the chaplain's views on the moral and religious condition of the men. The report concluded with miscellaneous comments and recommendations for means to improve the general moral, social, and religious condition of the regiment.[15]

In addition to submitting quarterly or monthly reports, regimental chaplains were expected to conduct public worship services each week, this duty certainly being their most conspicuous function.[16] The importance with which these services were generally regarded is evident in the many and repeated references to them by the chaplains. Chaplain Arthur B. Fuller of the Sixteenth Massachusetts Infantry described his Sunday services in camp as consisting of a Sunday school service at 9 A.M. and a preaching service at 5 P.M. In addition to these public services, he conducted a "social conference and prayer meeting" each evening, in front of his tent. These daily meetings were informal, involving a discussion of the latest news, general conversation, counseling, and concluding with prayer and a hymn. He related that in his public ministry every attempt was made to keep the services nonsectarian. He pointed to regular attendance of many Roman Catholics and Protestants of other denominations as evidence of his success in this endeavor.[17]

The chaplain of the Tenth Connecticut Infantry, Reverend Henry Clay Trumbull, conducted a variety of services each week, including a preaching service on Sunday morning and Sunday school services in the evening, followed by prayers in the later evening. On Wednesday evening he conducted a prayer meeting. Each weekday he also visited the regimental wards of the divisional hospital for devotional services and prayers. In preparing sermons for these services, Trumbull attempted to find texts and themes appropriate to the time, place, and circumstances of the regiment. He believed that a chaplain had an advantage over the parish minister in preparing sermons because chaplains' congregations were much more homogeneous.[18]

His activities as a chaplain did not cease even following capture by the enemy. Captured on Norris Island, South Carolina, on July 19, 1863, Trumbull was held at Castle Pinckney in Charleston until December 4, 1863, when he was released unconditionally.[19] While confined he stated that imprisonment did not shut him off from opportunities for service as a chaplain. Every evening he conducted prayers with his companions in misfortune before they lay down to sleep. On Sundays he led a service of worship in the officers' quarters and was granted permission by Confederate authorities to preach to the enlisted men imprisoned on the floor above.[20]

Trumbull also took the lead in organizing activities to sustain the men's morale: "There were prison amusements of their kind. . . . Now and then there was a lecture of some officer on a topic of interest to all. Moreover, there were well-attended prayer-meetings three evenings of the week. When there were any chaplains in prison, there were religious services, with sermons, twice each Sunday; and even when there was no chaplain, some non-clerical officer often performed this duty."[21]

Chaplain John R. Adams of the Fifth Maine Infantry, after describing the usual Sunday worship services, spoke of his other religious functions in a letter to his wife: "We have prayers daily with the regiment at 5 o'clock in the afternoon. . . . Every evening we have a good psalm-singing at the door of my tent, for the hymn-books are kept in my camp-chest." On one occasion he was requested to say a few appropriate words of dedication and offer a prayer at the raising of a new flagstaff in the regimental camp.[22]

The chaplain of the Second Massachusetts Cavalry, Charles A. Humphreys, emphasized the difficulties in attempting to hold regular worship services, the chief of which was locating a suitable place. Some of the sites he used included a barn (where his sermons were frequently interrupted by impious cattle), a clearing in a grove near camp (at Vienna, Virginia), and a large tent (when not in use for courts-martial).[23]

In addition to the regular services for the regiment each Sunday, he also held three services in the division hospital near the camp. Occasionally he was required to address the men on religious matters during dress parade. In defining the nonsectarian nature of his ministry, he said that his aim in preaching was to elevate rather than to convert.[24]

Father William Corby, who resigned his position on the faculty of the University of Notre Dame to serve as chaplain of the Eighty-eighth New York Infantry, referred to his duties while the regiment was in winter camp. He stated that during the winter he spent his time in much the same way as a parish priest did, except that he had no old women to bother him or pew rent to collect. He celebrated mass, heard confessions, and preached on Sundays and holidays. During the week many minor duties occupied his time. He was called on at times to instruct those who needed private lessons on special points of religion and everywhere to elevate the standard of religion, morality, and true patriotism. This formed the winter's work for all Catholic priests so engaged.[25]

Chaplain Corby conducted the mass in a variety of settings. At one time a large circus tent was used for daily services, the Sunday mass, confessions, and communion. This tent, which had cost $500 for the canvas alone, had to be abandoned during the Peninsular campaign when McClellan changed his base from the York River to the James River. On several occasions Corby conducted services outdoors, using an altar made of pine branches.[26]

During the winter of 1863, while in camp near Falmouth, Virginia, Father Corby was supplied by General T. F. Meagher with a detail of men to build a log church. It was completed just before Saint Patrick's Day, when it was dedicated with much fanfare.[27] To add to the attractiveness of the services and to provide a deeper significance in the military setting, Corby also developed a military mass, in which military forms of courtesy were used to express religious devotion. During the mass the troops would present arms at various solemn moments, military bands played at appropriate intervals, and at the climax—the consecration of the Host—cannons were fired. Corby reported that this service made a deep impression on all who witnessed it.[28]

Chaplain William W. Lyle of the Eleventh Ohio Infantry told of holding a regular Sunday service for his regiment while the Army of the Potomac was moving through Maryland to oppose the Confederate army of Northern Virginia at Sharpsburg. The service had hardly begun when it was interrupted by marching orders. There followed what was probably the shortest sermon on record. Said the chaplain, "Now, comrades, we have got orders to march, and I must stop. God bless you, and make you faithful soldiers for God and your country."[29] After the battle at Antietam he was requested to hold services for the entire brigade, which he did, as the other regiments in the brigade were without chaplains.[30]

Father Thomas H. Mooney, Roman Catholic chaplain, Sixty-ninth New York State Militia, saying mass before Bull Run. (Photograph by Mathew B. Brady)

Lyle also described a field service, held just before the Battle of Chickamauga: "The chaplain rode up in front of the line, and the colonel gave an order which, on being executed, formed the regiment in two divisions, with the chaplain in the center. Without dismounting, he addressed the troops in a clear, loud voice, that sounded strangely amid the loud explosions of the artillery and the rattle of musketry. . . . Every head was uncovered and bowed in reverence, while hands were clasped on the rifles, the bayonets on which were gleaming [in] the morning sun. . . . A low murmuring Amen was heard from the ranks as the chaplain closed."[31]

Chaplain Lyle also described the provisions made for religious services while in camp during the winter of 1862–63. He stated that after the quarters for the men had been "fitted up," a dismantled church was repaired and made quite comfortable for meetings. For several weeks, religious services were conducted nearly every night. Many interesting and encouraging meetings were held that, the chaplain believed, made a deep and lasting impression on the men who attended.[32]

In addition to conducting regular worship services, many chaplains helped to organize regimental churches and Sunday schools. Chaplain Fuller was instrumental in organizing an Army Christian Association in the Sixteenth Massachusetts Regiment, which, in the chaplain's opinion, produced many beneficial results. The services of this army church were held in a chapel tent donated by the citizens of Boston. As a special ministration, sponsored by the regimental church, the chaplain also organized a Sunday school for the former slaves and poor whites in the area surrounding the camp. Fuller was gratified by sizable attendance from both groups, as the Sunday school was integrated into its operation.[33]

Chaplain W. F. Harned of the Twenty-fourth Indiana Volunteer Infantry reported the establishment of a regimental church at Baton Rouge, Louisiana, where the regiment was stationed. Attendance at the non-denominational services was excellent, and the effect on the moral condition of the regiment was salutary, the chaplain reported.[34]

James Marks was another chaplain who organized a regimental church. The charter membership was 170, and according to the chaplain 60 of that number were new converts. Although this church was intended to give the men a definite feeling of religious unity, it was not meant to be denominationally exclusive or to take the place of former church affiliations. Marks believed that the organized group had a very beneficial effect on the entire regiment, and he cited its steady growth as evidence. The church services were held in a tent purchased for that purpose with funds donated by friends in the Pittsburgh area where the regiment (Sixty-third Pennsylvania Infantry) had been recruited.[35]

The chaplain's most solemn and heartrending duty was conducting funerals for those who died from sickness, wounds, or in battle.[36] Chaplain Fuller referred frequently to the many funerals he was called on to conduct. Often there were several in a single day, and seldom was there a day without at least one.[37] Chaplain Adams also mentioned the frequency with which he was required to perform this duty. While sickness took a heavy toll of lives, especially during the winter and spring months, the loss of life in battle was made very real to the chaplain as he performed the funeral services for those who had been killed in conflict. Often the funerals would be for groups of men buried in a common grave when time and conditions did not permit single services for each fallen soldier.[38] Chaplain J. Pinkney Hammond, in his *Manual* for army chaplains, listed as one of the chaplain's most important public duties the faithful performance of appropriate religious services for those who died for their country.[39]

Chaplains were also expected to share the heartbreaking news of a soldier's death with his family, usually by letter. Such letters must have been difficult to compose. One such note, from Chaplain Andrew Hartsock to the family of a soldier in the 133rd Pennsylvania Infantry, wounded at Fredericksburg, is typical. "Dear Friend: I truly sympathize with you in your bereavement. I can cheerfully testify to the upright conduct of your son. When I found him, after the battle of Saturday, he was praying, and as fully resigned as any man ever was when about to retire to rest for the night. There were no signs of fear, but he was perfectly calm. He lived until Sabbath about midnight, and during that time was perfectly resigned, and gave every evidence of a preparation for death. You may rest assured that his soul now rests with God."[40]

Another type of duty frequently performed by regimental chaplains was to serve as librarian and distributor of a variety of religious literature. Chaplain Fuller mentioned that the distribution of Bibles and religious reading matter occupied much of his time while the regiment was in camp. He commended the American Bible Society for generously supplying him with "excellent materials" that he in turn could pass on to the men.[41] Chaplain James Rogers of the Fourteenth Wisconsin Infantry found that distributing religious books, tracts, Bibles, and other literature was beneficial to the moral tone of the regiment. This was a more effective ministry, however, when centered in the division hospital where men recuperating from wounds or disease had time to devote to a serious consideration of such subject matter. Rogers praised the benevolent societies that so generously supplied the chaplains with the necessary materials for this work.[42]

Chaplain Trumbull frequently combined humor with the distribution of religious literature. On one occasion he approached a group of men who were about to begin a round of poker. Handing each man a tract, he remarked, "Tracts are trumps and it's my deal." Laughing at his witticism, the men accepted literature they might otherwise have refused, and the chaplain left convinced that he had eliminated at least one day's gambling. Trumbull's impression may not have been well founded, but his tact and wit in distributing literature were obviously appreciated by the men.[43]

Chaplain Adams found that the men tended to be more receptive to proffered religious literature if they were approached privately. For this reason he made it a practice to distribute tracts and New Testaments by visiting the men in their tents where they were less likely to be embarrassed by the presence of scoffing comrades.[44]

Chaplain Humphreys made a serious attempt to distribute religious literature keyed to the denominational preference of each man. Although he could not always obtain suitable literature for everyone, the men appreciated the obvious attempt to please and to avoid offense. Humphreys shared the belief of Chaplain Rogers that religious literature was most effective when distributed to convalescents in the division hospital, where enforced idleness made minds more receptive to such serious subject matter.[45] The chaplain also supervised a regimental library of modest proportions—two hundred volumes, supplied by a minister friend who desired to aid the chaplain in maintaining the morale of the regiment. There were volumes of poetry, literature, drama, history, and fiction, supplemented by a collection of magazines donated by parishioners. Humphreys noted that both officers and men seemed to appreciate the diversion made possible by such generosity.[46]

Chaplain J. Pinkney Hammond referred to the supervision of regimental libraries as one of the temporal duties of the chaplain. He also urged the establishment of reading rooms when practicable. By close supervision of these facilities, he explained, it would be possible for the chaplains to determine to a great extent what their men would read, a subtle and unobtrusive way of providing a wholesome influence on the regiment.[47]

Chaplain James Marks (Sixty-third Pennsylvania Infantry) considered the distribution of literature to be one of his most important duties. He reported: "My first care was to distribute Testaments and hymn books. The first week I appeared in camp I distributed to those who came to my tent four hundred copies of the New Testament, in four different languages,—English, German, French, and Italian—and during the same week, six hundred small hymn-books called the 'Soldier's Hymn-book'—drawing my supplies from the American Tract Societies of New York and Boston."[48] Marks also regularly distributed tracts and religious pamphlets each Sunday from the supply he had received from the various denominations and religious publishing houses. In addition, he collected a library of about four hundred volumes, supplemented by some three hundred magazines and reviews. The chaplain expressed his appreciation to the Soldiers' Aid Commission of Pittsburgh, the Sanitary Commission, and the American Tract Society for contributions to the library, which he believed had a positive influence on the men. The soldiers, he was convinced, were less inclined to waste their time at gambling or by seeking the excitement of intoxication when such beneficial diversion was available.[49]

Chaplain Lewis Hamilton of the Second Colorado Cavalry reported that the distribution of literature was an especially effective means of reaching a regiment engaged in garrison duty, where it was likely to be spread over a large area in small detachments. His own regiment was on such duty in and around Pleasant Hill, Missouri; consequently he observed from experience that "a very effective means of usefulness among our soldiers [was] the furnishing of them with good reading." This was so, he indicated, because literature could be sent to each post or station where members of the regiment were located. He employed this means of reaching the men quite freely because of the liberality of the Christian Commission in supplying needed literature. The men usually appreciated the reading matter thus supplied to them, for it helped them to pass tedious hours of camp life and guard duty more pleasantly. Literature had an added value, Hamilton asserted, in that it remained with men to be read and reread at leisure, thus exerting a continuing influence. The spoken word was more quickly forgotten.[50]

Chaplain Lyle noted that he had had the good fortune to "inherit," so to speak, from the chaplain who had preceded him a regimental library of modest proportions. He had been able to enlarge it, through donations by the Christian Commission, to some four hundred volumes. These books were kept during the months spent in winter camp in a small house that provided quarters for the chaplain, a prayer room, and a reading room. Lyle was convinced that the presence of high-quality reading matter was of great value to the men, for it tended, in his opinion, to elevate the moral tone of the regiment.[51]

Many chaplains served their regiments as financial agents. Although this function was not an official duty, it was widely undertaken as a service to the men and officers. This aspect of the chaplain's work involved making purchases for the men, collecting funds for transmission elsewhere, and on occasion granting loans in cases of extreme need.

Father Corby found the men of his regiment and brigade (the Eighty-eighth New York Infantry of the "Irish Brigade") deeply concerned about the welfare of the poor in Ireland. They took frequent collections for this charity, which they entrusted to Chaplain Corby for transmission through the archbishop of New York to Ireland. This responsibility required that the chaplain apply for frequent leaves in order to journey to Washington where he could dispatch these funds to their intended destination. Corby was deeply impressed with this evidence of concern and compassion on the part of those who were themselves in constant danger.[52]

Chaplain Lyman Ames of the Twenty-ninth Ohio Infantry found himself bearing a similar responsibility at the request of his regimental commander. In October 1864, the commander, Major Byron Wright, requested that Chaplain Ames be granted a leave for the purpose of delivering funds belonging to members of the regiment to their families in Ohio. At the time, the regiment was in Atlanta, Georgia. The request was granted, and the chaplain experienced an uneventful but profitable autumn excursion for the benefit of families back home.[53]

Chaplain Lyle also traveled to Ohio on numerous occasions on behalf of the men of the Eleventh Ohio Infantry. In a request for a leave from duty for one such journey, which was approved as a matter of routine, his commanding officer, Colonel P. P. Lane, explained that "Chaplain Lyle has something over twenty five thousand dollars ($25,000) in his hands for distribution among the families and friends of the Soldiers of this reg't., and it has been the custom of the regiment for the past eighteen months to deposit all surplus funds with him to be sent to Ohio, and he has acted as financial and general business agent for the reg't."[54]

Chaplain Hammond indicated in his discussion of the temporal duties of chaplains that requests for such financial transactions would frequently be pressed on them. It was his opinion that when responsibilities of this nature could be avoided graciously it was better not to assume them.[55] Chaplain Brown concurred with Hammond in this sentiment, urging chaplains to avoid financial entanglements. "As a rule," he said, the chaplain "should avoid all matters not legitimately pertaining to the duties of his office."[56]

Chaplain Humphreys also recorded his financial activities undertaken on behalf of his men. In addition to collecting money from the men, which he in turn forwarded to their families, he made it a point to urge those people at home who were in a position to help, to do so when a soldier's family was in dire need. This sort of benevolence was to him simple Christian charity. He practiced what he preached, moreover, for he made numerous loans to needy soldiers in the regiment. He was not dismayed, apparently, by the fact that many of these loans were never repaid. "I used to have several hundred dollars thus floating around in the regiment," he stated, "and, though much of it got waterlogged and sunk never to return, I felt that it had done good service." Whether or not the chaplain's optimism was well founded, his evidently cheerful nature and willing spirit must have made a good impression on his men.[57]

Many chaplains assumed a type of function that could not be classified as religious but nevertheless bore directly on the moral problems the men encountered. This was the promotion of temperance within the army. Father Corby recalled that he was frequently requested to administer "the pledge" to individuals who had been indulging too freely. Because of the prevalence of this problem in the regiment and the brigade (the Eighty-eighth New York Infantry of the Irish Brigade) Corby, with two other chaplains of the brigade, Fathers Dillon and Thomas Ouellet (of the Sixty-third New York and the Sixty-ninth New York, respectively), formed a temperance society. The approximately seven hundred members were provided with medals indicating their membership and their pledge to sobriety. It was not intended to promote total abstinence—a near impossibility with Irish fighting men, Father Corby observed—but rather moderation and the elimination of drunkenness.[58]

Chaplain Lyle conducted for the men of his regiment a regular lecture series concerning the problems of alcoholism, urging them to temperance as good soldiers. He was encouraged by the large numbers who attended the lectures and noted a gradual but definite improvement in the moral condition of the regiment.[59] Chaplain Humphreys was also convinced of the need for temperance societies in the army. He stated that while in the field away from temptation the men were abstemious; in camp, however, it was quite another matter as proximity to the tents of the sutlers frequently overtaxed even the strongest of good intentions.[60] Chaplain Adams conducted a lecture series similar to the evening lyceums so popular throughout the country during that era, devoting several evenings to a frank discussion of the problems of drunkenness. He expressed pleasure at the tangible display of interest and concern on the part of the men as evidenced by the goodly numbers in attendance at these lectures.[61]

Chaplain Fuller undertook the organization and sponsorship of a division of the Sons of Temperance in his regiment (the Sixteenth Massachusetts Infantry). This task would have been difficult under ordinary circumstances in an army camp, but the chaplain proceeded with the added handicap of holding the organizational meeting on New Year's

Eve.[62] In all probability more men appeared for the second meeting the next week. Chaplain Harned (Twenty-fourth Indiana Infantry) reported that his commanding officer, Colonel W. T. Spicely, had aided him immeasurably in curbing intemperance through both personal example and rigorous discipline. In fact, the colonel had encouraged him to establish a temperance society, which he did, with the result that the moral atmosphere of the regimental camp was vastly improved.[63] Chaplain Hamilton (Second Colorado Cavalry) stated that though intemperance characterized a few, a good number of the men had taken a pledge of total abstinence and were observing it strictly.[64]

Father James Dillon of the Sixty-third New York Infantry had, apparently, greater success than most in promoting temperance among his men. He was able to persuade several officers to assume offices in the regimental society as an example to the men. He also had a supply of medals specially cast to distribute to the members, which served to remind them of the pledge they had taken. When, during the Peninsular campaign, the commissary issued whiskey because of the foul water in the Chickahominy swamps, the "wet" members of the regiment claimed the allotments of the temperance men. For some undisclosed reason, a dispute occurred between a Sergeant Quinn and a Private Rutledge over the portion of Sergeant Dwyer, a "dry." When both men claimed Dwyer's share, their comrades insisted that they fight to settle the issue. The private, a small man, flattened the burly sergeant in a short contest and was declared the rightful holder of Dwyer's share of whiskey for as long as the commissary continued the ration. The name by which the regiment was known in the army is probably the best tribute, however, to the efforts of Father Dillon in promoting temperance; it was called the "Temperance Regiment."[65]

Chaplains also performed a variety of services that cannot be precisely classified as duties; these were evidence of a desire to accommodate and were usually well received by the men. Such activities included everything from writing letters for illiterate or disabled soldiers to organizing classes of academic instruction in Libby Prison. Chaplain Trumbull, for example, frequently wrote letters for men who could not, for one reason or another, stressing the vital importance of regular mail from home in maintaining morale in the army. He found that this service provided an opportunity for close conversation with the men, promoting a trust that made the task of providing spiritual counsel easier.[66] Chaplains Hammond and Brown both asserted that helping soldiers in their correspondence, that is, letter writing, franking of letters, and distributing mail from home, were duties to which the chaplain should pay special attention.[67] Chaplain Humphreys stated that he served as postmaster for his regiment (the Second Massachusetts Cavalry) and that in addition to franking letters for soldiers who could not prepay, he also distributed paper and envelopes freely to those who requested them.[68]

Chaplain George Bradley (Twenty-second Wisconsin Infantry) encouraged his men to pursue constructive hobbies rather than waste their time and money on gambling or strong drink. One especially popular hobby in which a number of men became quite adept was wood carving. Another popular diversion that both officers and men enjoyed was shellwork. Many objects of interest, beauty, and value were fashioned by the men of Bradley's regiment in these and other practical hobbies.[69] Chaplain Hammond, in his discussion of the temporal duties of chaplains, included an extended treatment on the value of recreation and entertainment in maintaining morale. He urged chaplains to encourage musical groups (both vocal and instrumental); games such as checkers, chess, dominoes, and backgammon (but not cards); and the organization of literary societies and classes.[70]

Several chaplains organized courses of formal instruction in a variety of subjects for the benefit of the men whom they served. Chaplain Marks used the chapel tent for organized classes in Latin, German, and arithmetic. He also formed a debating society in which he took great pride.[71] Chaplain Lyle conducted a writing class and supervised a lecture series devoted to philosophy, literature, and history, using the chapel as a meeting place. He was convinced that opportunities such as these were appreciated by the men and were of great benefit to them.[72] Chaplain Fuller organized a school for which he recruited five teachers from among the noncommissioned officers and men of the regiment (Sixteenth Massachusetts Infantry). He also formed a School Teachers' Association in cooperation with other regimental chaplains to expand the areas of teaching competence.[73]

To help maintain morale, Chaplains McCabe and Trumbull organized classes while being held as prisoners of war. In a letter to his wife from Libby Prison in Richmond, McCabe stated that "we have classes in French, Spanish, Latin, Greek, Rhetoric, English Grammar, Arithmetic, Algebra, Geometry, Natural Philosophy, etc." This school was commonly called the "University of Libby Prison"; the men who taught the French and Spanish classes were native in those tongues, and each of the instructors was reputed to be highly competent in his field. McCabe himself became fairly fluent in French while at Libby.[74]

Trumbull did not have the resources for such an ambitious undertaking at Castle Pinckney where he was imprisoned, but he was able to persuade some of the officers to lecture occasionally on topics of general interest. He also organized other types of activity, such as games and debates, and distributed supplies from the boxes the Sanitary and Christian Commissions had forwarded for the prisoners. All these efforts helped sustain the morale of the men during the dreary months of imprisonment.[75]

The battlefield and the emergency field hospital were together areas in which regimental chaplains could render the highest in spiritual service to the men they served. If ever men felt a need for the solace of religion it was in combat when they came face to face with the imminence of death, or in the hospital recovering from a wound or facing the reality of death.

Many chaplains gave careful accounts of the manner in which they sought to aid their men during those hours of crisis. Among those who did so was Father Corby. While accompanying his regiment on the march from South Mountain to Sharpsburg, Corby stopped by the roadside many times to hear confessions and give Extreme Unction to wounded and dying Confederates of the Catholic faith and to baptize any Protestant "Rebels" who wished it. Words of assurance to dying men were deeply appreciated, even when spoken by an opponent. At Antietam, the chaplain rode his horse to the front of the Irish Brigade as it advanced into battle "at double-quick." Hurriedly he told the men to make a sincere Act of Contrition as they moved to meet the enemy. Within less than thirty minutes, 506 of those men lay dead or wounded. Corby was on the field during the major part of the engagement—frequently under heavy fire—while he heard confessions, administered last rites and baptisms, and aided the wounded in any way possible.[76]

At Gettysburg Chaplain Corby again addressed the men of the Irish Brigade just before its entrance into battle on July 2, in defense of Little Round Top. "The Chaplain of the Brigade, Rev. William Corby, proposed to give a general absolution to all the men before going into the fight." An eyewitness described the scene: "Father Corby stood on a large rock in front of the Brigade. Addressing the men, he explained what he was about to do, saying that each one could receive the benefit of the absolution by making a sincere Act of Contrition and firmly resolving to embrace the first opportunity for confession of his sins, urging them to do their duty, and reminding them of . . . the noble object for which they fought. . . . Every man, Catholic and non-Catholic, fell on his knees with

Officers and chaplains of the "Irish Brigade." Back row, left to right: unidentified visiting priest and Colonel Patrick Kelly; front row, left to right: Captain Clooney, Father Dillon, Father Corby.

his head bowed down. Then . . . Father Corby pronounced the words of the absolution."[77]

Chaplain Rogers was another who spoke of his activities on the battlefield. At Shiloh he made it his duty to find shelter for the wounded by commandeering houses in the vicinity. When he had found adequate shelter for as many as possible, he rode back and forth over the fields searching for Union dead and any wounded who might have been overlooked. He aided the surgeons where needed, prayed with the wounded and dying, and when all was quiet he set about the sad task of providing the dead with a Christian burial.[78]

Chaplain George Pepper of the Eightieth Ohio Infantry found that his most difficult but important responsibility was to counsel with dying men who had no professed faith. There was about them, he noted, an utter despair. Yet many of them found an inward peace and outward composure by professing faith in Christ. Experiences such as these brought joy amid sorrow to the chaplain, especially when he was able to inform a bereaved family that the soldier had died in the "Most Holy Faith." Pepper also aided the surgeons and nurses in relieving the physical discomfort of the wounded in any way he could.[79]

Chaplain Trumbull was another who considered the task of comforting dying men to be a difficult one. Yet, Trumbull recalled, it was often a very rewarding task. He wrote of one occasion when he was called to the bedside of a lad of eighteen dying from a battle wound. The young man had run away from his home, and his irreligious attitudes had deeply grieved his parents. The chaplain had been asked to prepare the boy for the knowledge that he was dying. This information broke the young man's rebellious spirit, and he tearfully confessed a faith in Christ, asking that his parents be informed of his conversion. Trumbull was more than willing to comply with this final request. Weeks later he received a note of appreciation from the bereaved but grateful parents.[80]

Trumbull also told of his activities on the field of battle. In addition to encouraging the men to do their duty, he carried water and ammunition, comforted the wounded, Union and Confederate alike, and took down the final messages of the dying to be transmitted to the homes of the bereaved.[81]

Chaplain Humphreys was frequently called on to give comfort and counsel to dying soldiers. On one such occasion he began by reciting some Psalms of penitence and then asking the man, an infantry captain, if he was willing to die for his country. Although the captain stated his willingness to die for his country, he feared death because he had been an evil man and asked the chaplain to administer a sacrament. The chaplain struck a responsive chord when he stated that no sacraments were necessary because "the sacrifices of God are a broken spirit." The mortally wounded captain finished the text: "a broken and a contrite heart, O God, thou wilt not despise," and a few moments later died in full confidence that all was well with his soul. Scenes like this were frequent in Humphreys's experience and never failed to move him deeply.[82]

Chaplain Lyle recorded many details of his activity during and immediately following battles. His attentions were devoted around the clock to the needs, both spiritual and physical, of wounded and dying men. It was, he found, heartrending but rewarding work. Often he found himself comforting wounded rebels who had been left on the field by a retreating enemy. On one such occasion, he began to comfort a wounded man by speaking of the gallant cause for which he had fought, not realizing that the man was a Confederate. The chaplain reported that when he learned of his error, he had to change his line of comfort.[83]

Chaplains McCabe, Humphreys, and Marks each reported being captured by Confederate forces while remaining behind to attend to the wounded and to conduct burials when the Union forces withdrew. Marks had remained behind with several other chaplains and a group of surgeons when Heintzelman's Corps of McClellan's Army of the Potomac withdrew from the front after the battle at Savage Station during the Peninsular campaign. He explained that he felt it to be his duty to remain with his men as long as his presence was of value to them.[84] McCabe was captured at Winchester in the Valley of Virginia when he remained behind after General Milroy withdrew his forces in the face of Lee's advance down the valley to invade Pennsylvania. The chaplain spoke for a group of surgeons and chaplains who had remained to care for Union wounded, in an interesting exchange with Confederate General Jubal Early. McCabe reported the encounter as follows: "General Early," he said, "we are a company of surgeons and chaplains who have stayed behind to look after the wounded; we have finished our work and would like very much to be sent through to our regiment[s]." Early smiled and addressed McCabe, "You are a preacher, are you?" The chaplain answered that he was. "Well," said Early, "you preachers have done more to bring on this war than anybody and I'm going to send you to Richmond. . . . They tell me you have been shouting 'On to Richmond' for a long time, and to Richmond you shall go."[85]

The experience of the third to be captured in such circumstances was not unlike that of the previous two. Chaplain Humphreys was with his regiment, on patrol, when one of the men was killed by a sharpshooter's bullet in a minor skirmish near Aldie, Virginia. The chaplain remained to bury the man and provide a brief funeral as the regiment (the Second Massachusetts Cavalry) rode on. Captured by Mosby's guerrillas, he was not permitted to complete the burial but after being forced to walk some thirty miles leading his horse, which he was not allowed to mount, he was sent south to Charleston. He was kept in prison at Castle Pinckney for nearly three months before his exchange was effected. Although the chaplain's determination to do his duty resulted in a rather trying experience, he expressed no regrets, and within one month after his exchange he rejoined his regiment for service in the field.[86]

No discussion of the activities of regimental chaplains could be considered truly exhaustive, but the great variety and extent of their duties should be obvious. Chaplains were called on to provide spiritual consolation for deserters and spies awaiting military execution;[87] they served as stretcher-bearers; they fought in the ranks; they recruited replacements for their regiments; they baptized converts, conducted revivals, served Communion, and received new members into their denominational fellowship; some wrote for a hometown newspaper; others served artillery pieces when the gunners had been killed. It would be impossible to detail the full range of experiences these men knew, but years after the war Chaplain Eastman reminisced:

> In battle, the chaplain had no orders and went where he could do the most good. He seemed naturally to belong with the doctors. He could render intelligent help in bandaging wounds and at the operating table, and his opportunity of service to individual sufferers was absolutely without limit. It was his hour of duty. Some of the surgeons were posted well up toward the front to give first aid. More of them were in the large field hospitals of division in more secure places at the rear. The chaplain might be at either place or at both by turns. Some made a point of watching for any wounded man who might come staggering back, who perhaps could be helped up into the saddle and ride back to the hospital. When the demand for help became urgent the chaplains were nurses. As the rows of wounded men grew longer, chaplains went from man to man to see what could be done to relieve their pain, perhaps to take a message or write a letter. All day and far into the night this work would continue. A drink of water, a loosened bandage on a swollen limb, a question answered, a surgeon summoned, a whispered word of com-

fort marked their course. While surgeons and nurses were busy and weary, the chaplains gleaned after them. Each night at sundown the men who had died during the day were buried, with a short prayer, side by side in one shallow common grave, each in his uniform with canvas wrapped about his face and a strip of paper giving his name and regiment in a bottle buttoned under his blouse.[88]

The duties of the hospital chaplain, a large number of whom were regimental chaplains on detached assignment, were in many respects similar to those of regimental chaplains. The battlefield scenes were missing, but the effects of battle were in evidence in every hospital. The chaplains who served in military hospitals were eyewitnesses to scenes of human suffering that at times defied description. The maimed and dying were their charges, and their attempts to provide spiritual solace and physical relief are by themselves a chapter in the history of the Civil War.

Hospital chaplains were required, as were regimental chaplains, to submit regular reports of their work.[89] These reports were submitted each month to the surgeon in charge of the hospital where the chaplain was assigned and were transmitted by him to the Office of the Surgeon General. The reports, although they varied greatly in length and in the detail of information, were similar in form. They usually began with a statement indicating the chaplain's station, the address, and the date. There followed a brief explanation concerning how and when the assignment had been made. Next was the number of patients in the hospital at the time of the report. The size of the hospital library, if any, and any additions or changes that had been made, was the next item. After this the chaplain enumerated the number of religious services conducted, their type and location, and the usual attendance. Then the number of deaths, burials, and funerals was given, with an explanation of the chaplain's part in dealing with these matters. This was followed by the chaplain's analysis of the moral conditions in the hospital. An account of visitation in the wards, the distribution of literature and mail, the writing of letters, and any suggestions for the improvement of the conditions at the hospital usually concluded the report.[90]

Hospital chaplains, like regimental chaplains, were also required to conduct weekly public worship services.[91] Chaplain William Brown, who served at the Douglas Hospital in Washington, D.C., at the request of President Lincoln,[92] described these services in his manual on the military chaplaincy.[93]

In Brown's opinion, the hospital chaplain's duties centered on the room in the hospital designated as the chapel. He emphasized the need for a room suitable for this use in all army hospitals because, in his opinion, the wards were not well adapted to preaching services. There were to be formal worship services, involving a sermon, hymn singing, and the reading of Scriptures, at least once each week. Brown stressed the need to prepare carefully for these services, as the audience was often rather critical. The sermons, he said, should be short, to the point, and of a nondenominational approach, avoiding any appearance of theological polemics. The chaplain did have a singular advantage, Brown indicated, in the peculiar nature of his congregation. The men were there because of illness or injury, and many had experienced narrow escapes from death. Most of them were homesick, and many had observed, at first hand, the death of comrades. Many of them were destined to return to active duty and, hence, renewed danger in the near future. For these reasons, Brown believed that there was a readiness to listen that could be found nowhere else.[94]

Numerous other chaplains supported Brown's emphasis on the importance of these weekly worship services. Chaplain Alfred Nevin described the Sunday services he conducted at the Satterlee General Hospital in West Philadelphia. He conducted two services each Sunday plus a prayer service each Monday evening, a lecture (subject matter undisclosed) each Wednesday, and a Bible class each Friday evening. "In addition to these services," he reported, "a German minister, with our permission, preaches to the German Soldiers on Tuesday evening, and holds Bible class for them on Saturday afternoon."[95] The chapel at Satterlee Hospital was evidently a very busy place.

Chaplain M. Ambrose reported that he conducted two Sunday services each week, and a regular prayer service and Bible lecture on Thursday evenings. Other weekdays there were evening prayers in the chapel for all who were able and who desired to attend.[96] Chaplain J. J. Abbott, in his reports, indicated that there were numerous services in the hospital chapel at his station. Prayer meetings and Bible lectures were a regular practice as well.[97] Such was the substance of hundreds of monthly reports submitted by hospital chaplains to the surgeon general. They indicate that the men who served in this capacity took seriously their responsibility of providing public worship for the men confined in army hospitals.

Another responsibility of the hospital chaplains was keeping accurate records of all deaths, burials, and funerals that occurred at their posts. The information contained in these burial records was rather detailed. Included were the name and number of the soldier, the number and location of his grave, his hospital number, his regiment, company, and rank, his marital status, age, nativity, any references and remarks, and finally the date of death and burial. This involved much rather painstaking bookkeeping, and the chaplain was assisted in this task by the hospital's clerical staff. Chaplain Brown recommended that each hospital chaplain maintain a personal chaplain's register with all the vital statistics known to him of each man in his care. This would, he stated, aid the chaplain in filling out the burial record in the event of a soldier's death; it would also facilitate notifying the next of kin, a responsibility that devolved upon the chaplain at most army hospitals.[98]

The reports of the chaplains almost invariably referred to this function of recording deaths and burials, and the related duty of providing Christian or religious burial services. Frequently in these reports the chaplains mention attempts to forward mementos, last messages, and information concerning the circumstances of the soldier's death to his loved ones. Chaplain J. J. Abbott, in reporting the deaths in his hospital, attempted to assess the spiritual state of each man at death, a rather difficult task to say the least. Chaplain L. D. Ames reported that for each soldier who had died, he had conducted a "decent burial," in a well-marked grave, with appropriate funeral services. (This included one Confederate soldier who had died after capture from wounds received in battle.) Chaplain Joseph Anderson also reported his duties in connection with the deaths, and subsequent burials and funeral services, stating that he had taken measures to inform family and friends of all particulars whenever the information at his disposal permitted it.[99] This theme prevailed throughout the reports of hospital chaplains. Although it must have been distressing to have such repeated close contact with death and sorrow, this responsibility was accepted and faithfully performed by the men who served as chaplains in army hospitals.

Many hospital chaplains found their most effective ministry to be visitation at the bedside in the hospital wards. Chaplain Brown believed that men confined to their beds were frequently in a frame of mind receptive to matters of religion, much more so than were the ambulatory convalescents who had passed the medical crisis and were virtually assured of recovery. Under such circumstances, he asserted, men facing the possibility of death would respond to the tactful religious instruction of the chaplain. Brown urged that tact be exercised in conversing with the patients to guard against embarrassing them in the presence of their fellows.[100]

Chaplain Hammond was another who emphasized the importance of visitation in the wards. This bedside ministry was more deeply personal than the public worship service and hence promised greater results. The fact that a chaplain stopped to speak with the patients individually promoted a confidence that in turn evoked a good response to the Gospel. In the privacy of bedside conversation the men frequently asked questions and sought counsel, something they might have hesitated to do otherwise.[101]

The value of bedside visitation was understood and appreciated by the medical director of the Department of the Susquehanna. By Special Order Number 139, Rabbi Jacob Frankel was appointed as a visiting chaplain in Philadelphia, with the specific responsibility to visit the bedsides of the Jewish soldiers confined in all area hospitals.[102] Although not greatly detailed, the hospital chaplain's reports indicate that ward visitation was considered an important and regular function.

Another duty that occupied a large amount of the hospital chaplain's time was letter writing and the related tasks of franking letters, distributing writing supplies, and serving as a hospital postmaster. Brown emphasized the importance of regular communication with his family to the recovery of the patient. Regular communications, he said, relieved anxiety both at home and in the hospital and thus had a salutary effect on the men. It was, in his opinion, the chaplain's duty to urge his charges to write when they were able and to write for them when they were unable to write for themselves. Since it was a physical impossibility for the chaplain to accomplish this alone, he recommended that others be solicited to aid in this task. These volunteers could be convalescents, members of the surrounding community, clerical workers, or nurses.

Brown also urged chaplains to distribute writing supplies from the various agencies (the Christian Commission, the Sanitary Commission, and so on) that freely provided such items. Outgoing letters should be franked, he said, to prevent delay in homebound mail. Brown believed, however, that the chaplain should avoid, when possible, any duties as postmaster for the hospital in which he served. Acceptance of this duty tended to reduce the chaplain to the status of a clerk and should be left to hospital stewards and clerical workers.[103] Chaplain Hammond agreed with Brown in regard to the importance of regular correspondence with the home in maintaining morale and promoting recovery of the patient. In addition he urged that chaplains consider the feasibility of direct

communication with the families and friends of those who were criti-
cally ill or badly wounded. He also emphasized the fact that materials
for distribution among the men were available and should be utilized
by the chaplains.[104]

The chaplains serving in the hospitals within the Department of the
Cumberland (eastern Kentucky and Tennessee) were directed by depart-
mental headquarters "to write the letters of such of the Patients as are
unable *from any cause* to write their own letters." Furthermore it was
the duty of the chaplain "to attend to the Post Office Department of
the Hospital, a reliable messenger being detailed by the Surgeon in
Charge, as his assisstant [*sic*]."[105] The reports generally indicate that
this function was regularly undertaken by hospital chaplains regardless
of location. Although it was a time-consuming task for them, it must
have been appreciated by the men and their families.

Both Brown and Hammond urged that hospital chaplains make a
strenuous effort to provide suitable recreational facilities for their patients. They were opposed to gambling but believed that "good games"
(checkers, backgammon, chess, and so on) had both recreational and
therapeutic value; these games should be supplied and the men encouraged to participate. Musical activities were also proposed as diversion
during the dreary hours of hospital confinement, and practical hobbies
were encouraged. Lectures, reading classes, and instruction in various
fields of common interest were suggested as a positive means of sus-
taining the spirit of the men while they convalesced.[106]

Library facilities and good periodical literature, religious and secular,
were considered indispensable to chaplains, and they were advised to
consider the supervision of hospital libraries and reading rooms to be an
important duty. Chaplain Alfred Nevin reported that he supervised a
library containing more than 2,400 volumes for the use of patients in the
hospital where he was stationed. In addition to these volumes, which
circulated on a loan basis, he was able to distribute large amounts of religious reading material, donated by the Christian Commission and religious publishing houses.[107] Chaplain Rodney Gage reported his interest
in obtaining additions for his modest library. Although the library contained "a good variety, for the various intellectual tastes," it was barely
sufficient for the number of men who used it. He also distributed magazines and pamphlets freely when he could obtain them and stated his
strong belief that such reading matter had been instrumental in elevating the moral condition of the hospital generally.[108] Chaplain M.
Allington reported the acquisition of 300 volumes of "major importance"

and 4,000 "lesser volumes" to form a hospital library. He had also been able to distribute more than 2,500 "copies of literature of a religious nature" donated by an unnamed benefactor.[109] These are but a few examples of many such reports by hospital chaplains. Brown and Hammond in their handbooks for chaplains both endorsed the idea of hospital libraries supervised by chaplains. Both also stated that aid in forming libraries and in procuring literature for free distribution could be sought from the United States Christian Commission.[110]

Like their regimental counterparts, hospital chaplains expressed an interest in promoting temperance in the army. Several reported that they had formed temperance societies in their hospitals. Chaplain Alfred Nevin noted that he had organized a temperance society for the patients at his hospital and that the programs it produced (lectures, literature, and so on) were financed by the contributions of interested citizens of the surrounding community.[111] Chaplain Nelson Brakeman reported that he conducted a temperance meeting each Wednesday evening for those who were interested. He stated that "485 men and officers within the fort [had] pledged themselves to abstain from the use of all intoxicating drinks as a beverage."[112] Chaplain C. Brewster, stationed at an army hospital in Readville, Massachusetts, reported his efforts to promote temperance and complained of the people in the vicinity whose influence was thwarting him. "There are persons," he stated, "who infest the neighborhood and have at times actually made their way into the wards, who furnish liquor to the soldiers, and whose influence in other aspects is corrupting in the extreme." He objected strongly to the presence of such people in an army hospital and urged that they be denied admittance.[113] Reports such as these are common among the regular monthly reports filed in the records of the Surgeon General's Office.

It is evident that the chaplain was expected to be a clerical jack-of-all-trades. Probably no chaplain, regardless of competence, could have been satisfactory to every regiment or in every hospital. The characteristics that pleased the men of one regiment might well have been considered undesirable by the men of another command. If any single quality was necessary, however, for chaplains in the Union armies who desired to perform competently the multiplicity of duties confronting them, it was flexibility. Although the duties of the chaplaincy demanded endless energy and unlimited patience, devotion to duty, and constancy of conviction, the man who could not bend to the extra-ordinary circumstances produced by a great civil war could not gain the confidence of his men and ultimately found himself rejected by those whom he had hoped to serve. Many resigned, disappointed, disgusted, or disillusioned. Far greater, however, was the number who remained to serve and who, by their service, captured the affections and the respect of their comrades.

3

THE SHEPHERD AND HIS FLOCK

To assess the extent and effect of the chaplains' ministry in the army and its hospitals, it is important to know what they thought of the men they served and, in return, how they were regarded by those men. In their memoirs and reports the chaplains recorded their views, favorable and unfavorable, of the officers and men to whom they ministered. They frequently referred to obstacles encountered in their service as chaplains as well as to occasional encouragement. They also mentioned the cooperative spirit that prevailed among chaplains of many denominations. By the same token the soldiers frequently recorded in their journals, some of which were later published, their impressions of the "army preachers."[1] From a sampling of these sources it is possible to reconstruct a fair picture of the general relationship between chaplains and men during the Civil War. The danger here lies in the tendency to adopt a stereotypical view when, in all probability, no such thing as a "typical example" of such relationships exists.

Most of the men who entered the army of the United States as chaplains between 1861 and 1865 did so in the spirit of service. Since their duties involved, basically, attendance to the religious needs of the men and the promotion of morality, they tended to view the men accordingly. In fact, chaplains were required to include in their reports a statement concerning the moral condition of the regiment or hospital they served together with suggestions for improvements. As a result, much of every report and many pages of memoirs written later concern vices prevalent in the army. Also mentioned frequently is the chaplain's understanding of his personal relationship with the men he served and the manner in which he attempted to promote that relationship. Naturally each chaplain had a somewhat different view of such circumstances; consequently the best means of determining the chaplains' attitudes toward their men is by examining their memoirs and official reports.

Many chaplains reported that one of the chief obstacles to successful performance of their duties was resistance on the part of many officers to all religious activities. Complaints concerning such hindrances abound in the chaplains' reports and memoirs. Chaplain James J. Marks (Sixty-third Pennsylvania Infantry), commenting on the persecution many chaplains endured at the hands of antagonistic commanding officers, stated that "so far as the appointment of chaplains [was] concerned, it was evidently a concession made to the religious sentiment of the country—one of those formless, shapeless things thrown in to fill up a vacuum." He went on to say that in many regiments chaplains were tolerated only because the use of their names gave a moral tone to the regiment and aided in securing enlistments.[2]

Others echoed the theme. An outside observer, the Reverend P. V. Ferree, a minister in the Ohio Conference of the Methodist Episcopal Church, wrote of the obstacles his fellow ministers faced in the army. "In the majority of cases," he said, "the chaplain is only *tolerated* in the army, not appreciated or assisted. Numerous obstacles are thrown in his way." According to Ferree, many chaplains were actually driven from the army by the determined opposition of officers.[3] Chaplain George S. Bradley (Twenty-second Wisconsin Infantry), in a discussion of the hindrances he encountered and the difficulty of living a Christian life in the army (as either a soldier or a chaplain), listed as the number one problem the irreligious nature of the officers. "Most of the officers," he stated, "are irreligious men, and make light of religion. . . . It would seem frequently as though officers took especial pains to fill up the day [Sunday] with marching, camp duties, reviews or fighting." Open antagonism such as this, he believed, discouraged many professedly Christian men from even attempting to maintain their religious standards in the army, thereby further increasing the difficulty of the chaplain's task.[4] And not every regiment was guided by religious concerns in the selection of a chaplain. One New York regiment composed largely of men of German descent selected a surgeon as chaplain, preferring to have an additional doctor to having a man of the cloth.[5]

Hospital chaplains too felt the opposition of surgeons in charge of the hospitals. One such instance involved Dr. John Campbell, the surgeon in charge at Satterlee General Hospital in west Philadelphia. The doctor had adopted a set of rules governing the activities of the chaplain that were apparently very restrictive. Complaints of the physician's hostility reached the office of the surgeon general in Washington; this led to the appointment of an experienced chaplain, the Reverend Alfred Nevin, and to a letter from Joseph K. Barnes, then acting surgeon general, to Campbell directing him to be more accommodating to chaplains in the future. Barnes wrote: "I desire to call your personal attention, to the necessity that exists, for more liberty of action in the execution of ministerial duties within that hospital." The surgeon general continued: "The rules adopted by the Surgeon in Charge, are complained of by the entire Presbytery of Philadelphia as exclusive, the chaplain only being allowed to visit the bedside of a patient, upon his request. Experience has shown that the labors of an earnest and zealous Chaplain, add to, rather than diminish military discipline, and harmonize with all necessary regulations." The reports of Chaplain Nevin following the incident indicate that the doctor became a more amiable commander after receiving the missive from the surgeon general.[6]

Chaplain M. Allington, who served at Army Hospital No. 14 in Nashville, Tennessee, experienced a vast change in his relationship with his surgeon in charge. On October 21, 1864, the chaplain submitted a precise and encouraging report detailing the duties he had performed, concluding with a statement that the services were well attended and that he had experienced no obstacles to the performance of his responsibilities. Just three months later, on January 21, 1865, Allington's report was of a different tenor. The room he had used as a chapel had been taken from him, dances were held in the wards (he objected to the impropriety of clapping hands and stamping feet in the presence of dying men), and he had been threatened by the citizens sponsoring the dances and by the surgeon in charge, who "surpassed them if possible in blasphemy." He concluded by stating that he hoped the time would come when "a chaplain may rebuke gross inconsistency of a surgeon & citizens with out being removed from the scene of his labors." No explanation is given for this change of climate, but apparently a personality conflict of major proportions had developed during the fall and winter months.[7]

The dispute between Chaplain Henry N. Hudson (First New York Engineers) and General Benjamin F. Butler was probably the most widely publicized example of friction between a chaplain and an army commander. Hudson was fairly well known in New York as an authority on Shakespeare, and because of his abilities as a writer he frequently sent letters concerning military matters to the New York *Evening Post.* After Butler's failure to take the city of Petersburg, Virginia, during the spring campaign of 1864, the chaplain wrote a lengthy letter to the *Evening Post* praising two of Butler's subordinates and criticizing But-

ler for timidity and incompetence. The letter was published anony-
mously with editorial comments to the effect that Butler's blunders had
cost the army a chance for a stunning victory.[8]

A short time later Hudson was sent to New York on a special assignment and was granted permission to visit his family. While he was there
his son died of illness, and both he and his wife became seriously ill.
When he received orders directly from General Butler to rejoin his command immediately, he reported to his colonel who was also then in New
York. As the colonel had no further orders for him, Hudson submitted
his resignation, which the colonel approved and forwarded through
channels to Butler. General Butler's immediate response was an order
to the chaplain to give his parole to return to the army at once or be
sent in arrest and under guard. Hudson gave his parole and returned to
the army camp at Bermuda Hundred, where he was interrogated by
Butler about his writing career, rebuked, and subsequently confined for
fifty days in the stockade. When the chaplain demanded either a trial
or release he was returned to his regiment but was not permitted to leave
it for any cause. General Grant investigated the case at this point, at
the request of Hudson's friends. The chaplain was given a leave of absence to extend throughout the period left in his term of service.[9]

Subsequently Hudson published an account of his difficulties with
General Butler. In it he charged Butler with attempting to blame subordinates for personal blunders and with punishing him because he
would not make statements to support these contentions. Butler replied
in a broadside of forty-eight pages, accusing Hudson of fabrication and
stating that the chaplain had confessed to absence without leave.[10]

It is not possible to untangle the maze of conflicting evidence presented in this bitter exchange, but neither man emerges blameless from
the encounter. This is, however, a rather extreme example of the friction that was a possibility, and occasionally an actuality, between a
chaplain and his commander.

The blame for difficulties with the officers did not always lie with
the officers. The Reverend George Leakin, a hospital chaplain at
McKim's Mansion Hospital in Baltimore, experienced difficulty in drawing his pay because the surgeon in charge, Dr. S. D. Freeman, would
not sign an affidavit stating that the chaplain had been present for duty
during the period in question. When Leakin reported this to the surgeon general's office, an investigation revealed that he was also the
pastor of a local church and that he spent much of his time away from
the hospital. A note from the surgeon general's office stated that since

the doctor would not and the chaplain could not, in good conscience, state that he had been present for duty, the remedy was "in the proper performance of his duties for the future." The suggestion bore fruit, as the chaplain's service record indicates the regularity of his duty from that time forward.[11]

Chaplain Charles McCabe (122nd Ohio Infantry) got into difficulty with his colonel through his own doing. The chaplain held a "protracted meeting," which ran over the scheduled time for dress parade, and was rebuked for it by the colonel. His initial reaction, anger, turned to chagrin when he reconsidered the situation, and on the following day he sought out the colonel to tell him, "Colonel, you were right and I was wrong; henceforth I will obey orders." With the air cleared the chaplain experienced no further conflict with his commander.[12]

But if some chaplains experienced much difficulty, deserved or undeserved, with their commanding officers, many others reported that their commanders lent them full support and encouragement. One of these was Father William Corby (Eighty-eighth New York Infantry), who enjoyed the full cooperation of the colonel commanding the regiment and also of the brigade commander, General T. F. Meagher. The general frequently assigned men to assist Corby in setting up a chapel or an altar or to such other work necessary to the proper religious functions of the chaplain. Such a spirit of cooperation was gratifying to Father Corby, and he expressed his high opinion of officers of this caliber.[13]

Chaplain Charles A. Humphreys (Second Massachusetts Cavalry) believed that though his youth and inexperience (he had been ordained as a chaplain directly from Harvard Seminary) were something of a handicap in his ministry, he nevertheless enjoyed a good relationship with the officers of the regiment. "My relations to the officers," he said, "are of the pleasantest kind. I have their respect and so far as I know their confidence."[14] Chaplain John R. Adams (Fifth Maine and 121st New York) was another who commented on the cooperative spirit of the officers with whom he served. He was especially grateful, he remarked, for the example of sobriety set by the officers of the 121st New York. None of them used whiskey, and their temperance in language and their general demeanor proved to be a positive asset to the chaplain in his promotion of morality in the regiment.[15]

The chaplain of the Tweny-fourth Indiana Infantry, the Reverend W. F. Harned, believed that strict camp discipline was of great assistance to any chaplain, and he commended his commanding officer, Colonel W. T. Spicely, for his strictness in "restraining intemperance and immorality and encouraging the men to attend church." The fact that the colonel and many other officers attended worship services regularly promoted attendance generally, in the chaplain's opinion.[16]

Chaplain Henry Clay Trumbull (Tenth Connecticut) gave an unusually fine tribute to the cooperative spirit of both officers and men as he reviewed his duties with the regiment. "In all my work," he reported, "I have had the hearty cooperation of the officers and the grateful appreciation of the men, and I give God thanks for the pleasantness of my sphere here."[17]

Nor were commanding generals entirely insensitive to the difficulty of promoting religion and morality in an army. The incompatibility of war and religion was in reality the basic difficulty all chaplains faced. The mission of the army in war is to defeat the enemy, to conquer by force, which inevitably means death and destruction; hence it makes few plans for means by which a clergyman in uniform can advance the religious ideals of love, peace, and mercy. Yet on certain occasions recognition of the nation's dependence on God was granted.

One such occasion was on September 6, 1861, when General George B. McClellan, commanding the Army of the Potomac, issued General Order Number 7, directing all officers and men to exhibit a greater respect for the Sabbath. Commanding officers were advised to suspend all work and avoid any unnecessary moves on Sunday. Officers and men were also urged to attend the regular worship services following the regular Sunday morning inspection. The order concluded: "One day's rest in seven is necessary to men and animals: more than this, the observation of the holy day of the God of mercy and of battles is our sacred duty." A few weeks later, on November 27, McClellan reinforced this order by specifically directing that the Sunday inspection be terminated by the time set for public worship, with an added warning to officers against hindering the men's attendance.[18]

President Lincoln too urged the careful observance of the Sabbath in the army. On November 15, 1862, an executive order was published directing that all Sunday labor be reduced to "the measure of strict necessity." The president said, "The discipline and character of the national forces should not suffer, nor the cause they defend be imperiled, by the profanation of the day or name of the Most High." He went on to quote George Washington as an example of a commander with proper concern for the welfare of his men: "At this time of public distress men may find enough to do in the service of God and their country without abandoning themselves to vice and immorality. The General hopes and trusts that every officer and man will endeavor to live and act as becomes a Christian soldier defending the dearest rights and liberties of his country."[19] Support such as that of McClellan and Lincoln was certainly welcomed by the chaplains of the army, and though the effect on officers who had been inclined to hinder is not measurable, it is probable that overt opposition to the chaplains was sharply curtailed.

Chaplains frequently commented on the vices prevalent in an army camp—profanity, drunkenness, gambling, and Sabbath-breaking were most frequently mentioned—occasionally attempting to explain such conduct and the difficulty of eliminating it from army life. In his final monthly report, written while his regiment (the Twenty-first Wisconsin Infantry) was waiting to be mustered out of service at the conclusion of the war, Chaplain O. P. Clinton commented on the moral condition of his men, noting that their conduct while in the army was determined largely by their background and previous associations. Those of good character previous to their duty as soldiers maintained it, and vice versa. Few, he thought, were greatly changed by their army experiences. Clinton concluded the report with a word of praise for the faithfulness and bravery his fellow officers and the men exhibited. His report said: "In regard to the moral condition of this Regiment, I am warranted in saying, the men of generous impulses and manly purpose before entering the service with [few] exceptions have conducted themselves with propriety, maintaining their self respect as good soldiers; and will return to their friends with good names and a matured manhood. The reverse is true of those whose early associations were unfortunate; who had lived to no legitimate purpose, and never care to rise above the lower strata of humanity." Clinton concluded: "Too much praise cannot be accorded to the officers and men of this command for faithfulness and bravery as true soldiers. Their work is now done; and they return to their homes and peaceful avocations with the pleasing consciousness of having done what they could for their afflicted country."[20] He apparently understood the influence of background on men's character and did not expect or insist that all men conform to his concept of proper deportment.

In composing his monthly report for January 1864, Chaplain Humphreys stated his uncertainty as to the religious sentiment and status of the regiment. He was concerned about the profanity rife in the ranks and also among the officers. "Regard or respect for my office," he said, "restrain profanity in my presence; I would that regard for God would restrain it everywhere." He nevertheless considered the moral condition of the regiment generally good, especially when the men were removed from temptation, chief of which was alcohol.[21]

Chaplain James B. Rogers (Fourteenth Wisconsin Infantry) stated his belief that profanity and Sabbath-breaking were the two chief vices of the men who composed the Union armies, and of all groups the teamsters were by far the most profane. He criticized the officers for failing to repress the evil and even encouraging it by their own profane example.[22] Chaplain Adams admonished profanity tactfully by tapping the offending individual on the shoulder and remarking, "I hope God will not hear that prayer of yours." This gentle approach proved far more successful than a stern lecture, and his "influence upon the regiment was marked. Profanity was much less frequently heard."[23]

Chaplain Trumbull reported that the addition of new recruits to fill out the regiment, many of them paid substitutes, had a detrimental effect on the moral condition of the regiment. The newer men were inclined to desertion, robberies (never a problem previously) were frequent, "and gambling and profanity . . . called for frequent checking." His method of checking profanity was clever: he told the men that he had been authorized by the colonel to do all the swearing necessary and urged them to send for him if there was a need for profanity. This approach did not eradicate all swearing, but the men responded favorably to the chaplain's tact and wit.[24]

Thomas Drumm, a hospital chaplain in Alexandria, Virginia, reported that one of the two hospitals he visited regularly was remarkably free from profane language while the other was foul with it, a situation he couldn't explain. Both hospitals were plagued by rampant gambling, however, and the chaplain regretted the poor example of the staff.[25] Chaplain Rodney Gage (Third Division General Hospital, Alexandria, Virginia) reported that profanity was rampant in the wards of the hospital, although it tended to diminish when his presence was known. "There is much profanity among a portion of the men," he stated, "and I am sorry to say, all the officers are not freem [*sic*] from this sin. There have also been a few cases of intemperance of an alarming character." Gage also noted the prevalence of gambling, which he believed should be prohibited. "It is my opinion that if some restrictions could be placed on 'Card playing,' it would improve the moral tendencies of the hospital. . . . It can no longer be pleaded as an excuse 'that they have nothing else they can do.' The 'Library' . . . now contains a good variety, for the various intellectual tastes."[26] Chaplain Joseph Anderson (Barrack and St. Mary's Hospitals, Detroit) believed that profanity was the glaring vice in the army. Although no gambling or intemperance plagued the hospital, profanity met him everywhere.[27]

The chaplain of the Second Colorado Cavalry, the Reverend Lewis Hamilton, in reporting on the moral status of his regiment, stated that though only a small minority of the men professed to be Christians, there were few, if any, he considered immoral. Both officers and men were, he reported, addicted to constant profanity and were indifferent to the sanctity of the Sabbath. Intemperance, though it did exist, was a relatively minor problem, but gambling at cards was common, to the great distress of many soldiers' needy families. But despite the size of the challenge he faced, Hamilton was convinced that the preaching of the gospel would be effective if only more men could be induced to attend the services.[28]

Yet many chaplains were convinced of the efficacy of their ministry, in spite of the vices so prevalent in the army. Chaplain L. S. Chittenden (Twenty-fourth Indiana Infantry) reported a great religious revival in his regiment. In less than a month there had been one hundred conversions, and thirty-seven men had been baptized. Nightly meetings were crowded, and the revival continued until marching orders brought the meetings to an end.[29] Chaplain Marks recounted his regiment's enthusiastic response to the gospel during the winter months of 1862–1863. He stated: "During these months, hundreds in the camp found the highest joy in religious meetings, and with ever new pleasure they came together to hear the gospel. . . . It was a time of great searchings of heart, and for many weeks my tent was crowded at all hours, when the men were off duty, by those wishing to know the way of life."[30] Chaplain Lafayette Church, Twenty-sixth Michigan Infantry, reported that he held prayer services in the men's quarters four evenings a week at *their* request. The interest in these meetings, already high, was on the increase, he reported, and there was a general surge of religious interest in the regiment. Some had experienced conversion, and others were asking how they too might gain salvation.[31] Private Wilbur Fisk of the Second Vermont Infantry also commented about the effectiveness of such nondenominational religious meetings. He said: "No sectarianism or bigotry marred the harmony of the meetings. Nobody inquired of another if he was a Methodist, a Baptist, or an Episcopalian, and no one seemed to care for religious preferences. If a man was Christian, it was enough. The first Sabbath of this month the sacrament of the Lord's Supper was partaken of by about thirty communicants. Eleven made a profession of faith, and three were baptized."[32]

Chaplain Gage never failed to determine, if possible, the spiritual condition of every man who passed through the hospital he served. In reporting the deaths, he recorded his personal impression as to whether each soldier had been prepared to die, and in every case he did his utmost to provide every soldier with the opportunity to hear the gospel carefully explained, to accept or reject as each might choose. A random sample from such a report stated: "Robert Johnson, Co. E., 138 PA., died at McVeigh Branch, Dec. 20th, 1863. After he was wounded he sought the Lord; & I believe he died trusting in the merits of Christ's atonement."[33]

Chaplain A. S. Billingsley (101st Pennsylvania Infantry, serving on detached duty at the First Division General Hospital, Fortress Monroe, Virginia) was convinced that the men confined in the wards of the hospital where he served appreciated his efforts on their behalf, and he saw positive evidence of spiritual change in many of them. He reported: "I often read the Bible, exhort, sing, and pray with them. [I] have many precious interviews with them, often leaving them bathed in tears. They appreciate it highly and are grateful. Conversions are frequent. Many of the soldiers die happy, triumphant deaths."[34]

Such accounts are commonplace. Perhaps Chaplain Francis McNeill most nearly perceived the difficulty of determining the character of the "inner man" in another man, and yet accurately read the deep longing of the soldier's heart: "It is difficult to report upon the moral and religious conditions of the men. . . . One feeling possesses all minds, controlling every purpose of heart and soul—to be mustered out of the service and permitted to go home."[35]

Although sectarian differences could have hampered the chaplains' work, remarkably few instances of denominational friction were reported. For several decades before the Civil War, the Methodist Episcopal and Baptist Churches had enjoyed phenomenal growth in this country, especially in the Midwest. The members and pastors of these churches, who were accustomed to an emotional evangelism with minimum emphasis on form, ritual, and sacraments, tended to distrust the churches that did emphasize a liturgical worship, especially the Roman Catholic Church, with which they had had a very limited contact. The growth of the Catholic Church had been, during the same period, largely due to immigration, which to many Protestants made Catholicism seem somehow un-American. On the other hand, Catholics, Episcopalians,

Lutherans, and members of other liturgically oriented churches tended to distrust the informal worship of their critics.[36]

An example of such mutual skepticism was recorded by Father Corby. The chaplain had been called to counsel with a deserter who had been condemned to death and was awaiting execution. Corby wished to prepare the man for death through the sacraments of baptism, confession, communion, and Extreme Unction. He was resisted, however, by a Protestant chaplain (name and denomination not known) who insisted that ritual was unnecessary, that faith alone was sufficient for salvation. When it became apparent that a mutual distrust was about to deprive the unfortunate soldier of any religious solace, Corby asked the other chaplain if he believed that baptism would *harm* the man. When the chaplain replied negatively, Corby then asked if there was any objection to his baptizing the man since it would do no harm. Faced with this proposal, the Protestant chaplain withdrew his opposition, and Corby proceeded to baptize the condemned man.[37]

Far more frequent, however, are the references to a spirit of cordiality and cooperation in the army chaplaincy. Chaplain Trumbull described a joint service that he and an unnamed Catholic chaplain conducted for the men of their regiments. It was a simple but dignified service without sectarian characteristics; both he and the priest addressed the men, receiving a good response. "In the long run," he recalled, "there was no practical hindrance to my work as a chaplain as growing out of the differences between Catholics and Protestants." Cooperation among the various faiths, in his experience, was the general rule.[38]

Chaplain William Lyle (Eleventh Ohio Infantry) also noted the cooperation that generally prevailed among chaplains of the various faiths. It was most evident, he believed, in the manner by which regimental and brigade churches were formed. Forms of baptism, confirmation, and other subjects likely to cause controversy if rigidly defined were posited on a broad interdenominational or, rather, nondenominational basis, thus avoiding the possible bitterness of denominational rivalries.[39] Chaplain Arthur B. Fuller (Sixteenth Massachusetts Infantry) attested to the cordial relationship he enjoyed with chaplains who represented other faiths. He stated that in his own ministry he attempted to avoid any sectarian characteristics in deference to the many faiths represented in his regiment.[40]

Chaplain Adams reported that he conducted a joint communion service with a chaplain from another regiment (and denomination). Both strove to keep the service nonsectarian, and men of many denominations freely partook without hesitation. He frequently attended the services of other chaplains, inviting them in turn to attend his own. On one occasion, he attended a joint hospital service, conducted by twelve chaplains in cooperation, and expressed his belief that it had been a profitable experience to see such harmony in the ministry.[41]

Chaplain Rogers spoke warmly of the spirit of cordiality that prevailed in his relationship with chaplains of other faiths. He recalled that "some of them were of denominations different from my own, yet they were Christ's true followers and . . . I am happy to say that this union of Christians on the platform of their common faith is no unusual thing in the army. It were well if all Christians had more of this mutual love; not limiting themselves by the bounds of their own church associations."[42]

The friendships that developed from the close associations of men who fought, marched, and lived together during the war years did much to allay suspicion and religious bigotry. Father B. C. Christy of the Seventy-eighth Pennsylvania Infantry believed that "the few years of the war did more to allay the bigotry of the protestant minds, than fifty years of civil life could have possibly done." Although Protestant soldiers (and chaplains) at first distrusted the Catholic chaplains, they gradually developed a respect and affection for the priests that were carried home at the war's conclusion, helping to promote religious tolerance.[43] Corby, despite his trying experience described earlier, reported that generally his working relationship with Protestant chaplains was excellent, and he believed that the war had promoted interfaith understanding. He quoted an unnamed Protestant captain as saying, "One good result of the Civil War was the removing of a great amount of prejudice. When men stand in common danger, a fraternal feeling springs up between them and generates a Christian, charitable sentiment that often leads to excellent results."[44] Corby was in full accord with the captain's statement.

Nearly fifty years after his service in the chaplaincy, the Reverend William R. Eastman recalled with fondness the cooperation among the ministers who served the soldiers. He illustrated this spirit, which would then have seemed truly remarkable to the denominations at home, by relating the experience of two of his friends in the chaplaincy, Joseph Twichell and Father Joseph O'Hagen. These two men, one a Catholic priest and the other a New England Unitarian, were sleeping together for warmth at Fredericksburg one cold December night just after the battle, when Father O'Hagen began to laugh. "'What are you laughing at?' demanded Twichell. 'At this condition of things,' was the reply. 'What? at all this horrible distress?' 'No! No! but at you and me; a Jesuit priest and a New England Puritan minister—of the worst sort—spooned close together under the same blanket. I wonder what the angels think.' And a moment after, he added, 'I think they like it.'"[45]

One assessment of the chaplains who served the Union armies was essentially negative. "Relatively few became honored and indispensable pastors to their regiments." And again: "Except for a few able and dedicated ministers, the army was forced to take either the young and untried or the civilian cast-offs."[46] In opposition to that gloomy characterization it seems more nearly accurate to say that information sufficient to determine the details of a chaplain's ministry is available about relatively few of those who served in that capacity. What is most likely is that the "average" chaplain performed his duty conscientiously if not spectacularly and like the "average" soldier returned to the relative obscurity of civilian life when the war ended and the muster rolls were closed. Only those who wrote memoirs and those whose service attracted the attention of others are known sufficiently to judge the degree of esteem with which their men regarded them. Certainly the chaplains who recorded their experiences have not agreed with the contention that relatively few of them were successful in their ministry, a criticism, incidentally, with which they were forced to contend during the war.[47]

Chaplain George Whitfield Pepper (Eightieth Ohio Infantry) bitterly assailed those who denigrated the chaplaincy. He asserted that "those who have had the best opportunities for observing army life, pronounce emphatically in favor of the chaplaincy. A set of reckless newspaper reporters and hypocritical legislators, have used every method to misrepresent and ignore the services of Clergymen in the field."[48] Worthless officers who for the first time in their lives were clothed with authority were given credence when they spoke contemptuously of dedicated army ministers. Pepper continued: "It is false, meanly false, to denounce all Chaplains as worthless." There was not a class of men in the army who commanded the respect, *without* the aid of rank, that the chaplains did. His rebuttal concluded with these stirring words: "*It is true, and it is a pity that it is true,* that there have been drones among the army chaplains—a class of uneducated impostors, who have easily yielded to the demoralization of camp life, associating with officers in their habits of profanity, drunkenness, and other like vices. But to measure the whole class by these exceptions, to deny all the good the order has performed, to detract from the benign influence it radiates through the land, and to undermine the confidence of the people in these conservators of the public heart, is cruel, uncalled for, and iniquitous."[49]

The possibility of the appointment of "drones" and "uneducated impostors" as chaplains stemmed from the early legislation governing qualification, selection, and appointment. The Act of July 22, 1861, required only that appointees be ordained Christian ministers.[50] Many denominations, in fact practically every Protestant group, found it necessary to rely on lay preachers because of the shortage of fully educated clergy. Variously referred to as "lay readers," "local preachers," "lay preachers," or "lay pastors," these men were especially numerous in rural or undeveloped areas of the country that proved unattractive to clergy with regular training. Some denominations, most notably the Baptists and Methodists, had no set educational requirements for ordination in that era; in such churches, anyone who could convince an ordination council called by a local congregation that God had called him into the ministry could obtain ordination. In one instance, "certain local preachers (lay preachers) of the Methodist Episcopal Church, in Pennsylvania especially, had obtained ordination at the hands of an independent Congregational Church, for the sole purpose of becoming chaplains in the army." Regular church officials deprecated this situation and refused to recognize the ordinations as valid.[51]

By the end of 1861 the War Department had received some reports concerning unsatisfactory chaplains. On December 5, 1861, Benjamin F. Larned, paymaster general of the army, wrote to Senator Henry Wilson of Massachusetts regarding the situation, stating: "I regret to say that very many holding this position are utterly unworthy, and while I would not deprive our regiments of the service of a minister of the gospel, I think none should be appointed who did not come recommended by the highest ecclesiastical authority with which they are connected."[52] Subsequently Congress raised the qualifications for appointment. The Act of July 17, 1862, required that before a prospective chaplain could be mustered into the army he must present either recommendations from the ecclesiastical body with which he was connected or the endorsement of five accredited ministers of his denomination.[53] With this elevation of the standards for qualification as a chaplain, it would seem that any dissatisfaction with a chaplain on the part of the officer who made the appointment—after consulting his men and subordinate officers—was the fault of the officers and men themselves for having chosen poorly.[54]

Individual chaplains were not above legitimate criticism, however, as not every chaplain was a model for the men he served. James Kidd, who served in General George Armstrong Custer's Michigan Cavalry Brigade, noted that his chaplain was "not at all fitted for the hardships and exposure . . . and it was much as he could do to look after his own physical well-being, and the spiritual condition of his flock was apt to be sadly neglected." The problem was that "soldiers were moving away from chaplains as rapidly as they charged that chaplains were drifting away from them. Combat could no longer be fitted easily within Christian precepts, and in men impelled to resolve that tension, religious ordinances could be suppressed as the daily experience of war could not."[55] Criticism continued throughout the war, however, and in May 1864, Chaplain S. K. Berridge, in apparent exasperation, wrote to the surgeon general demanding to know why, "if chaplains were of no value as frequently charged," did not Congress repeal the legislation providing for their appointment.[56]

Chaplain William Young Brown believed that despite the criticisms leveled at the chaplains, the chaplaincy was "the greatest instrument by which the moral and religious forces of the Church" sought to influence for good the men of the army. Without chaplains, he believed, other agencies would do something for the soldiers, but their efforts would be "occasional, fitful, and of little permanent value." The practical issue, then, was not to attack the chaplains but to determine whether they were worthwhile, and then either to sustain them or permanently terminate religious services in the army. Criticism of the men who were doing their utmost to provide for the spiritual welfare of the soldiers was not, in his opinion, the proper means of curing the alleged ills in the chaplaincy. He concluded that "if its present organization is deficient let the law be amended. If he is subjected to unreasonable control of irreligious men, and his services liable to be interfered with by them, let him be disenthralled from such a position. If his legal status is anomalous and uninfluential, give him rank and official position, suited to his high character as a man, and the dignity of his ministerial office. If he is not held to sufficient accountability, give him a responsible head, and hold the department accountable for the efficiency of each of its members. But let him be sustained."[57]

Without doubt there were chaplains who failed to live up to the standards expected of ministers. Chaplain Lyle contrasted the conduct of two chaplains he knew. One of them (whom he did not name) was lazy; he was unwilling to expose himself to danger during engagements and would not soil his hands to aid the wounded. Instead, he was contented to deliver his one sermon a week and to watch the battle from the safety of the rear while enjoying a good cigar. The other, a Chaplain Grimes of the Ninety-second Ohio Infantry, worked constantly on behalf of his men, aiding the surgeons, carrying water and ammunition, and comforting the dying at all hours, in addition to all his other duties. He was finally forced to resign, Lyle reported, when his health was broken. For the first man, Lyle noted, he had nothing but loathing; for Chaplain Grimes he had a deep admiration and appreciation.[58]

The men respected the chaplain who did his best for them, and they detested those who seemed callous and unconcerned. One soldier stated that the men judged a chaplain in four ways. First, was he religiously fit? Second, was he physically fit (a chaplain should be able to care for himself)? Third, was he "acquainted with the animal 'man'"? And fourth, did he possess honest "horse sense"? Each chaplain, he explained, was measured by these qualities, which the men believed were desirable. Chaplain A was a good man, but he lacked tact. He was always looking about the camp for things to correct, and he could not understand why his stern lectures on cursing provoked derision. Chaplain B was lazy. He delivered "an army sermon on Sunday and nothing else the rest of the week." Chaplain C was too conscious of his rank. He was afraid to see life as the soldier viewed it, remaining aloof and cool. "Of the three, the boys hate the first, despise the second, and d__n the third." Upon hearing one chaplain say of himself that he was decomposed, the soldier commented, "Now a drunken General and a 'decomposed' Chaplain are about as useless lumber as can cumber an army." Chaplain D, however, though he got along poorly at first and was the butt of many jokes, found the proper point of contact with the men when he helped them by carrying water during the Battle of Chickamauga. The men did not forget the concern displayed by the chaplain, and his ministry among them became deeply appreciated.[59]

The men also appreciated the "down to earth" chaplain. One such army preacher demonstrated a practical concern about the diet of the men in his regiment and often went foraging for supplies to supplement the military diet. An officer commented: "He is a terrible forager, this valiant young son of the prophets. He makes frequent pilgrimages after provisions for his flock and helps personally towards devouring the substance of the enemy. Some days ago he presented himself at regimental headquarters and said, 'Colonel, the health of this battalion requires sweet potatoes, and I should like permission to take up a contribution. By the way, it is Sunday, I believe. If I get back early enough, I shall preach this afternoon.' Off he went with a couple of soldiers, impressed a plough and a pair of mules at a plantation, and returned with a load of vegetables."[60] Certainly this "shepherd" cared for his "flock."

Ezra Sprague, a Universalist minister who had enlisted in the 119th New York Infantry as a private soldier, was promoted to the chaplaincy of that regiment when the former chaplain resigned. He had served in his new capacity slightly longer than six months when charges and specifications were brought against him for (1) failing to make the required quarterly reports, (2) slander of another officer, (3) stealing oats, and (4) misuse of government property. Unfortunately the records of the court-martial proceedings are lost, and the disposition of this case is unknown; however, the charges are an indication that chaplains were held as strictly accountable for their behavior as any other officer.[61]

Charges and specifications were also brought against Chaplain Hermann Bokum who served at Turner's Lane General Hospital. Dr. Robert Cushman, the surgeon in charge, charged Bokum with overstaying a thirty-day leave granted on August 27, 1864. The chaplain did not return to duty until November 4, 1864. Charges were brought on the following day; however, the War Department, for an undisclosed reason, extended the leave to include November 15. Consequently, the charges were returned to the surgeon, who in turn ordered that they be dropped.[62]

Chaplain C. J. Bowen, who served at the Camden Street General Hospital in Baltimore, was reported by the surgeon in charge for repeated tardiness for scheduled funerals at which it was his duty to officiate, and also for ordering the sergeant not to detail a military escort for the funeral procession as the surgeon had ordered. There is no record of proceedings against Bowen, however, and he was honorably discharged on June 10, 1865, when his services were no longer needed.[63]

Henry Hudson, for all his difficulties with General Butler (described earlier), resigned and was given an honorable discharge on February 10, 1865, by Special Order Number 66, paragraph 20, from the Adjutant General's Office, a fact indicating, perhaps, that the chaplain was not quite the scoundrel that Butler had declared him to be.[64]

These examples demonstrate that not all chaplains were above reproach. There were the weak, inefficient, incompetent, and dishonest among them, just as there are in every profession. But for every poor example, for every instance where a chaplain was charged with misfeasance or malfeasance or nonfeasance, there are many times over the good examples. Most of the men who served their country in the chaplaincy made an honest effort to do their duty, and a careful examination of their service records indicates their general success in that endeavor.[65]

George Pepper, who helped to raise the Eightieth Ohio Infantry and served as a captain in that regiment before ill health forced him to resign active military command for the slightly less strenuous work of the chaplaincy, briefly sketched the character of several chaplains with whom he had been associated and about whom he had heard the men comment.[66] The first of those was the Reverend John R. Eddy, chaplain of the Seventy-second Indiana Infantry. Chaplain Eddy was not a man distinguished by many outstanding characteristics but was known despite his brief term of service as a friend to every soldier. He was killed instantly when struck by a cannon ball at Hoover's Gap, near Chattanooga, Tennessee, just two weeks after leaving his Indiana parish to minister to the spiritual wants of the Hoosier soldiers who had requested that he be appointed regimental chaplain.[67]

Chaplain L. F. Drake (121st Ohio Infantry) was considered by the soldiers of his regiment to be a model chaplain, for his greatest abilities lay in two areas the men considered vital—hospital work and preaching. When a man was in the hospital, uncertain about his future, the chaplain's words of comfort and assurance meant most. And to have a chaplain whose sermons met the needs of men who regularly faced death, who could challenge them with more than platitudes, made this presence desirable. Drake was both of these things to his men, demonstrating a "breadth of education and Christian experience" that made him a welcome member of the regiment.[68]

The chaplain of the Sixty-third Ohio Infantry, Benjamin St. James Fry, was not a remarkable man in physical appearance but performed his duties with a vigor that attracted men to him. To the usual work of his office he added the task of serving as the correspondent for the local newspaper in Ohio, and the men enjoyed having in their midst a man who saw to it that their names frequently found their way into print for friends at home to see.[69]

Chaplain R. B. Bennett (Thirty-second Ohio Infantry) gained the respect of his men before ever serving as chaplain. He had joined the regiment as a private soldier and fought in the ranks for months before he was appointed to fill a vacancy in the chaplaincy at the request of his fellow soldiers. As chaplain, Bennett was respected quite as much for his former activity as a soldier as for his preaching, for he approached both responsibilities with the same vigorous spirit.[70]

John M. Springer, who had also served in the ranks before his appointment to the chaplaincy of the Third Wisconsin Infantry, was impressed indelibly upon the memories of his men by his fine example of personal courage. When his regiment was hard-pressed by Confederate forces at Resaca, Georgia, during Sherman's Atlanta campaign, Springer took up the musket of a fallen soldier and took his place in the line. The chaplain fought bravely until he was carried from the field, dying from multiple wounds. At the field hospital, "he rounded out his noble life in prayers for the success of Hooker's splendid corps, then busily engaged with the enemy. Thus died Chaplain Springer. His last words presented a beautiful and sublime finish to his memorable life. The deep drawn sigh, the copiously falling tears of his comrades in arms, thrillingly attested the veneration in which he was held. . . . 'It is all well.'"[71] Following his death the men composed a memorial to Springer. To them he had distinguished himself as a Christian, by his piety; as a minister, by his devotion, diligence, and practicality; as a laborer and visitor, he was distinguished for his faithfulness and understanding; and as a fellow soldier, he was "beloved by his brethren in Sherman's army."[72] The chaplaincy of the Third Wisconsin was passed to another, who, coincidentally, bore the same surname, a young man (twenty-five years old) named Isaac E. Springer.[73]

Father Peter Cooney (Thirty-fifth Indiana Infantry) served with his regiment throughout its entire service. Despite the fact that Cooney was an older man (he was well past fifty, but his exact age is not known), he was noted for his vigor and was extremely popular with the men. Not the least appreciated of the priest's characteristics was his sharp Irish wit. Cooney was understandably proud of a report submitted by his colonel commending the chaplain for faithfulness in the performance of his duty. The report was quoted in a letter from Father Cooney to his brother: "To Father Cooney, our chaplain, too much praise cannot be given. Indifferent as to himself, he was deeply solicitous for the temporal and spiritual welfare of us all. On the field he was cool and indifferent to danger and in the name of the regiment I thank him for his kindness and laborious attention to the dead and dying."[74] Surely a man thus described by his commander must have enjoyed the approbation of the officers and men of his regiment.

John R. Adams was sixty years old when he accepted the appointment to the chaplaincy of the Fifth Maine Infantry and was mustered into service on June 24, 1861. Despite the fact that Chaplain Adams contracted malarial fever during the Peninsular campaign in 1862, he served his regiment until it was disbanded on June 24, 1864, at the expiration of its three-year term of service. On July 4, 1864, he accepted from the governor of New York a commission as chaplain of the 121st New York Infantry, the men and officers of which regiment were anxious to obtain his services. At the time he was sixty-two years of age. He served the 121st throughout the duration of the war, and in his entire service, illness notwithstanding, his only personal leave came in April 1863, when he was given a twenty-day furlough to attend the marriage of his only daughter. His pass, signed by Major General John Sedgwick, commanding the Fifth Corps of the Army of the Potomac, bore that officers's endorsement designating the chaplain as "a good officer."[75]

Adams died on April 15, 1866, at the age of sixty-four, less than a year after he was finally mustered out of the service of his country. The men he had served wrote of his service:

> From his quiet and beautiful home in Gorham he went forth to the war with the going out of the Fifth Maine, in which he was commissioned as chaplain. In nearly every march he participated with the regiment, and upon nearly every battlefield he rendered noble and efficient service in administering to the wants, bodily and spiritual, of the soldiers. He loved the men; the men loved him. In him they found a friend, earnest, true, sympathetic, unobtrusive; he had the esteem and respect of the highest in rank. . . .
>
> In every duty he was prompt and faithful. By the couch of the sick, the wounded, and the dying, his frequent presence inspired, soothed and made hopeful the sufferer. His quiet dignity, yet humility of manner, checked the wild and thoughtless. Every Sabbath, when it was possible, the regiment were assembled for religious worship; and many of the discourses to which they listened from him were models of earnestness and beauty. He delighted in preaching the word. A revival accompanied his chaplaincy.
>
> Precious was his association in life; sweet and fragrant his memory in death.[76]

Charles M. Blake rendered service considered so desirable by the surgeons in charge of the hospitals at which he was stationed that he became the object of a military tug-of-war. In December 1862, Major General J. D. Cox, on learning that Chaplain Blake was to be transferred from a hospital in his department (at Charleston, Virginia, now West

Virginia) to a hospital at Gallipolis, Ohio, wrote to Secretary Stanton recommending two other ministers for the Gallipolis post, as he wished to keep Blake in his department. In his letter Cox included a short testimonial for the hospital chaplaincy. "As it is my opinion," he said, "that chaplains are far more useful at hospitals than they ever can be in the field, I am desirous that these places should be supplied." Cox's wish was not granted, however, and Chaplain Blake was transferred to the post at Gallipolis.[77]

The chaplain was a man who wished to be active in his work, as is evidenced by a letter addressed to the Adjutant General's Office on January 3, 1863, less than a month after his transfer to Gallipolis. Blake wrote: "I would respectfully request that I be ordered from this to some locality, as Nashville, Tennessee, nearer active service, where I may be more useful to our suffering soldiers." The hospital at Gallipolis was very quiet, with few patients, he indicated, and the local pastors could easily do the very limited amount of visitation required. He wished to be where he could be constantly active on behalf of those suffering from wounds or illness.[78] Such a chaplain could hardly be considered a shirker.

Another chaplain who did not seek to evade responsibility or to avoid work was the Reverend C. B. Thomas, who served at the Washington Street Hospital in Alexandria, Virginia. When Thomas learned that a fellow chaplain was to be discharged from the army, his term of service having expired, he immediately informed the surgeon in charge of his willingness to conduct services in the other man's stead until the vacancy could be filled more satisfactorily. Thomas wrote: "I am just informed that Mr. Newell who had been acting for several months in the capacity of Chaplain at King St. Hospl. this division, has been discharged from service & will soon finish his very satisfactory labors there. Should there be any delay in the appointment of his successor I will volunteer to preach there every Thursday evening & at the McVeigh House every Tuesday evening until some other arrangements more satisfactory to you can be made."[79]

When Chaplain Nelson L. Brakeman (First Indiana Heavy Artillery, formerly the Twenty-first Indiana Infantry) resigned his commission to accept a presidential appointment to serve as a hospital chaplain, the officers and men of his regiment adopted a resolution commending him for the faithful service he had rendered to the regiment.[80] Although they rejoiced "in his prosperity and preferment," they stated their sincere regret at his removal from them. The officers adopted a resolution that states: "and it gives us peculiar pleasure here to review, *with empha-*

sis, the *valor, fidelity and ability*, when in July, 1861, he was unanimously chosen our Chaplain. He leaves us as he came to us, and has lived among us with an unblemished character as a man and Christian minister, and bearing with him the *benediction of the entire regiment.*"[81]

Evidence of personal bravery on the part of a chaplain always elicited the admiration of the men who witnessed it. Captain John G. B. Adams, historian of the Nineteenth Massachusetts Infantry, recalled such an incident he had witnessed in Andersonville Prison. He wrote: "There was a chaplain confined with us who was a very earnest Christian. Every night he held services on the steps of the main buildings, and, with a voice that could be heard throughout the prison, would pray for our country and flag, and for damnation and disaster to all rebels. The commanding officer came in one day and ordered him to stop, but he said they put Paul in prison, yet he prayed, and while he had a voice he should pray to his God, and use language best suited to the occasion. Courage always tells, and when they found that they could not frighten him they let him pray unmolested."[82] When Chaplain McCabe was confined in Libby Prison, he antagonized his captors but kept up the morale of his fellow prisoners by singing the words of the poem "Battle Hymn of the Republic" (which he had memorized when it first appeared in the *Atlantic Monthly*) to the popular marching tune "John Brown's Body" and inviting the men to join him. This brought threats from the guards, but intimidation did not frighten McCabe, and the defiant spirit of the chaplain did much to lift the flagging spirits of the men confined with him.[83]

The historian of the Second Division, Army of the Cumberland, William Sumner Dodge, recalled the bravery of the chaplains who served the regiments in that unit. The heroism of the chaplains was especially conspicuous during the Battle of Stone's River, fought in Tennessee on the last day of 1862. In praising the gallant conduct of those men, Dodge singled out two for special mention: "None are more entitled to the gratitude of the soldiers and their friends, and the unfeigned admiration of the country, than Chaplain Michael Decker, of the 34th, and Chaplain C. G. Bradshaw of the 79th Illinois regiments. They were where the fighting raged thickest, and aided the unfortunate off the field, sometimes supporting one on each side. Many a life was saved by their efforts on that day."[84] The men *did* appreciate chaplains who bore the brunt of battle with them.

Father Thomas Ouellet (occasionally spelled Willett) of the Sixty-ninth New York Infantry made a lasting impression on the men of his regiment through his brave conduct during the Battle of Malvern Hill (July 1, 1862). Moving about the lines, comforting wounded and dying men, Father Ouellet was constantly exposed to Confederate fire. Each man was asked if he were Catholic and if he wished absolution. One man replied, "No, but I would like to die in the faith of any man who has the courage to come and see me in such a place as this."[85]

Chaplain James H. Bradford (Twelfth Connecticut Infantry) was commended for personal bravery by his commanding officer, Lieutenant Colonel Frank H. Peck, in a report preserved in the *Official Records.* "Chaplain Bradford is deserving of great praise for the fearless activity with which he ministered to the suffering during the battle and the night following," the colonel reported following an engagement near Opelousas, Louisiana, April 17, 1863.[86] Colonel H. M. Plaisted, a brigade commander in Sherman's army, cited Chaplain Henry Clay Trumbull for distinguished service in the fighting with Hood's army in October of 1864, just before the "March to the Sea" was begun: "I cannot fail to mention Chaplain Trumbull, Tenth Connecticut, who was constantly at the front with his regiment, as is his wont at all times. He was conspicuous on this occasion, with revolver in hand, in his effort to stay the crumbling regiment. An hour later he officiated at the burial of our dead, while the skirmish line was still engaged and every moment a renewal of the attack was expected. The sound of prayer mingled with the echoes of artillery and musketry and the crash of falling pines for hastily constructed breast-works. His services to the brigade, not only on this but on so many other like occasions, are gratefully acknowledged."[87]

One of the finest examples of conviction and constancy to duty was Chaplain Arthur B. Fuller. The son of a prominent leader of Massachusetts and a brother of Margaret Fuller of Brook Farm fame, Fuller was a well-known clergyman in the New England area. In the army he had earned the respect of the officers and men of the Sixteenth Massachusetts Infantry, successfully establishing a regimental church.

Chaplain Fuller resigned because of poor health after sixteen months of field service, but only after he was promised an immediate appointment to hospital chaplaincy where he could continue his service. His resignation, submitted at Falmouth, Virginia, on December 8, 1862, was accepted, and he was honorably discharged two days later. Aware that a great battle was soon to take place at Fredericksburg, just over the Rappahannock River, Chaplain Fuller determined to stay until after the battle to render all possible assistance. On December 11 (the day after his discharge and two days before that bloody battle), he volunteered to cross the river, armed with a musket, to help drive Confederate sharp-shooters from the houses of Fredericksburg so that the engineers could lay the pontoon bridges necessary for the army's crossing. That after-noon he was killed in the streets of the village, one of the first of the thousands of casualties of the "Battle of Burnside's Blunders."[88]

Fuller was technically out of the army at the time of his death. Con-sequently, his wife and three children (a fourth was expected) were not entitled to pension under the law. His death was widely noted and mourned in New England, however, and Governor John A. Andrew of Massachusetts supported Richard F. Fuller, the chaplain's brother, in a petition to Congress, in the name of Fuller's widow, to enact special legislation granting a pension to the chaplain's family. Accepting the recommendation of its pension committee, the Senate adopted a reso-lution that reads in part: "though Chaplain Fuller was technically out of the service of the United States, still he was really in the service of his country and in the line of duty while bravely leading on the soldiers, and dying on the field of battle." Congress passed this act on February 25, 1863.[89] No soldier offered a greater sacrifice in the service of his country than did Chaplain Fuller.

In truth, however, not every Massachusetts man spoke well of Chap-lain Fuller. Major Henry Abbott of the Twentieth Massachusetts wrote of the chaplain to his father in November of 1862, "so [we] gave our valises in charge of Rev. Dr. Snob and Toady [the chaplain's son] Fuller of the 16th" as the regiment left Falmouth for a return march to Warren-ton Junction. Whether Abbot's impression of Chaplain Fuller changed after Fuller's death is not known.[90]

The chaplains mentioned are not a rare few who served commend-ably. The list could be much longer. A careful examination of the service records of the men who served as chaplains in the army of the United States during the years of the Civil War reveals that poor chaplains were the small minority and that the vast majority served commendably.

When an attempt was being made in the Senate to reduce the number of chaplains as a means of economy, Senator Daniel Clark of New Hampshire argued against the proposal. It was his opinion that the chap-lains' influence was of great value to the army, and to eliminate even a few would be false economy. He concluded his arguments with these words:

I think a good chaplain is the most effective man in the regiment, and I can now point to men who are doing more good as chaplains than almost any [other] man in the regiment. Though they do not fight, they do a great deal toward keeping the regiment ready to fight; they are with the sick, they are with the suffering, they do a great deal to keep your army such as it ought to be. In my judgment, you had better not take away from the regiment the man to whom the soldier goes in his time of suffering, or when he needs advice. You had better let him be with the men, and let the men be close to him, and about him, and let them see him every hour of the day, and let them come to him readily and ask his advice, and let him be a friend to them, and a close friend, and about them all the time.[91]

The perceptive chaplain was aware that his life was influential, perhaps more so than his words. Chaplain Trumbull noted this fact, stating that "the chaplain lives among the men. His life and everyday conversation are as much a part of his ministry as his Sunday service, for the men see him constantly." Trumbull was aware that his every deed was observed, his every word noted, and that inconsistency in his life could damage irreparably his opportunity to influence his men for good.[92]

Chaplain Joseph Anderson was another who realized that his greatest asset in dealing with the soldiers who passed through the hospitals he served was a consistent life. He remarked: "A chaplain's influence must be largely moral rather than official. His power for good depends entirely upon character. This must be his chief passport to the respect and affections of the men, and the foundation of his usefulness." The chaplain who had the best interests of his men at heart, who honestly desired to win them for God, would find it wise to "merge the officer in the friend," to lead rather than push.[93]

Chaplain Rogers commented on the influence a chaplain could exert by his presence alone if his example before the men had been consistent with what he preached. He asserted: "The services of chaplains avail more than many think to promote religion and morals in the army. There is a restraining influence in the very presence of a minister of Christ."[94] And finally, in the words of Chaplain Bradley: "Chaplains, who have been the men for the positions, have found the most ready access to the hearts of soldiers, and no more respectful or attentive congregations could they anywhere find."[95]

4

A FUTURE FOR THE FREEDMEN

Still another aspect of interest and importance in a study of the Union chaplaincy during the Civil War is the relationship between chaplains and former slaves. Many chaplains in recording their experiences of the war years referred to the multitude of problems—social, political, religious, moral, and economic—raised by the abolition of slavery. They attempted to evaluate the character and potential of blacks, to assess their prospects in a predominantly white society, and, in many instances, to lend assistance in the monumental task of elevating blacks through education, both religious and secular, to a level commensurate with their new status.

As the Union armies penetrated the Southern states, increasing numbers of blacks came into the camps of the federal troops. Although contact with the former slaves under these circumstances undoubtedly gave a rather different impression than had they been observed in servitude, there was yet ample opportunity for the chaplains to see the causes of the degraded condition of the ex-slaves and to provide badly needed assistance to them as they faced the challenge of their new status as free members of society.

Chaplain Arthur B. Fuller (Sixteenth Massachusetts Infantry) considered the problem of how best to provide for the former slaves to be one of national concern. Noting the depressed state of these unfortunate people, he blamed the system that had for generations exploited them. He was delighted, however, by their eagerness for freedom, for education, and for elevation socially. The nation, he urged, must take bold measures to meet the pressing needs of these people. It was essential to create a viable future for the freedmen.[1]

Chaplain James B. Rogers (Fourteenth Wisconsin Infantry) scorned those who pointed to the degraded circumstances of the former slaves as evidence of their inferiority. It was true, he acknowledged, that they were degraded, but why should anyone expect them to be otherwise? They had never been permitted to assert their individuality, to exercise free will, to choose their own position. How could former slaves be expected to stand tall when they had been forbidden the enjoyment of rights claimed by the white race as inalienable? This perpetual denial of right, and not any inherent inferiority, was the cause of the depressed state of these people.[2]

Despite the terrible handicap of enforced ignorance with which blacks were encumbered, Rogers spoke highly of their basic character and optimistically of their aptitude for learning. Blacks were, he said, a courteous people by nature, more so than their "superior" white brethren; furthermore, they were open to religious teaching and were faithful to their responsibilities when given an opportunity to demonstrate it. Concerning the former slaves' ability to learn, Rogers stated that they compared very favorably with the poor Southern whites who were, in his opinion, less intelligent than ever the slaves had been. It was his belief that their "capacities for education [were] equal to those of white children, and their thirst for learning rather greater."[3]

Because of these rather definite views, Rogers strongly urged a governmental program of education for blacks, to hasten the day when they could attain equal status with and full acceptance by whites. He pointed out that as long as the ex-slaves remained ignorant, they were ready targets for exploiters of all types. As a chaplain he had observed occasional mistreatment and deception of freedmen by Union soldiers. Taking advantage of ignorance in this manner was to Rogers a despicable act that would be repeated over and over were blacks not promptly educated.[4]

If any one thing should prove to be an insurmountable barrier to the attainment of racial equality, it would be incipient racism, Rogers asserted. There were, even in the North, hundreds of thousands who believed the Southern doctrine of white supremacy and black inferiority. It was this group that was proposing colonization of blacks outside the United States, said the chaplain, a proposal he considered cruel and unjust. Blacks had labored as hard as, indeed harder than, any other Americans to build this country and to wrest them from it and colonize them elsewhere would be as evil as the institution of slavery itself.[5]

Chaplain George Pepper (Eightieth Ohio Infantry) also commented on the charge that the evident ignorance of the former slaves was proof of inferiority. It was meanly false, he said, to point to a race that had been held by force in a frightful state of degradation and blame the ignorance that inevitably resulted from such bondage on inherent inferiority. He observed that the poor white population of the slave states was quite as ignorant in many respects as the slave; hence it was not an innate inferiority in the case of either poor whites or blacks, but the stultifying influence of slavery on the society of the South that accounted for the ignorance there prevailing.[6]

Pepper observed that blacks were "gifted with more than ordinary intellect, more exercised than cultivated." There was in the former slaves an aptness to learn and a thirst for knowledge that would enable them, the chaplain believed, quickly to attain an equality with whites *if* opportunities for education were provided. For these reasons he urged Congress to consider immediate and appropriate legislation to cope with this vast problem, for only a massive educational program financed and controlled by the national government could offer a fair prospect of success.[7]

James J. Marks, chaplain of the Sixty-third Pennsylvania Infantry, was another who considered former slaves to be unfortunate victims of circumstances rather than inferior creatures. It was his opinion, based on personal observations in Virginia, that blacks were in many ways superior to poor whites. They were, he believed, more ambitious than poor whites despite the absence of opportunity for advancement. Among their many virtues he listed patience, hope, a responsiveness to appeals to their better nature, and above all else an absence of the spirit of vindictiveness one might have expected to find in an oppressed people.[8]

Lieutenant George H. Hepworth of the Fourth Louisiana Native Guards, a former chaplain, stated that after the Emancipation Proclamation the most common question Northerners asked of those who had traveled in the South was: "Are the blacks ready for freedom?" It was, he said, a question fraught with difficulties, yet he, for one, was not fearful of trying the great experiment. The usual arguments about black inferiority were patently false, and the oppressed blacks were far more fit to be free than many people who already enjoyed that inestimable privilege. Blacks were "fitter to be free than to be slaves." Of one thing, Hepworth said, there was absolutely no doubt. The slaves everywhere in the South had an intense longing for freedom; they wished "to possess their own bodies, and to govern their own fortunes."[9]

One chaplain, the Reverend Burr Baldwin, stated his desire to be stationed near Washington to aid in the colonization of former slaves, a project he understood was about to be launched by the government. He had high hopes for this enterprise, which he believed would result in the elevation and improvement of the African race. Colonization, he thought, would benefit not only the ex-slaves but also the nation. This scheme would remove from the American population a minority race that Baldwin was convinced could never be fully assimilated, thus removing a source of social friction detrimental to both races.[10]

Chaplain Baldwin's interest was not typical.[11] The more general consensus was to regard the United States as the natural home of the black just as it was of the white population. Consequently the usual response among the chaplains in a position to render assistance was to encourage the former slaves to seek education, and several voluntarily served as teachers in this regard.

The problem of what should be done with the freedmen was seriously considered by Chaplain Stephen A. Hodgman (Seventy-fourth U.S. Colored Troops). Unlike Chaplain Baldwin, he totally rejected the idea of colonization outside the United States. It was an idea formed by those who rejected the doctrine of natural law as stated in the Declaration of Independence—"All men are created equal." Colonization was, he argued, cruel and visionary. The South should be the former slaves' home; they had certainly earned it! Why, he asked the proponents of colonization, if it was not disagreeable to have blacks in the South and to mix with them when they were degraded as slaves, should it be so disagreeable to endure their presence when they had been educated and elevated in freedom? Why, he asked, should the former slaves be required to move from the land they had worked or even from the section that had exploited them? Blacks were Americans, and as such deserved the same guarantees that all other Americans enjoyed.[12]

Chaplain Henry Clay Trumbull (Tenth Connecticut) discussed at great length the problems of the freedmen and their attitudes toward slavery and emancipation. He took sharp exception to the argument that blacks were contented with perpetual servitude, that they were inferior beings who could not attain equality and were not interested in emancipation. Blacks universally welcomed emancipation, Trumbull asserted, including those who were faithful to their masters. They deemed the Union armies to be God's instrument for the liberation of the oppressed. They were ready and eager to grasp their freedom when and as they could.[13]

The chaplains frequently referred to the vast number of former slaves who flocked into the Union camps as evidence of their dissatisfaction with the "benevolent and Christian institution" of slavery. There was always an upsurge in the number of blacks coming into federal lines when an advance was made into an area previously unpenetrated. The consensus was that to the black the Union army represented freedom. But the presence of a large number of former slaves in the army camps, a number ever increasing, created obvious and monumental problems, problems that the federal government must face decisively if the status of blacks was not to be even more unfortunate than it had been in slavery.[14]

Frequent references to the blacks' abilities as soldiers were made by the chaplains. Chaplain Charles McCabe (122nd Ohio Infantry) commended the manner in which the "chattels" fulfilled their military trust. Black troops held a substantial sector in the Union lines outside Petersburg, Virginia, during the siege of that city in 1864 and 1865, a rather grave responsibility, the chaplain indicated. Had they failed it would have spelled disaster for the entire army. "But no one [expected] anything from them like unfaithfulness. They [would] be true." Despite the knowledge that their capture would almost certainly mean death, as the Fort Pillow incident indicated, black troops continued to fight well, and enlistments remained high. McCabe believed that this spirit was evidence of a determination to fight for liberty and social position.[15]

Chaplain Hodgman and Lieutenant Hepworth both attested to the superb fighting qualities of the freedmen. They were brave, well disciplined, and able marksmen, said Hodgman, and less likely to question their officers or to act insubordinately than were whites. Hepworth attributed the former slave's fighting spirit to his knowledge that he was fighting for freedom and against his "beloved former master." Both men believed that the performance of the ex-slaves as soldiers demonstrated rather conclusively their manhood and disproved the claims of black inferiority.[16]

Although one might have expected a spirit of vindictiveness among black troops, the chaplains saw nothing to indicate its presence; instead black soldiers exhibited a kindness toward their enemies that they had rarely received as slaves. Chaplain G. T. Carruthers (Fifty-first U.S. Colored Troops) described the aftermath of a military encounter in which his regiment took part in Alabama. The rebel lines were taken by a charge spearheaded by black troops. "In the works old masters surrendered to former slaves. A commanding officer [was] reported to have surrendered his sword to an old slave and [to have] besought his protection." There were no acts of violence "committed beyond those necessarily incident to a charge. [They] proved themselves as magnanimous to the vanquished as courageous in the charge."[17]

Thomas Calahan, the chaplain of the Forty-eighth U.S. Colored Troops, also reported on the charitable attitudes of his men toward the rebels. He stated that his regiment had been assigned to guard a sizable group of Confederate prisoners. Their kindness toward their captives won warm expressions of gratitude from those who had expected retribution. No rebel, said Calahan, was in any way injured by a black soldier after resistance had ceased.[18]

Both Carruthers and Calahan resented the different treatment accorded to black and white troops. Carruthers stated that at Selma, Alabama, the white troops had bivouacked in the city while the black regiments were ordered to encamp in a pasture on the opposite side of the Alabama River. Later, at Montgomery, the same thing had been repeated. The chaplain acknowledged that this may have been a coincidence, that the commanding general may have been innocent of intentional discrimination, but the apparent implication of inferiority by this segregation of the army was "not unfelt by officers and men of the division and not unnoticed by the unfriendly eyes of [the] enemy."[19] It seemed to him an unfair and unwise policy, unfair to the men who had fought as valiantly as any other Union soldier, and unwise to appear as guilty of race prejudice as the former slaveholders. Calahan was as aroused by discriminatory treatment of black troops as was Carruthers. To him this violated the spirit of the Union war effort, the spirit of equality and brotherhood. Despite the obvious bias with which his black regiment had been treated, however, Calahan observed that his men were deeply religious and were willing to trust God to square their account.[20]

Although the chaplains were optimistic, generally, about the former slaves' character and capacities and were hopeful of their prospects for a vastly improved status through education, they were not blind to the many problems yet to be solved to realize these possibilities. They did not regard the army's employment of blacks—as laborers at menial wages or as soldiers fighting to procure by arms what was their natural right— to be the answer to these problems. Much more would be required.

Probably the most eloquent expression of these opinions by any chaplain came from the pen of Chaplain H. H. Moore, a Methodist, who wrote for the *Western Christian Advocate* an article that vividly portrayed the plight of former slaves and his hopes for their future. Moore said that the power and influence that had effected the blacks' emancipation must and would assume the responsibility of making them a respectable and homogeneous element of the American social and political community. No visionaries or theorists should aspire to the task of elevating blacks, for in this task a true realization of the effects of slavery was essential. The former slaves needed guidance and supervision. "The elevation of the black men to citizenship, intelligence, virtue and prosperity," he argued, would "be an addition of . . . worth, and honor, and power to the republic." The government should assure "not only emancipation, but paternal care and elevation. Churches, aided by benevolent societies, and having the sympathies of the people, [would] bend their best energies to this work."[21]

Many chaplains acted unofficially, on a voluntary basis, to assist the freedmen in their struggle to attain three basic goals: education, economic stability, and social equality and acceptance. Their approaches to the problems confronting former slaves varied, but their emphasis was almost invariably on the need for elevating a depressed people by educating them and thus equipping them for their new role in society.

Chaplain Norman Badger reported on several occasions that he was conducting a school for black soldiers confined because of wounds or illness at the hospital in which he was stationed. His basic concern was to teach them elementary reading, writing, and arithmetic. He considered it absolutely essential that the freedmen have at least a basic elementary education if they were to adapt to their new status successfully. There would not now be the guarantee of economic security, however minimal, that slavery had provided; thus former slaves, to become economically self-sufficient and to avoid the danger of exploitation by former masters, needed an education. Badger continued this work after the war had ended until he was mustered out of military service in September 1865.[22]

Chaplain Fuller organized a Sunday school for blacks and poor whites in the vicinity of the camp where his regiment was stationed (near Warrenton, Virginia). Secular subjects such as reading and writing were taught in addition to the regular religious emphasis, and the chaplain was encouraged by the aptitude of his black pupils. There was, he stated, sufficient reason to believe that education would bridge the gulf between slavery and freedom.[23]

William K. Talbot, a hospital chaplain stationed at Beaufort, South Carolina, reported that though his regular duties kept him constantly occupied, he was still able to spend time each day with black convalescents, teaching them to read, write, and figure. It was a fascinating and rewarding endeavor, he indicated; the avid thirst for knowledge demonstrated by these "dusky soldiers" was evidence of an ambition denied fulfillment under slavery. He noted a remarkable improvement in their "loyalty and morals" and indicated that most of them were very attentive to religious instruction. Education, he believed, was the key to a successful transition from slavery to freedom.[24]

The chaplain of the Twelfth U.S. Colored Troops, the Reverend William Wentworth Eaton, provided educational opportunities for his men despite the difficulties that arose from their assignment. The regimental duty involved guarding more than eleven miles of railroad, which spread the men out over such an area that it was difficult to maintain a regular class schedule. Eaton reported that "notwithstanding these peculiar circumstances [he kept] up a daily school with encouraging results." He was aided in this undertaking, he stated, by educational pamphlets and books from both the Christian Commission and the Pennsylvania Freedman's Aid Commission. The school was conducted in the tent of the sutler accompanying the regiment. Eaton was convinced that this effort was of immense value, for in his opinion education for the former slaves was essential if they were to attain the social status they so earnestly desired.[25]

Another aspect of the voluntary efforts to aid the former slaves stemmed somewhat indirectly from the work of the army chaplains. This involved the appropriation of church properties, in areas of the seceded states occupied by Union forces, for use as centers for religious and secular education of the former slaves. "Sometimes the chaplains with the forces of the occupation would commandeer a vacant church edifice and use it for their services." On such occasions, "a congregation would be invited to join in worship with the soldiers." As this situation became known to officials of Northern churches, "they recognized that here was an opportunity to further their missionary program."[26] These churches were utilized extensively for denominational educational programs, once the War Department authorized such takeovers.

One of the early examples of this type of endeavor involved the Beaufort Baptist Church, a large congregation on Port Royal Island, South Carolina. Before the war the congregation had been composed of masters and slaves; the latter comprised the large majority but, as slaves, were without voting privileges. Chaplain Frederic Denison (Third Rhode Island Heavy Artillery) and the Reverend Solomon Peck, secretary of the American Baptist Missionary Union, together cooperated with the black congregation that had remained behind when their masters fled the island at the threat of Union occupation. It was their purpose, by using the church for a schoolhouse during the week, to provide the former slaves with an opportunity for a basic education in addition to the regular worship services. Peck wrote President Lincoln requesting permission to proceed with this undertaking and received from the president an approving letter, in which he pointed out that the congregational form of government practiced by Baptists gave the blacks, a majority, every right to take charge of the church.[27]

Even before this, Reverend Peck had addressed a "memorial" to the president, dated September 26, 1862, in which he requested that "the beneficent labors" of ministers assigned by the Union to work with the former slaves (cooperating with the chaplains) in and near Port Royal, South Carolina, "be suffered to proceed without unnecessary interference." He also urged "that the churches & congregations spoken of [several were included] be allowed to assemble & worship as heretofore in their respective meetinghouses without 'let or hindrance,' except as the use of the said house be imperatively required by military exigencies." Lincoln forwarded the request to Secretary Stanton with an endorsement noting the danger of denominational clashes in the sort of work Peck had outlined. Each church, so Lincoln believed, should follow its own forms and avoid interference in the work of other churches similarly engaged.[28]

This activity did involve denominations other than the Baptists, and although there were a few incidents of interdenominational friction, traceable mainly to a "competitive spirit," the work of education progressed rather harmoniously and with considerable success.[29] The American Baptist Missionary Convention (frequently referred to as the Missionary Union) also encouraged black ministers to accompany the Union forces for the purpose of working with the former slaves. A committee of black Baptist ministers was appointed by the Missionary Convention to present a request to Lincoln for permission to pursue this work. This was done, and the president responded favorably, giving to the ministers a letter endorsing their proposal. "Today," said President Lincoln, "I am called upon by a committee of colored ministers of the Gospel, who express a wish to go within our military lines and minister to their brethren there." The president continued: "The object is a worthy one, and I shall be glad for all facilities to be afforded them which may not be inconsistent with or a hindrance to our military operations."[30]

On January 14, 1864, the Home Mission Society of the American Baptist Church was granted permission, in a circular published by the War Department under the signature of Edward D. Townsend, the assistant adjutant general, to occupy churches belonging to the Southern Baptist denomination in which loyal ministers were not then serving. These buildings were to be turned over to loyal ministers, designated by the Society, for the encouragement of "the loyal sentiment of the people." The officers commanding in the various departments of the

South were instructed to comply with this circular and to aid the Society in any way practicable. It was implicit in this directive that these facilities be used to the benefit of the former slaves as well as to encourage Southern whites to return to their former loyalty.[31] Later that same year, the Missionary Society presented to President Lincoln a set of resolutions, which had been adopted at a session held earlier in Philadelphia, commending him for his course of action relative to the abolition of slavery and thanking him for his support in their efforts to establish loyal churches and elevate the former slaves in the areas of the South occupied by Union forces. Said the president, "I can only thank you for thus adding to the effective and almost unanamous [sic] support which the Christian communities are so zealously giving to the country, and to liberty." He continued:

> Indeed it is difficult to conceive how it could be otherwise with any one professing christianity, or even having ordinary perceptions of right and wrong. To read in the Bible, as the word of God himself, that "In the sweat of *thy* face shalt thou eat bread,["] and to preach therefrom that, "In the sweat of *other mans* faces shalt thou eat bread," to my mind can scarcely be reconciled with honest sincerity. . . . When brought to my final reckoning, may I have to answer for robbing no man of his goods; yet more tolerable even this, than for robbing one of himself, and all that was his. . . . When, a year to two ago, those professed holy men of the South, met in the semblance of prayer and devotion, and, in the name of Him who said "As ye would all men should do unto you, do you even so unto them" appealed to the Christian world to aid them in doing to a whole race of men, as they would have no man do unto themselves, to my thinking, they contemned [sic] and insulted God and His church, far more than did Satan when he tempted the Saviour with the Kingdoms of the earth. The devils attempt was no more false, and far less hypocritical. But let me forbear, remembering it is also written "judge not, lest ye be judged."[32]

The permission granted to the Baptists and the type of activity that grant intended were preceded, in November of the previous year, by a similar grant to Bishop Edward R. Ames of the Methodist Episcopal Church. It is probable that the possibilities for work of this sort were impressed upon Bishop Ames by Chaplain Lyman D. Ames (Twenty-ninth Ohio Infantry), a relative, during one of the chaplain's many trips to Ohio in charge of funds belonging to men of his regiment. It was Bishop Ames who first broached the idea of using loyal Northern ministers in Southern churches to promote loyalty and Union sentiment. Stanton responded enthusiastically to the proposal and directed his assistant, Townsend, to issue a circular to commanding officers in the various Southern departments ordering their cooperation with the bishop in the enterprise.[33]

This order was expanded in scope early in 1864 to include three other departments in which Bishops Osmon C. Baker, Edmund S. James, and Matthew Simpson were permitted the same type of activity as had been granted Bishop Ames. Ames himself in the early part of 1864 toured the areas of the Southern states that were occupied by federal troops, and as a result of his journey numerous appointments of loyal Northern ministers were made to Methodist Episcopal churches in that area.[34] Men serving in this capacity were both willing and eager to cooperate with chaplains in the same area who were also interested in promoting the elevation of former slaves through education.

When other denominations learned of the action of the War Department on behalf of the Methodists and Baptists, they naturally sought similar consideration for themselves. On March 15, 1864, the Church of the United Brethren in Christ addressed a petition to Secretary Stanton requesting permission to occupy vacant rebel churches "for the purpose of establishing Schools and missions among the Freedmen." The petition pointed out that since the denomination excluded slaveholders from church membership, it had no organized churches in the slave states, with the exception of a few in the border states. The request cited work already being done in Vicksburg and Davis Bend, Mississippi, where day schools and Sabbath schools for the former slaves were already in operation. This work, which was being done in cooperation with the army through its chaplains, was threatened by the encroachments of other denominations, and the Brethren thus desired protection for what they had done and permission to continue their work.[35]

What Lincoln had feared might develop from the request of the Reverend Peck of the American Baptist Missionary Union in connection with his work in South Carolina—a clash, or "collision" as he put it, of different denominations engaged in this type of work—became a reality in Vicksburg, Mississippi.[36] The United Brethren established a congregation of blacks for religious worship in an abandoned Baptist church during the winter months of 1863–1864. In addition to the regular Sunday services, they conducted an elementary school in the church edifice during the week. A rather touchy situation arose when in April of 1864 the agents of the American Baptist Home Missions Society took over the building for services each Sunday as permitted in the circular that Stanton had approved. Although the Baptists permitted the Brethren to continue their day-school operations during the week, the Brethren protested to Stanton, believing that a congregation of some four hundred members was being stolen from them. In two letters to the secretary of war, the spokesman for the Brethren, the Reverend D. K. Flickinger, promised that his people would be more careful in occupying buildings in the future if only they were permitted to retain the one in which they were presently conducting the school. They had, Flickinger said, spent a sizable amount of money to repair the building, and it was costly to staff the school. When Stanton refused to make an exception in this instance, Flickinger wrote a third and, apparently, final letter. He stated that the Baptist agent, a Mr. Corse, had turned the building over to an army chaplain, an act that in Flickinger's judgment indicated that the Baptists were not yet ready to occupy the building. In the light of such circumstances he urged once more that the Brethren be permitted to retain this one building. On June 7 Stanton refused finally to change his previous circulars to permit this exception, and the incident was closed, albeit not without some bitterness.[37]

The Presbyterian denomination had been rather severely divided on theological and sociopolitical issues by the time the war broke out, but the three larger Northern groups—the Old School and New School Presbyterian Churches and the United Presbyterian Church—each sought the same privileges as those granted to other denominations. The United Presbyterians were first to receive such favorable consideration from the War Department. On February 15, 1864, in response to a letter from the Reverend John L. Pressly, Secretary Stanton directed that a circular, similar to those previously issued for the Baptists and Methodists, be forwarded to all departments in the South on behalf of the United Presbyterians. Because there was no United Presbyterian Church as such in the slave states, due to the schism over slavery that had divided the church into northern and southern branches in the 1830s, the circular indicated that in the South the property of the Associate Reformed Presbyterian Church could be occupied by loyal United Presbyterian ministers. The New and Old School missions boards were given a joint grant of permission to work in Union-occupied territory in March of 1864, but it did not include the privilege of occupying Southern churches.[38] The general trend of Presbyterian aid to blacks was to work through the home missions boards of the denominations in cooperation "with such existing agencies as the United States Christian Commission, the United States Sanitary Commission, the chaplains, the army, and the Federal Government."[39]

It is probable that other denominations engaged in similar activities among former slaves in Union-occupied areas of the South. The Lutherans, the Congregationalists, the Unitarians, the Catholics, and the Quakers, however, did not seek to appropriate properties belonging to the Southern wing of their denominations; hence, no circulars were issued specifically in connection with those denominations. Chaplains belonging to these denominations (excepting the Quakers) did serve with the army, although their total number was proportionately small.[40] Chaplain Edward O'Brien (Seventeenth Illinois Cavalry) was the only Roman Catholic chaplain about whom it was possible to verify any labor with blacks. All that is known of his service is that he held the post of superintendent of refugees for the Rolla district of Missouri for some months in early 1865.[41]

The Quakers, who were conscientious objectors, did not supply chaplains to the army but did voluntarily aid former slaves. When Congress passed the draft act of February 24, 1865, belated recognition was given to Quaker scruples. Legal provision was thus made for their employment in hospitals or caring for former slaves if they did not choose to pay a substitute.[42]

Disputes between and within denominations engaged in work on behalf of blacks did arise as mentioned earlier. Occasionally denominational agents would preempt a Southern church only to have the congregation and former minister protest to the War Department that they were indeed loyal to the Union. In one such instance, in which a Methodist congregation in Missouri protested the seizure of their edifice by agents of the Methodist Episcopal Home Missions Board, the president directed the secretary of war to exclude Missouri from the previous circular that authorized such action.[43] Lincoln pointed out that Kentucky had never been included in the area designated in the earlier circular, that Missouri should not be included (neither state had seceded), and that the true purpose of such authorization was not to promote denominational feuds or schisms but to rally sentiment for the Union.[44]

While it is not possible to establish a conclusive tie between denominational efforts with former slaves and similarly voluntary activity by the chaplains of the army, it is nevertheless highly probable that close cooperation did exist. The evidence contained in the chaplains' monthly reports to the adjutant general indicates that this was an activity widely practiced by chaplains of all denominations.[45] The records of the religious denominations include few direct references to chaplains, but the general tone in each instance was to encourage the efforts of all who were working for the elevation of former slaves, clergy of their own or other denominations, and representatives of benevolent societies alike.

In addition to the work among former slaves undertaken voluntarily by the chaplains, there was a far more extensive enterprise for their aid, operated under army auspices and in some areas administered by chaplains. There are three major obstacles to a discussion of this enterprise relative to chaplains. The first is the fact that chaplains' reports dated prior to April 9, 1864, are almost totally nonexistent, due to the requirement prior to that date that chaplains submit *quarterly* reports to the officer commanding the regiment in which they served. The regimental commanders were not required to resubmit these reports to the adjutant general's office; hence, an invaluable source of official information has been lost to the historian.[46] A second obstacle is the fact that almost without exception, chaplains assigned to duty with former slaves for more than brief periods resigned their commissions as chaplains to accept rank with command in black regiments. This step was taken to facilitate the fulfillment of their duties, not because of a loss of interest in the chaplaincy; nevertheless, it technically removes these individuals from a treatment devoted to the chaplains.[47] The third obstacle, less imposing but yet restrictive, is that references to chaplains in the *Official Records* are minimal to say the least; in fact, most of the references to chaplains who worked with former slaves speak of them in their later military command rather than in their previous position as chaplains. For these reasons it is necessary to go slightly beyond the limitations of a discussion concerning the work done among blacks by chaplains *as chaplains*, in order to develop a coherent picture of this very important activity.

The first official recognition of the problem posed to the army by the large numbers of former slaves flocking to its lines came in May 1861, when General Benjamin F. Butler, commanding at Fortress Monroe, Virginia, refused to give up fugitive slaves who had come within his lines, declaring that they were contraband of war, that he needed workmen, that the enemy was employing blacks to construct fortifications, and that the Fugitive Slave Act of 1850 did not apply to a foreign country, which Virginia claimed to be.[48] With the approval of the secretary of war (then Simon Cameron), Butler proceeded to inaugurate a system

The Poplar Grove Church, Petersburg, Virginia. Built by the
Fiftieth New York Volunteers Engineers, March 5, 1865.
(Photograph by Timothy O'Sullivan)

under which able-bodied blacks were employed on a wage basis, destitute and unfit blacks were supplied with rations by the army quartermaster, and the needs of nonlaboring blacks were supplied from the
earnings of the laborers. This policy marked the army's first attempt to
find a suitable and practical means, consistent with a war effort and
humanitarion values, for the care of former slaves.[49]

According to Chaplain John Eaton (Twenty-seventh Ohio Infantry),
Butler's system contained the essential features that were to be found

in subsequent efforts to aid former slaves. The officers who followed
Butler in this post, moreover, continued his policies. General Butler later
began a similar program in Louisiana as commander of the Gulf Department at New Orleans, a program continued by his successor there,
General Nathaniel P. Banks.[50]

In the fall of 1861, General Thomas W. Sherman, who commanded
the Union forces occupying the Sea Islands off the coast of South Carolina and Georgia, was authorized by the War Department, under authority of the Confiscation Act of August 6, 1861, "to employ all loyal
persons offering their services for the defense of the Union." Although
Sherman himself did not organize a system for aid to, or utilization of,
blacks, E. L. Pierce, an agent of the Treasury Department (which
the Confiscation Act had designated as the custodian of abandoned
lands and slaves), inaugurated an experimental program for blacks
at Hilton Head, South Carolina. Pierce had worked in the Butler program at Fortress Monroe before being sent to South Carolina, and the
ideas he had seen in operation there gave him a starting point for his
own program. His system called for the leasing of abandoned lands to
loyal persons who would in turn employ former slaves at a fixed wage.
Pierce had barely begun his task when the responsibility for the abandoned slaves was transferred from the Treasury Department to army
officials.[51]

It was General Rufus Saxton, as a military commander of the Department of the South, who enlarged the program for aid to former slaves.[52]
In August of 1862, he was authorized by Secretary Stanton to recruit
and arm blacks (under the provisions of the Militia Act of July 17, 1862),
with the same pay, rations, and equipment provided white volunteers.
This provided an occupation for able-bodied black males thus enlisted
in the army, and it must be regarded as a major step in the process of
recognizing blacks as equals. Saxton was also directed to occupy abandoned plantations and to employ the former slaves for cultivating land
thus confiscated and harvesting the crop. The system was followed of
leasing lands to loyal persons and requiring them to employ blacks at a
fixed rate. In November 1862, a black regiment, the First South Carolina Volunteer Infantry, was sent on a coastal expedition south from
Beaufort, South Carolina. Accompanying the regiment, which was later
commended for its coolness and bravery under fire, was Chaplain
Mansfield French, who also served the men as a teacher.[53]

The Reverend French is the only chaplain who can be conclusively
linked through the *Official Records* and chaplains' reports with the
operation of this system in the Department of the South, and nothing

beyond the fact that he served this regiment is known. It is possible, however, and even probable that the activities of the American Baptist Home Missions Board, under the Reverend Solomon Peck, and the work of Chaplain Denison fell within the program of education and welfare that General Saxton organized and encouraged.

The preceding discussion outlines the type of activity undertaken by army commanders in areas of the South where Union penetrations freed slaves. Those mentioned do not constitute a complete list of such attempts, but since in only one department—the Department of the Tennessee (which included Arkansas and was later expanded to include the Departments of the Ohio and the Cumberland as the Division of the Mississippi)—can a clear connection between these efforts and the chaplains be established, a more thorough discussion of the activities involving former slaves in that department is enlightening.

The problem of how to handle blacks who flooded Union lines at every point of penetration into the slave states was especially acute in the Mississippi Valley. Union military advances were more extensive here than in the East, and the progressive southern movement of the federal armies in the great valley brought them into an area with one of the heaviest concentrations of blacks in the nation. Union commanders, threatened with a practical inundation by blacks, had to solve the problem of caring for them if the forces they led were even to fight. The proportions of this problem could hardly be grasped, or so it seemed to Chaplain John Eaton of the Twenty-seventh Ohio Infantry. Several years after his service among former slaves, Eaton tried to convey the immense complexity of the problems confronting those given the responsibility of caring for the ubiquitous newly freed in the Valley of the Mississippi. He wrote: "Imagine a slave population, springing from antecedent barbarism, rising up and leaving its ancient bondage, forsaking its local traditions and all the associations and attractions of the old plantation life, coming garbed in rags or in silks, with feet shod or bleeding, individually or in families and larger groups—an army of slaves and fugitives, pushing its way irresistibly toward an army of fighting men."[54] It was like the arrival of whole cities in their midst, Eaton continued, like an exodus without a Moses to lead it. Although no apparent reason brought them, and despite the fact that in the armies they often encountered a prejudice more bitter than that left behind, they were sure that their interests were identical with the objects of the Union armies. Had such a destitute and unfortunate people been permitted to enter the camps of the Union armies without care and supervision the effect on the Union cause would have been disastrous, he believed.[55]

Without a definitive governmental policy for dealing with blacks freed by army advances, Union commanders in the Valley were forced to meet this problem on an ad hoc basis. The clearest picture of work on behalf of former slaves undertaken by chaplains at the assignment of a commanding officer involves that of Chaplain Eaton.[56] Eaton's first encounter with the problem former slaves posed to the army came early in 1862 when his regiment was a part of the small army with which General U. S. Grant achieved his victories at Forts Donelson and Henry in West Tennessee (the chaplain's reaction to this situation is described later in this chapter). Despite the fact that Grant was operating under orders from General Henry Halleck, which excluded fugitive slaves from Union army camps or lines, he recognized that the blacks posed a problem that could not be solved simply by denying them sanctuary in federal camps.[57] Consequently Grant issued a general order that barred private citizens hunting fugitive slaves from the camps. He also ordered that blacks who had been used as laborers by the Confederates would be held by the army and employed by the quartermaster. All officers in the command were to deliver to the quartermaster any blacks who had been at Fort Donelson at the time of its capture, and under no circumstances were any fugitives to be returned to their masters.[58] Until the fall of 1862, it was the quartermaster's duty, in Grant's command, to see that blacks coming into Union lines were employed for the benefit of the government; thus, while the letter of Halleck's order was obeyed, its spirit was evaded.

During that period (from February to November 1862), Chaplain Eaton, with other chaplains and officers, had done what he could "to relieve the most urgent and immediate cases of distress" and to check potential danger to the welfare of the soldiers. It was his experience, however, that individual efforts were futile in coping with a problem as immense as that posed by the situation the army confronted in its southern advance.[59]

One assignment the chaplain was given during that period made him a likely candidate for work with the former slaves, although apparently he did not suspect it then nor even realize it later. This was Eaton's assignment by Colonel J. W. Fuller, his regimental and brigade commander, to the position of brigade inspector. In this capacity, the chaplain was to inspect weekly the camps of each regiment in the brigade and to report to the colonel regarding "their police, the cleanliness of the men, and the character of the cooking." The practical experience Eaton gained in the months following this order (July 24, 1862) was probably the decisive factor in Grant's choice of the chaplain to serve as superintendent of the contrabands.[60]

With winter fast approaching and no suitable system organized to meet the needs of the increasing number of blacks who crowded his camps and impeded his progress toward the proposed move against Vicksburg, Grant appointed Chaplain Eaton to serve as superintendent of freedmen for the Department of the Tennessee. Grant, through the chaplain, thus launched the most systematic and continuous organized effort on behalf of former slaves undertaken throughout the war, and he acted on his own initiative, without presidential, congressional, or War Department authorization. It was an act of unusual foresight and courage.[61]

In explaining his instructions to Eaton (November 12, 1862), Grant stated his intention to turn a potential menace into positive assistance to the Union armies. Former slaves could perform many of the camp duties then being done by soldiers and also lend assistance in road building, bridge repairs, the construction of fortifications, and so on. Women could be employed as laundresses, hospital aides, and cooks. He mentioned the possibility of using the former slave as a soldier, eventually even making him a citizen and a voter.[62]

Grant's concern was probably both military and humanitarian. To prevent demoralization and disease in the Union army and to maintain its fighting trim, it was necessary to care for these thousands of destitute, confused, and homeless people. Thus it was his desire to remove them from the army camps, and by using their labor make them self-sustaining if possible, for he had no authority in law for the expenditure of one penny in their behalf.[63]

Eaton was instructed to organize camps for the contrabands, the first at Grand Junction, Tennessee, about five miles from where the army was encamped, providing shelter for them and organizing them for profitable labor. Deserted houses and old army tents were used to shelter the contrabands, with those most endangered by illness, age, or infirmity receiving preference. The sick, including a few smallpox victims, were isolated from the larger group to minimize contagion. The surgeon of the Twenty-seventh Ohio, Dr. W. B. Thrall, was appointed medical director of the contraband camp under Eaton's supervision. Able-bodied blacks were immediately organized in labor forces and put to work harvesting crops from abandoned plantations, cutting wood, and performing various other duties about the camp.[64]

This marked the beginning of Chaplain Eaton's labors with and on behalf of former slaves in the Mississippi Valley. John Eaton was personally responsible for the administration of their affairs in the Department of the Tennessee (which later included all of Mississippi, Arkansas, Kentucky, Tennessee, and parts of Louisiana, as the Division of the Mississippi), from November 1862 until the spring of 1865 when the Freedmen's Bureau assumed the task.[65]

Despite General Grant's full cooperation and support, Eaton found his new assignment fraught with difficulties. A major and continuing problem was obtaining sufficient and competent personnel to work with and protect blacks. Since few soldiers and fewer officers would volunteer for work with the former slaves, Grant had to order a regiment temporarily detailed to guard them and to direct the chief quartermaster of the department to issue to Eaton tools, clothing, and other articles of subsistence.[66]

A still larger grant of authority was provided for the chaplain in December 1862, when Grant authorized him to appoint assistants, subject to his orders, to aid him in his duties, and specifically outlined areas in which Eaton's authority was final.[67] With such support Eaton was able, gradually, to bring a semblance of order out of the chaotic situation that had prevailed in the Union camps and to prevent fresh arrivals of former slaves from impeding the efforts of the armies henceforth.

The original camp at Grand Junction had to be abandoned after the destruction of Grant's base at Holly Springs (December 20, 1862) postponed his move against Vicksburg. The new center was at Memphis, Tennessee, where another camp was established on a similar basis. Suffering was acute during the winter months, but it was far less severe than it would have been had no organized relief effort existed. In the meantime, the government was moving toward a more positive policy for dealing with former slaves. The Emancipation Proclamation, which became effective January 1, 1863, in which Lincoln stated that blacks would be received into the armed forces of the United States, indicated the direction governmental policy was to pursue. The evident acceptance of blacks as laborers and soldiers foreshadowed their ultimate acceptance as citizens.[68]

Eaton and his assistants labored throughout the war to alleviate physical, moral, and social distress among former slaves in the Mississippi Valley. They established camps, or "home farms" as they were also known, at numerous strategic locations including Vicksburg, Cairo, Natchez, Davis Bend, Memphis, and others. They organized a system of labor, aided by General Lorenzo Thomas, the adjutant general, whereby all blacks not enrolled in the officially designated "colored" regiments then being recruited by the army were grouped in five separate classes. The five classes were (1) new arrivals and those employed as laborers by the army; (2) those residing in cities where special skills were of value (this group included barbers, blacksmiths, shoemakers, seamstresses, etc.); (3) woodcutters employed on islands and secure points along the river; (4) plantation laborers, most of whom worked for others who either owned or leased land, while others themselves leased land; and (5) the sick, the young, and the aged. Background, abilities, age, sex, and health were all taken into consideration in determining the individual category, and employment was suited to particular capacities.[69] From these groups the lessees of abandoned lands could hire laborers by contract at a set wage rate low enough that it made the use of black labor profitable. This system, which Thomas and Eaton felt was workable and practical, was sharply criticized in the fall of 1863 by an agent of the Western Sanitary Commission, James E. Yeatman, who felt that it favored the lessees at the expense of the former slaves.[70]

The result of this criticism was the formulation of a system for the leasing of abandoned lands by Yeatman and William P. Mellon, a special agent of the Treasury Department, which was by law authorized to control abandoned land. Under the Mellon-Yeatman proposal the wage scale would have been drastically increased (from $7 to $25 a month at top rate), and the size of the leasehold reduced to minimize speculation. Had this plan been implemented in the Valley, it would have removed from army control the labor of blacks in that department. Since Eaton was convinced, and army commanders supported him, that divided control would produce chaos, a compromise was effected that retained a lower rate of wages, with Treasury agents supervising the leasing of lands, while Eaton and his assistants continued to supervise the former slaves.[71]

Despite this compromise, friction between Eaton's Department of Freedmen and the Treasury Department continued intermittently throughout 1864. In July of that year Eaton journeyed to Washington to prevent the Treasury Department from taking over control of the former slaves as it was attempting to do at that time. Through an interview with Lincoln and George Harrington, the assistant secretary of the Treasury, the chaplain succeeded in retaining control of the former slaves for the army.[72] This system was undisturbed until March 1865, when the Freedmen's Bureau began its operation.

To General Grant belongs the credit for recognizing the serious condition of former slaves in the Mississippi Valley and for assigning to

Chaplain Eaton the task of developing, implementing, and directing the vast program that directly addressed their needs. Various social and religious agencies also contributed to the educational improvement of the former slaves; a few examples indicate the sort of aid upon which Eaton was able to draw.

The poverty and helplessness of many of these black people were almost beyond belief, but their ignorance was even more appalling. Although Eaton's efforts on their behalf at Grand Junction and Memphis eliminated the worst physical distress, there was still much suffering in the contraband camps. The chaplain had barely time to organize the camp at Memphis in late 1862, when the concentration of Grant's army (in January 1863) for its final move toward Vicksburg caused Confederate planters by the score to abandon their plantations, taking their able-bodied slaves with them to Texas and leaving behind to fend for themselves the very young and the very old. It was the chaplain's duty to collect these people into contraband camps and make provision for them from the resources available to him. Grant provided rations and what tents and old army clothing he could. Other aid came from various aid societies to which Eaton wrote asking assistance.[73]

After the surrender of Vicksburg on July 4, 1863, which left the entire length of the Mississippi in the control of Union forces, Bishop William Elder of Natchez, the Roman Catholic prelate of Mississippi, was contacted indirectly by Chaplain Eaton. The intermediary was a Catholic physician on Grant's staff, a Dr. Hewit. Elder enlisted the aid of a recently arrived Belgian priest, Father Charles von Quekelberge, who devoted his entire time to work among the contrabands in the home farms at Natchez and Vicksburg. The priest continued this work for several months in cooperation with Eaton's assistants until his health was broken, forcing an end to his labors. "While Bishop Elder was chiefly concerned about the spiritual welfare of the emancipated Negroes, he was not insensible to their material wretchedness." Yet he was reluctant to make any friendly gestures to the Union officers of the forces occupying the Valley in view of what the planters, Catholic and non-Catholic, might think, "To assume the role of champion of the freed Negroes who only a few months before represented the wealth of so many of his flock would have left Elder open to the charge that he was insensible to the Catholic planter's present economic distress, perhaps even to the charge that he had been a secret abolitionist all the while."[74] In the summer of 1863, Dr. Hewit suggested to the bishop that a religious order be invited to open an orphanage in Vicksburg. Elder replied that he would not oppose the idea but that he could in no way cooperate positively in the matter. The doctor contacted the Fathers of the Holy Cross at Notre Dame but was unable to arouse interest in the project. Finally the bishop wrote to fellow prelate Archbishop Purcell of Cincinnati suggesting that as a Northern spokesman for the church he should initiate the project. This too met with failure.[75]

Within two years Elder and another associate, Archbishop Jean Marie Odin of New Orleans, were both appealing to religious orders to supply teachers and open schools for the blacks in their districts. Elder saw the former slaves, "especially the youngsters, as potential converts." In the spring of 1865 a great number of black children were going to school and this for the first time in their lives. "It was unfortunate," he continued, "that so many of them were going to 'New England Teachers' who were circulating among their pupils 'all sorts of puritan papers & tracts.'" Elder specifically requested that an order of black nuns, the Oblate Sisters of Providence, be sent to Vicksburg and Natchez to teach the black children in those cities, but was unable to secure their services.[76]

Bishop Odin also sought aid for an educational program for the black population of Louisiana in the spring of 1865. He appealed "to the religious orders within his jurisdiction to open schools for blacks" but received no answer for several months. "So intense was southern feeling against educating blacks that the religious orders," many of whom shared the sentiment as loyal Southerners, "shied away from the task for fear of alienating white patronage." By the time the prelates of the North and South were in full communication and cooperation once again, the opportunity for work had been largely forfeited as other churches and agencies assumed the task of educating the former slaves. Thus "a combination of racial prejudice, timidity, and a scarcity of manpower and resources" cost the Catholic Church "the chance for large-scale conversion of the Negroes to Catholicism [during and] after the Civil War."[77]

Although the Roman Catholic Church proved reluctant to contribute to the education of the former slaves, other churches and social agencies were able and eager to provide Chaplain Eaton with supplies and teachers.[78] It was Eaton's belief that though the first responsibility of his Freedman's Department was to provide material necessities, employment, and protection to the blacks, this was first "in order only— not in importance." He believed that the mental and moral enlightenment of former slaves was the truly great object of his labors and that the achievement of at least a rudimentary school system for their education would ultimately produce the greatest benefits for the former slaves and the nation. "Accordingly from the very first, efforts were made to secure the assistance of army chaplains, and such other men as were likely to feel the importance of this matter." The aid of benevolent persons, either individuals or groups, was also welcomed by Eaton. Some of those he singled out for praise were the American Missionary Association, the Western Freedman's Aid Commission, and the Society of Friends.[79]

Progress was at first slow, uncoordinated, and very limited, because of the instability of the military situation in the Valley and the lack of real central authority over these efforts. Eaton's control was informal and hence minimal, and success depended on the cooperation among the many independent agencies and individuals working under different auspices to achieve the same ends. An increase in the number of volunteer workers followed the capture of Vicksburg and subsequent occupation of Natchez, which guaranteed Union control of the territory bordering the Mississippi and improved the security of those involved in this charitable work.[80]

To these volunteer teachers General Grant proffered welcome, if at first unauthorized, assistance in the form of transportation, quarters, rations, and classroom facilities whenever military considerations made it possible for him to do so. This achieved a dual purpose: in addition to facilitating and encouraging the work of those engaged in educating former slaves, it also brought the agents of the societies into closer contact with Eaton, for it was through his Freedman's Department that requests for such aid were channeled. In September of 1863, Secretary Stanton formally authorized the aid program that Grant had undertaken on his own authority.[81]

Despite this aid and the increasing size of the volunteer teaching force, much effort was duplicated. A shortage of funds and facilities also hampered the work. Still further, there were difficulties arising from the jealousies and friction unavoidable when so many independent agencies are working on the same problems in the same area. This situation prevailed until September 1864, when the War Department recognized the need for a centralized authority to control and systematize all efforts for the education of blacks. Accordingly Eaton, in his capacity as general superintendent of freedmen, was designated to serve as the coordinator of all educational efforts in the department.[82]

On the basis of this order Eaton appointed seven district superintendents, four of whom were ministers and had been army chaplains.[83] He then called them to his headquarters in Memphis for a joint conference with the representatives of the aid societies and church missions boards. At the conference there occurred an extended and frank discussion of the problems in providing former slaves with an opportunity for education. From this exchange of ideas, participants reached a general agreement concerning the need for a carefully regulated system, and on October 20, 1864, Eaton's office issued a circular outlining the system agreed upon and the rules by which it would be operated.[84]

This circular, which went to all those engaged in educational work and to all commanding officers in the department, instructed each school superintendent to report to the local superintendent of freedmen (Eaton's assistants), who were charged with the task of procuring and regulating all school property. Eaton would furnish clerical help for the district when the local superintendents of freedmen considered it necessary. Cities and towns were subdivided into school wards, and pupils were required to attend the school located in their district except in cases of special permission from Eaton. Local school superintendents and agency representatives would decide who would teach where, and the district school superintendents would be responsible for determining school hours, textbooks, organization, classification, and discipline. A minimal tuition fee, in lieu of property taxes, which were impossible to collect under wartime circumstances, helped to defray the cost of the program and had the added value, Eaton believed, of developing in the blacks a sense of responsibility and dignity. The maximum fee was $1.25 per month per pupil to be paid by the parents or guardians. The fee was flexible, however, and was based on the ability of the parent to pay. No child was denied education because of a parent's inability to pay, and many attended these schools on a tuition-free basis. Although Eaton did not support the fee system in theory but only out of necessity, he was convinced that it had a positive effect on the blacks, for it gave them a feeling of having contributed to their own improvement. Night schools were also inaugurated under Eaton's aegis to provide adults an opportunity to obtain an education in the hours not given to labor.[85]

At the same time the circular was issued, Eaton, in his capacity as general superintendent of freedmen, wrote a lengthy report to Secretary Stanton in the form of an open letter, detailing the work being done, the intent behind it, and prospects for the future. He concluded the letter with these words: "Sensible of the trying circumstances under which this action is taken, and the great responsibilities involved, we appeal under God to the considerate judgment of every friend of universal education."[86]

Exact figures on the number of blacks who benefited from these educational programs are not available because some agencies and individuals were unwilling to cooperate with the Freedman's Department. The available statistics are reasonably accurate, however, and do indicate the size of the program inaugurated and supervised by Chaplain Eaton. For example, in one calendar year (from January 1, 1863, to January 1, 1864), Eaton's Freedman's Department cared specifically for 113,650 former slaves in a department that according to the 1860 census had 770,000 blacks.[87] Multiply this by the increasing number of slaves liberated by the deeper penetrations of the Union armies during 1864 and the spring of 1865, and an appreciation of the immensity of Eaton's task is possible. It is true that Eaton was not a chaplain after October 9, 1863, for he was given rank as colonel of the Ninth Louisiana Native Guards to strengthen his hand in dealing with other military commanders at that time.[88] Yet this in no way detracts from the fact that this vast undertaking was directed by a man who entered the army to serve God and country as a chaplain and who continued that work on behalf of a people whose bonds, having been broken by the army, could turn nowhere but to the army in their distress.

Although these examples are not an exhaustive record of the work done by Union chaplains in educating former slaves, they do indicate the general nature of their efforts and reveal the chaplains' optimism regarding the beneficent effect of education on blacks. It is unfortunate, in a very real sense, that the United States Army was not better utilized as a training school for the freedmen. Perhaps a policy such as that suggested to his distinguished father by Charles Francis Adams, Jr., who commanded a black regiment, might have warranted official consideration. "As soon as quieter times for soldiers shall come I should hope to see Chaplains and schoolmasters attached to each regiment. . . . My hope is that for years to come our army will be made up of mainly blacks and number many thousand. I would have at least a four year term of enlistment and yearly send out of the Army from fifteen to twenty thousand black citizens, old soldiers and masters of some form of skilled labor. Such is my philanthropic plan for the race and I do not know that I can do better than to devote to it some few of the passing years of my life." Earlier, Adams had doubted the wisdom of recruiting blacks, but his service as an officer in the Fifth Massachusetts Cavalry, a black regiment, had caused him to revise his estimate of former slaves as soldiers and as potential citizens.[89]

One cannot estimate precisely the value of the learning that the former slaves attained from army chaplains and other concerned individuals. Certainly many blacks were aided greatly in the traumatic transition from dependent bondage to independent and responsible citizenship by the education thus obtained. And education was an enduring contribution, a truth aptly expressed in the words of Chaplain Eaton: "Whatever education has been accomplished among the people cannot be taken from them."[90]

5

THE CAUSE OF IT ALL

Nearly all chaplains who wrote about their service with the army recorded both their personal reactions to the war and their beliefs as to its causes, and many of them also attempted to determine the feelings of the men in the ranks regarding the same issues. It is likely that some chaplains were not deeply concerned with the slavery issue, as there were in the Northern states denominations and clergy that had not yet seen slavery as a great moral issue by 1861. Yet it is improbable that in recording his experiences after a war that had abolished slavery a former chaplain would disclose any proslavery sentiments. Almost universally, however, as revealed in the accounts of chaplains who did write, both chaplains and men evinced a strong antislavery sentiment coupled with a firm conviction that the institution of slavery was at the root of all causes to which the war had been attributed. Such convictions, based on the belief that Christianity and slavery were totally antithetical, were in vivid contrast to the thinking of Southern clergy. Slavery was to them a political question of local rather than national concern, and it was being attacked by a hypocritical Northern clergy that they believed had perverted the gospel of Christ. Secession was held to be the inherent right of any state.

The Reverend Joseph Cross, who served in the Confederate army as a chaplain, said of the Union armies, "our invaders have been utterly regardless of every principle of the Christian religion and every sentiment of enlightened humanity."[1] Cross believed that Northern churches preached a corrupted Christianity and that God, having ordained the separation of the Southern states from the Union, would establish them in independence. He also believed the Southern cause to be as holy as Christianity itself, and he was convinced that God would never abandon its supporters. Undoubtedly it was "the plan of Providence" that the Southern people would form a separate and independent nation. After this occurred, Southern pulpits would be freed from the corrupting influence of skeptical philosophy, and the people would be liberated from the contagion of New England "neology, puritanical fanaticism, and the whole hell-brood of vipers and vampires which have poisoned and drained the very life-blood of Northern Christianity."[2]

In stark contrast, when Chaplain James B. Rogers of the Fourteenth Wisconsin Infantry entered the slave states for the first time, traveling with his regiment up the Tennessee River into Kentucky from Paducah, he received the distinct impression that the surrounding countryside was inferior. He observed great barren areas, deserted when the soil had become exhausted by the continuous planting of the same crop. Schools, he stated, were also nonexistent. His impression was that the curse of the Almighty seemed to rest upon the land of slavery, extending to all interests alike. The very soil itself seemed cursed with barrenness, at least over wide districts, although it had been rich in its native condition.[3]

Rogers considered secession and its immediate result, civil war, to be acts of treason, a viewpoint he emphasized in his ministry as a chaplain.[4] A participant in the bloody battle at Shiloh, he viewed the carnage and speculated as to its cause. Only one truthful answer, he believed, could be given to this question. A single agent, standing in back of every other, had been instrumental in urging on the conflict and had supplied the rebellion with both motive and energy. "Its evil life could be prolonged only by dooming to death thousands upon thousands like those who lay there that morning stark and cold on the bank of the Tennessee. Slavery!" Rogers considered the thousands of men who were killed to be offerings on the "altar of slavery."[5]

The chaplain occasionally encountered antislavery sentiment among pro-Union men in the South. These exceptional people realized, apparently, that whites had been victimized by slavery quite as much as had blacks, although in a different manner. One of them, a Colonel Hamilton of Texas, was quoted as saying, "I know that slavery must perish, in order that liberty may survive. I know that the manacles must fall from the fettered limbs of the black race on this continent, in order that the white man may not be manacled."[6]

Chaplain Rogers expressed amazement at the credulity of the poor Southern whites, who appeared to him more ignorant than the slaves. Yet these people supported and labored to establish a government that would only perpetuate their wretched status.[7] Rogers favored a vigorous prosecution of the war and argued that slavery, rebellion, and secession should be ended once and for all by this means: "Timid measures are treason now. It is bold, active, decided men, men with nerve enough to neglect precedent and all the past, and with resolute hand reach forth to grasp the future, that we want."[8]

Arthur B. Fuller, chaplain of the Sixteenth Massachusetts Infantry, remarked that his earliest antislavery inclinations came from attending a series of lectures in Albany, New York. "I [had] been attending a course of antislavery lectures by Frederick Douglas, the fugitive slave, and [had] become greatly interested," he explained.[9] He stated his belief that there was a definite slave-power conspiracy that promoted disunion and prepared for war, especially during the administration of President James Buchanan.[10] Fuller viewed secession as treason, "a despicable act of cowardice," remarking in a letter to his family after having passed through Baltimore, "You can hardly imagine how much the evidence of a more stern dealing with traitors and a more vigorous prosecution of the war inspire the soldiers with fresh hope and confidence."[11] The chaplain's antipathy to slavery was reinforced as he served in Virginia, where he observed the effect of the institution everywhere. One incident he described as being especially distasteful to him involved reading in the *Day Book*, a Norfolk newspaper, the advertisement of a sale of free blacks at auction, for nonpayment of city taxes. The sudden awareness that this was an everyday event in the slave states outraged Fuller's sense of human decency.[12]

The chaplain of the Eightieth Ohio Infantry, George Whitfield Pepper, also viewed secession and civil war as treason. Shortly after the war he visited Richmond, where he had a brief interview with Robert E. Lee. Although he was deeply impressed by the evidently fine character of the former Confederate commander, the chaplain nevertheless remarked: "had it not been for that one dark spot upon his fame, treason, I would have left the presence of General Lee, impressed with his greatness and goodness of heart."[13]

When commenting on the condition of the countryside during Sherman's drive through northern Georgia to Atlanta during the summer of 1864, Pepper pointed to the depressed state of the poor whites who blindly accepted the dictation of the slaveholders. He expressed the opinion that the population evidenced similar characteristics wherever slavery existed: "the same detestable ignorance, the same degradation and stolidity, the same dullness and opacity of understanding, the same disinclination and feebleness as to all the nobler employments of the mind. . . . The people seemed to be devoted only to sensual pursuits and to desire merely to satisfy their animal appetites. And thus the curse of slavery plucks the crown from the head, and strips the soul of its beams of glory, and sinks it to a lower and vulgar abyss, where it lies in the utter wreck of its nobility and perfection."[14]

The chaplain also spoke of the terrible effect of slavery on blacks but was optimistic about their future in freedom. Pepper believed that the federal government was obligated to act on behalf of the former slave, and he also believed that blacks had been gifted with more than usual intelligence, developed through necessity for survival rather than formal instruction. Slaves had been kept in an abominable state of degradation, a fact that was common knowledge and merited the immediate attention of the federal government. But a quickness to learn and acquire knowledge had been demonstrated, he observed, in the cases of thousands of slaves who had mastered the subjects generally taught in the common schools in an incredibly short period of time. In this regard he expressed his hopes for the future: "I appeal not to the affections or humanity, but to the justice of every one . . . whether men so constituted present no character which a wise government can mould to the great purpose of augmenting the prosperity of the country, and the happiness of society."[15] Chaplain Pepper made no apologies for the depredations of Sherman's troops in Georgia. In his view the destruction of property was a better means to victory than was the destruction of life; furthermore, any destruction inflicted was richly deserved as the price of treason. This was especially true, he said, in South Carolina, for that state had plotted the treason that brought destruction to the rest of the South; South Carolina was reaping at last the consequences of its treason.[16]

A lieutenant in the Fourth Louisiana Native Guards, George H. Hepworth, who had previously served a Massachusetts regiment as chaplain, was appalled at the degrading effect of slavery on owner and slave alike.[17] He cited repeated encounters with slaveholders, expressing his shock at their duplicity. Slavery, he had become convinced, was the source of innumerable evils: adultery, fornication, incest, the sale of one's own offspring, general poverty at the attainment of wealth for the select few—these were but some of the fruits of slavery.[18] The true cause of secession, Hepworth asserted, was directly traceable to slavery; the idea of war gained support because the price of slaves was gradually increasing and had reached the point at which the profit on the crop was materially lowered. In his opinion, "Secessionism was little else than an immense financial speculation covered up by a vast cumulus of nebulous rhetoric about Southern rights. The only right they cared for was the right to turn human blood into bullion." The people of the South, according to Hepworth, were irritated not by the severity of the laws that had been passed but by the "humane sentiment of the age as represented by the people of the Free States." They candidly admitted that the independence of the Confederacy would have opened the African slave trade, which would have brought the price of slaves down, thereby increasing the profit on the crops cultivated by slave labor.[19]

The extremes to which Southern clergymen had gone in an effort to prove the inferiority of blacks, and hence the justice of slavery, were revealed to Hepworth as he chanced to find an old copy of DeBow's *Review*, containing an article by a Reverend Samuel Cartwright of New Orleans. The article purported to explain the *true* biblical account of the Creation. In both the King James and Douay versions of the Bible, the Hebrew had been incorrectly translated, according to Cartwright. God had created "living creatures" (blacks) and Adam (white man) at different times, he asserted. The "living creatures," being destined to serve the white man as slaves, were unhappy out of that condition. Cartwright carried the absurdity to its logical conclusion, Hepworth noted, by asserting that the serpent that had beguiled Eve was in fact a black gardener who seduced the innocent white woman. This reputed "scholarship" by a professedly "Christian" minister amazed the former chaplain, who found it difficult to believe that a clergyman could have become so perverted.[20]

Chaplain Henry Clay Trumbull of the Tenth Connecticut Infantry, in recounting his reaction to the Confederate attack on Fort Sumter, stated that when, on April 14, 1861, "the old flag was there hauled down under the hostile fire of those who had been trusted as its defenders, and the aroused North was in the white heat of a righteous indignation," he thought of the sermon he was to deliver on the following day.[21] Only one text seemed appropriate—the command of the Prince of Peace: "He that hath no sword, let him sell his garment, and buy one."[22] The chaplain had had definite antislavery views before the war. In a conversation with a friend from the South concerning the institution of slavery, he had remarked: "Well, my dear friend, if . . . *the system of slavery* requires that it be made a crime to teach one of God's children to read God's Word, and also requires God's ministers to perform the marriage service with a distinct proviso that man may put asunder those whom God has joined together, don't you think that system itself is, to speak mildly and reverently, a *damnable* system? I think it is."[23]

Trumbull related in detail his reactions on meeting the hundreds of contrabands who flocked to the Union armies wherever and whenever they penetrated the slave states. It was his impression that blacks almost universally welcomed emancipation, even if they were faithful to their masters, for they believed that the Union armies were God's instrument of deliverance. "Whether slaves were well-treated or ill, whether their masters were kind and considerate or harsh and severe, a desire for liberty seemed to possess the slave heart." The chaplain thought that all slaves were ready to attempt the escape from bondage whenever the opportunity presented itself, the only exception being those who were not able to take their families with them and were not willing to go without them. "When someone said to Mr. Lincoln that the slaves had no desire for emancipation, that as a class they were contented as they were, he replied that, if that were really so, it would furnish the best reason he had ever heard for thinking that they were unfit to be free." Trumbull, however, considered all of the slaves he met, or of whom he heard, as evidence contradicting this statement: "They all longed for liberty, and all were ready to grasp it when they could."[24]

George S. Bradley, chaplain of the Twenty-second Wisconsin Infantry, rejoiced in a change of army policy toward blacks brought about by the colonel of his regiment. The colonel, William L. Utley, had been ordered by the brigade commander, Brigadier General Q. A. Gillmore, to surrender four contrabands to their owners who were purported to be loyal. In his refusal to comply with this order, Utley said that although he recognized the authority of the general to issue commands regarding "all military matters pertaining to the movements of the army," he acknowledged no authority concerning the surrender of contrabands "save that of the President of the United States."[25] The colonel then mentioned in passing that his superior was "no doubt conversant with that proclamation dated Sept, 22nd, 1862, and the law of Congress on the subject." Utley stated in conclusion that he personally had had nothing to do with the entrance of the contrabands into the camp and would have nothing to do with sending them away.[26] There followed a rather heated discussion concerning rank, military protocol, and emancipation between the colonel and the brigade commander.

The next day General Gillmore informed Colonel Utley, with some embarrassment, that the proclamation of the president and the act of Congress had been reviewed and that a new policy would henceforth be effective: no more contrabands were to be returned to slavery. The chaplain endorsed the stand his commander had taken and rejoiced that the Army of the United States would no longer be reduced to the status of slave catcher.[27]

The test of the new policy came a short time later when the regiment passed through Georgetown, Kentucky. Colonel Utley warned the residents of that community, who had threatened to seize the blacks with the regiment, that his men would march with loaded rifles and fixed bayonets; he advised them that if any interference was intended, all women and children should be removed in advance. The Twenty-second Wisconsin passed through the community without incident, and when the regiment left Kentucky, the chaplain rejoiced that no black who had sought protection with it had been forced to return to bondage.[28]

Bradley quoted his predecessor as chaplain of the regiment, Caleb Pillsbury, with regard to the avid proslavery sentiment of the people of Kentucky. "On the subject of slavery the people are very nearly united—almost to a unit. The leading men of the State and the most influential classes of the people are resolutely, almost madly determined to sustain the institution at all hazards. They are ready to peril anything in its support."[29] Pillsbury declared that both the governor and the legislature of Kentucky openly and insultingly denounced the president, Congress, and all others who suggested the abolition of slavery as a means of preserving the Union. After professing his belief that "with Kentuckians slavery is the first object," Pillsbury intimated that "the state would join herself to the Southern Confederacy at once, had she no hope of a pro-slavery triumph in the North, and were she not to [*sic*] closely watched by the loyal armies."[30]

Chaplain Bradley's response upon hearing of the treatment of Union prisoners in Andersonville Prison was to blame such inhumanity on the institution of slavery with all its barbarity. Of those responsible for Southern treason and such crimes against defenseless prisoners, he said, "there should be no mercy toward Davis, Lee, and their tools. *Hang them!*"[31] The chaplain vehemently denounced the Copperheads of the North as the worst sort of traitors.[32] The men, he said, felt the same about those who tried to defeat them on the home front. He quoted a private soldier as follows: "There is nothing that will make me as mad so soon as to think of those Copperheads at the North." The soldier particularly resented the fact that the men in the ranks were fighting the rebels while some of the people at home were doing all that they possibly could to lend aid and comfort to the enemy. He threatened: "They better crawl into their holes before we return home, or there will be a savage time."[33]

On the march with Sherman's army through Georgia, from Chatta-nooga to Atlanta, Chaplain Bradley noted that the ravages of war were forcing former slaveholders and slave catchers to live in circumstances like those of the former slave. He found this to be simple justice and applauded. In commenting on the criticisms hurled at Sherman for the depredations of his "Bummers" in Georgia and South Carolina, he posed the following question, which he promptly answered: "Do you say it is terrible thus to destroy property? So it is, but better thus than to de-stroy life. . . . Let ruin bring them [the people of the South] to their senses, if nothing else will."[34] When conversing with a Southern clergy-man in South Carolina (March 1865), who told him that the people along the route of the army were becoming very bitter because of the destruc-tion of property, Bradley replied, "Well, let them rage. We have their hatred already, and they have sworn eternal separation, so that any little increase in hate will not materially affect matters. They have the alternatives before them in plain English—submission, or *coercion* and *subjugation*."[35]

Chaplain Bradley was convinced that slavery had caused the war, and he stated that even the people of the South with whom he had conversed had readily admitted that this was so. "People," he said, "have told me that they went to war for the purpose of making their institutions more secure."[36] Thus Bradley had not the faintest glimmer of doubt regard-ing the justice of the Union cause and the imperative need to conclude the war with total victory. The platform adopted by the Democratic party for the election of 1864, with its "peace plank," seemed to him an indication of surrender to the forces of slavery and a repudiation of the efforts of three and a half years of sacrifice. He stated this convic-tion emphatically in a letter to his family, asserting that he would in-finitely prefer to die on the field of battle than to "submit to the reign of *southern despots, or yield an inch to their infernal desires.*"[37]

Bradley felt it to be imperative that the right side prevail and affirmed his belief that the nation's flag, purified by the blood of the thousands who fought and died for the Union cause, would eventually wave in triumph over all sections of the country. "The rights of *all* shall be emblazoned upon her folds in letters of fire, and the United States of America will sustain a name not second to any nation on earth." The war, he declared, could not stop until the victory of the Union was assured and "every chain [was] broken that binds human limbs and reduces *man*, created in the image of his Maker, to the level of the brute." For lasting peace to be possible, Chaplain Bradley protested, "slavery, the curse of our nation, must be plucked out, *root and branch*, and the tree of Liberty firmly planted." Although unable to believe that McClellan would be nominated and elected to the executive position, he expressed his confidence that there would be no peace so long as the institution of slavery existed, for the army would never submit to the dictation of a weaker force. He stated: "But I will not dwell longer upon this subject. I have no fears but 'Honest Old Abe' will fill the chair at the White House another four years, and will *see* this thing through, despite southern foes and northern traitors."[38]

The Reverend John R. Adams, who entered the army on July 4, 1861, as the chaplain of the Fifth Maine Infantry at the age of sixty, served throughout the war, becoming the chaplain of the 121st New York Infantry when his first regiment was disbanded in the summer of 1864.[39] Chaplain Adams was not reluctant in expressing his views on the causes of the war. To him there was ultimately but one cause—slavery. He considered this moral evil to be the source of all issues that divided the nation, and he could not believe that a just God would bless those who defended it. He stated his conviction as follows: "When I read in the Scriptures of the marked expression of God's hatred of oppression, I feel that ultimately the Divine blessing will not rest upon a cause which (according to Alexander H. Stephens, of Georgia, the Vice-President of the Southern Confederacy) 'glories in making slavery the cornerstone of their anticipated republic.'"[40]

While accompanying his regiment during the Peninsular campaign in the spring of 1862, Adams commented on the vast numbers of "contented" blacks who flocked to the federal forces. "Slavery has received a blow from which it will not recover," he remarked. And again, "Slavery is receiving a death-blow! I am glad that it is so. . . . Whenever our army goes, contrabands abound."[41] When Lincoln issued his preliminary Proclamation of Emancipation (September 22, 1862), the chaplain defended the president's right to act as he had. "I told my friends that the war would kill slavery. Wherever the army has moved, there slavery is good for nothing. Negroes come into our lines of their own accord. . . . If by attacking slavery he [Lincoln] can withdraw aid and comfort from the enemy, he has a right to do it."[42]

Adams also made no apologies for the destruction of property inflicted on the slave states by the Union armies. Viewing the desolation of the countryside near Warrenton, Virginia, he remarked: "I have no sympathy whatever with the disloyalty of this part of the country. If the inhabitants have broken the solemn compact, they must not call upon our army to protect their property." Later, when the Shenandoah Valley of Virginia was systematically devastated to eliminate its value as a granary for the Confederacy, Adams stated his belief that the destruction of property in this manner was entirely justified both as punishment for rebellion and as a war measure.[43]

The chaplain believed that the enemies of the federal government at home and in the field were equally guilty of treason against the United States. Referring to the Peace Democrats, he said, "I hope the time will come when the Copperheads will swing." The Confederate argument that the government of the United States had been too oppressive was absurd in his judgment. It had been *their* government, he pointed out, as three-fourths of the administrations since the Revolution had been headed by Southern men or Southern sympathizers. Even such highly respected Southern leaders as Robert E. Lee in some way deserved the ruin they had brought upon themselves by their treason. Adams acknowledged that he had previously had a good opinion of General Lee but admitted that his estimate of the man had changed after the general had, in his parting address to his soldiers after his surrender, thanked them for their "fidelity to their country." The chaplain contended that "all who, having been educated at the expense of the nation, and having taken oath to defend the flag of their country, then desert it, deserve to be wiped out in some way."[44]

Another chaplain, Charles A. Humphreys of the Second Massachusetts Cavalry, became an abolitionist as a result of his experience in a Southern prison. Captured by Mosby's guerrillas while conducting a burial service for Union dead near Aldie, Virginia, he was confined at Camp Oglethorpe, Georgia, for nearly two months before being released.[45] During that time he witnessed the barbarities, as he described them, of the treatment of Union prisoners held there. In describing his reactions, the chaplain expressed his opinion that crimes such as these could be committed only by men "debased by long years of familiarity with the cruelties of human slavery." Although he maintained that it was necessary to forgive such people and that they should be looked upon more with pity than with anger since they had been "dehumanized by the institution under which they were nourished," Humphreys also stated that "we cannot forget the fearful price paid for its extinction not only in blood on the fields of battle but in exposure and starvation within the prison-pens of the South." In conclusion he asked that "Heaven save us from harboring again in our social or political system any such cruel injustice."[46]

Such a policy as that of Southern authorities toward Union prisoners, Humphreys believed, was probably dictated by military considerations. The Confederates received from Northern prisons well-fed, healthy men, ready to return to the field of battle, while in exchange the Union received broken, half-starved men, unfit for duty for months, if ever. To the chaplain, this was treachery inexcusable.[47]

Chaplain James J. Marks (Sixty-third Pennsylvania Infantry), captured by the Confederates when he chose to remain with the wounded of Heintzelman's Corps after the Battle of Savage Station, related a conversation with a Confederate Major Ker who had accused the North of starting the war.[48] Marks then proceeded to answer the charges. After remarking on the fact that the major, as an old army officer, must have seen service in the Northern states as well as in the South and therefore must have become familiar with the attitudes and desires of the people of the free states, Marks stated his belief that the major should realize that the war had been forced upon the North. He pointed out that it had not been the North that for years had been threatening hostilities and the division of the Union. The people of the North, Marks claimed, made the largest concessions, yielding everything the South asked in the spirit of compromise and peace. "*We* had no taste for war, the genius of our people did not run in that direction. The very thought of civil war was dismissed from our minds as a hideous dream, and no man amongst us dared to predict such a national calamity."[49]

On the other hand the South, according to Marks, had been preparing the mind of the public for this event by predicting war and urging the people to prepare for it. The chaplain emphasized the fact that even Southern schools were, essentially, military academies; children had been educated to look forward eagerly to the time when they would fight to force greater concessions from the North or win glory on the field of battle. He declared, however, that the major fully realized that this was not the spirit of the people of the free states. "*We* felt that in peace was our greatness, and that all the institutions we most dearly prized flourished under its shadow. You forced this war upon us, major, and having commenced it, you must take all the consequences."[50]

The major denounced the chaplain vigorously, stating that his chief desire was to see the South avenged. Some prominent men of the locality who were present and overheard the exchange endorsed the major's remarks and added that they wished to see no more prisoners taken. Peace could be restored, so they indicated, only if the United States restored or paid for their slaves, paid the entire cost of the war, divided the territories equally with the South, and permitted Maryland, Missouri, and Kentucky to join the Confederacy. Chaplain Marks responded by saying that if he went North and advocated peace on such terms he would be considered insane; at the same time, he rebuked the major and his friends for malice such as had never been heard in the North. He was saved from physical assault by the crowd of listeners only when the colonel of a North Carolina regiment joined Major Ker at the chaplain's side and the major calmed the crowds by reminding them that such treatment of a prisoner was not worthy of Southern chivalry.[51]

Marks echoed Humphreys's belief regarding the conditions in Southern prisons. Only a "civilization" that could condone slavery would permit such intolerable conditions, he asserted. "With all their boasted civilization and humanity, the Confederate government continues to immerse thousands of men in living tombs." It should not be considered surprising, he observed, that one-third of the men who had been imprisoned did not come out alive—and that all prisoners were marked by the results of breathing such contaminated air. "The treatment which our prisoners have received at the hands of the Rebel government displays, more than anything else, how completely it has thrown itself out of the pale of Christian civilization."[52]

The chaplain also commented on the effects of slavery in Virginia, as he viewed the people of that state. Blacks as a class, he thought, were superior in many respects to the poor whites whose ignorance and animality he found incredible. To his surprise, he found that blacks were seldom vindictive despite the oppression they had endured. One former slave in particular impressed Marks, a middle-aged man named Hanson Yerly, who although only one-sixteenth black had been forced into a life of perpetual slavery. This man, whose family had been sold away from him, was firmly convinced that God was punishing Virginia for permitting the interstate slave trade to ruin black families. The chaplain agreed.[53]

Father William Corby (Eighty-eighth New York Infantry) did not frequently speak concerning what he called political matters and sectional interests, but occasionally before a battle he would speak to his men, reminding them of the just and noble cause for which they were fighting. One such occasion was on the eve of an anticipated battle at Mine Run, Virginia. Recalling the scene, Father Corby said that he had spoken a few words of encouragement to the men, "exhorting them to remember that they were fighting in a just cause to preserve the integrity of the United States, which had never committed an act of tyranny toward any of its citizens." He reminded them that the battle they were fighting was that of liberty, justice, and the rights of humanity, and "that England, who largely fomented the Rebellion by her emissaries in this country, hypocritically crying out against the barbarity of slavery, was now aiding, by her cursed ill-gotten gold, the Southern people to maintain in perpetual slavery 4,000,000 human beings." The chaplain felt that all of this was being done to divide the nation and destroy the principle of self-government, "wrested from her tyrannical hand by the brave heroes of the Revolution, who won for us our inheritance of liberty."[54] Such an appeal must have been effective in preparing men to meet the perils of battle on the morrow.

Father Corby. This statue is at Gettysburg. A duplicate statue is located on the University of Notre Dame campus, where it is referred to as "Fair Catch Corby" by students because it resembles a football player indicating a fair catch punt return. (Photograph by author)

The chaplain of the Third Rhode Island Heavy Artillery, Reverend Frederic Denison, was yet another who was convinced that slavery had been the ultimate cause of the war; he was further convinced that the men of the ranks also believed it, viewing the war as a struggle for national unity and brotherhood. In his opinion, the states that seceded from the Union fought for its dissolution and for the permanent establishment of slavery on a legal basis. Those states that remained loyal, on the other hand, fought for the unity of the country and freedom for all within its boundaries. It was the chaplain's firm conviction that the men of the Northern armies had battled for the dual purpose of maintaining the Union and freeing the slaves.[55]

Denison was rather quickly disenchanted with the "aristocratic Old South" as the Union armies penetrated the slave states, giving him an opportunity to see for himself the "elegant" culture of which he had heard such lavish praise. It was to his eye but a facade, a superficial veneer that helped to cover but did nothing to correct the squalid existence of the Southern masses, white or black. The homes of the Southern planters were, according to Denison, "by no means prepossessing." Pencil sketches by various artists and impressions gained from his reading had led the chaplain to "expect something more tasteful and elegant." Denison had believed that "reputed wealth and cavalier pride naturally promised culture and excellence." The mansions of the slaveholders, however, did not live up to his expectations; in fact, he described them as being "quite unlovely; usually large, but coarse and unfinished, showing best from a distance; for sanitary reasons, without cellars, and raised a few feet from the earth on stone or brick piers, and largely furnished with coarse verandas; all revealing a lordly ambition without a lordly cultivation. . . . [Plantation homes were] as a general thing, the castles of haughty indolence and aspiring inability. Their background consisted of low, dark slave-barracks. Magnolias overshadowed misery."[56]

Denison was fascinated by the haunting melodies of the former slaves, whom he met by the score. The "relics of slavery" he called them: their composers had sung in the darkness of perpetual bondage, but even in their bonds had captured the true spirit of freedom in song. The chaplain expressed a strong desire to preserve these "songs from the dark."[57]

But despite his hatred for slavery and its offspring, rebellion, Denison was moved by a spirit of compassion as he viewed the wreckage of a culture now dead. "With all our opposition to rebels and to slavery, that inspired the rebellion, and with all our joy at the downfall of the Confederacy," we nevertheless "felt a kind of sympathy, strongly verging on compassion, for the people of the South who had madly, foolishly brought upon themselves such great losses and such painful destitution." In continuing his description of the end of a civilization, Denison stated that the foundation of Southern domestic and political economy had been completely destroyed with the abolition of slavery.[58]

The chaplain also spoke of the terrible cost of the war, in lives, in blood, and in property; yet he considered its results priceless. The complete overthrow of slavery in the nation and the decisive demonstration that the United States was a national government rather than a league of independent states were to Chaplain Denison invaluable gains for the nation. Denison considered the government of the Union, having been tested by war, to be the foremost example of a self-reliant federal state "ever known in the world's history."[59]

Lieutenant Colonel Samuel Fallows of the Fortieth Wisconsin Infantry had served previously as the chaplain of the Thirty-second Wisconsin for a brief interval, until forced to resign because of extended illness.[60] While serving as chaplain in the Thirty-second, Fallows had sounded a militant note in expressing his attitude toward the war. He regarded secession as treason, demanded its absolute extinction and with it the annihilation of slavery, the ultimate cause. It was his belief that until the last vestige of the rebellion was wiped out, the people of the North should not give up the struggle. He asserted that ministers as well as members of their congregations should join the soldiers in the field if necessary. Said Fallows: "our pulpit may have to be the seat of war; our auditors the rebellious South; the singing of our choir the battle cry of freedom; our prayers the skyward rocket and the whizzing shell; our sermons the sharp and piercing bullet; and our benediction the bending of the forest of glistening steel and the resistless charge of the bayonet." He also expressed strongly his belief as to the reasons for which the war was being fought: "This is a holy war, this war to free the slave and save the nation."[61] His service as a military commander was sufficient evidence that the chaplain was as militant in deed as in word.

Reverend William W. Lyle, who served as chaplain of the Eleventh Ohio Infantry for two and a half years, discussed the evils of slavery at length and on numerous occasions, concluding that it was *the* cause of rebellion, secession, and civil war. He charged that the American Tract Society had equivocated on this great moral issue, that when slavery had ceased, the agency could claim no credit. The chaplain declared that "when the last link of Oppression's chain is broken . . . and the nation is redeemed and purified from the vile sin of slavery . . . and the thrice-accursed fiend of slavery is forever driven from the earth, the claims of this mammoth publishing enterprise, for occupying an advanced position on the great question of human rights . . . will neither be great in themselves, nor reflect honor upon those who urge them."[62]

Lyle stressed repeatedly the horrors of war, lest any think of it as glorious. He reminded his readers that "even when engaged for a good cause—when it is for the defense of truth and righteousness, and is absolutely necessary to roll back the dark tide-wave of human oppression, and to destroy the foulest treason—war is still a terrible reality." After the Battle of Antietam, the chaplain viewed the carnage on the field as he worked among the wounded and dying and paused to reflect on the ultimate cause: "THESE WERE ALL SLAIN BY THE INFERNAL SPIRIT OF SLAVERY! AND THERE SHALL BE NO PEACE UNTIL OPPRESSION IS DESTROYED. THE SWORD SHALL DEVOUR TILL SLAVERY IS NO MORE."[63]

Lyle also recorded his reactions to the opinions expressed by slaveholders with whom he conversed as Sherman's army penetrated Georgia. In response to their contention that slavery was a Christian institution, he argued that in his opinion the church of Christ fell from a lofty position when slaveholders, "whose merchandise was slaves and souls of men," were protected by the name of Christianity. "Away with all cant about Christian slaveholders! Christian slaveholders! As well talk about honest thieves, benevolent murderers, loyal traitors, and pious devils." The chaplain protested that the first of these terms was no more absurd or self-contradictory than any of the others, "and had it not been for a time-serving ministry, corrupt political platforms, and a venal press, the absurdity would never have been palmed on the Christian world as a Bible truth."[64]

The observable effects of slavery everywhere contradicted the assertion that slavery was a Christian institution, according to the chaplain. After talking with a young black near Atlanta who had never heard the name of Jesus Christ, Lyle commented on the "Christianity" of slavery: "Talk about the heathan [sic] in Africa and India and the South Sea Islands! Talk about the divine, patriarchal institution of slavery, and the eminently Christianizing spirit which it manifested!" As he continued, Lyle mentioned that it was not surprising that the slaveholders and their "miserable servile apologists" in the Northern states had attempted for many years to disguise the iniquities of the system. The thought that ministers of the Gospel had openly "baptized the vile thing in the name of the God of truth and love" and had "thrown around it the sacred protection of the Divine Word," and that it had even been received into the church, appalled the chaplain. "But slavery is dead!, Thank God, it is dead!" He rejoiced: "What an emasculated Gospel, in the hands of corrupt ministers, failed to do for the South, the bayonet, in the strong hands of brave soldiers, has, in the providence of God, most signally and gloriously accomplished."[65]

The chaplain went on to describe the effects of this "Christian" institution on the Southern whites who supported it so militantly. The presence of "white slaves," evidence of the immorality of the masters and overseers, was to him an indication that the "Christian" master would enslave his own offspring to satisfy his greed for economic gain.[66] Chief victims of slavery and the slaveholders' greed were the poor whites. Lyle explained it thus: "The poor whites of the South—'the white trash,' as they are generally called—a poor, degraded, ignorant, thriftless people, who are at once the objects of the slaveholder's hate, and the ready tools with which to work his schemes of villainy—bear unmistakable evidence of the crushing, grinding effects of slavery on the poor non-slaveholding whites, while the everyday evidences of the bleaching process on the colored race testify to the fearful immoralities of slaveholders themselves."[67]

Slavery, he went on, had stifled the democratic right of free speech. No one was safe from physical harm who dared to oppose the institution. To preserve slavery, its supporters would subvert liberty and democratic government. He claimed that faithful ministers, who had dared to speak out against the evil institution that had spread desolation and sorrow, were "mobbed, imprisoned, scourged, banished, tarred and feathered, hanged or shot, while reproaches and curses were heaped upon their names and characters." All of these things and many more were done, he alleged, "to prevent agitation and hide from the outside world the loathsome, secret workings of the SUM OF ALL VILLAINIES."[68]

Lyle vigorously denounced those "Copperheads" of the North who were, in his view, meaner, more vicious traitors than those in armed rebellion. Referring to those newspapers that spoke for the "peace party," he said, "Like all pro-slavery sheets that have ever been published in the interest of human oppression, the papers . . . were full of unblushing falsehoods, filthy inuendoes [sic] regarding the motives of the friends of freedom, forged correspondence from the army, asserting that the President's Proclamation of Emancipation was fiercely denounced by the soldiers."[69]

Another chaplain, Stephen A. Hodgman of the Seventy-fourth U.S. Colored Infantry (originally mustered as the Second Louisiana Guards of African Descent), spoke as a Northern-born minister who had served Southern pulpits for thirty years prior to the war.[70] Hodgman, who had left Ohio in 1831 and had lived in the South ever since, maintained that he had always opposed slavery but that he had continued to believe it could and would be overthrown by moral reformation rather than force.[71] The firing of Confederate batteries on the flag of the United States at Fort Sumter had convinced him that his former view was mistaken, and from that point on he was an abolitionist.[72] The chaplain interpreted the proceedings of the Charleston Convention of the Democratic Party (1860) as a deliberate Southern move to divide the party and hence, by defeating Stephen A. Douglas and splitting the vote among several candidates, ensure the election of Lincoln, which they then hailed as just cause for secession.[73] In Hodgman's view, the war was the punishment of God on the nation for having tolerated slavery for so long. He hailed Lincoln for the Emancipation Proclamation, stating that his act had rendered the president immortal, second only to Washington in the annals of American history.[74]

The chaplain also assessed the terrible cost of the war in money and lives. In his opinion, the Civil War, at the lowest possible estimate that could be made, would cost the nation, North and South, "four thousand millions of money, one million of valuable lives, and a badge of mourning hung on nearly half the dwellings in the land" before it ended. According to the chaplain, "These [were] some of the fruits of the grand rebellion—and the cause of all [was] slavery!"[75]

Some of the chaplains recorded their reactions to the news of Lincoln's assassination, a reaction shared by the men of the ranks. The overwhelming emotion experienced at that time of national tragedy mingled grief with anger, shock and disbelief with indignation. To Chaplain Denison this crime was the last insane act of treason: "Insane secession commenced its career with theft, and closed it with assassination." The murder of the president was "the last barbaric throe of the spirit of Rebellion." According to the chaplain, the act was "in keeping with the spirit that had rule at Andersonville." In his opinion the occurrence was even more unfortunate for the South than for the North, "for the great fatherly heart of Mr. Lincoln would have been . . . generous—possibly too much so—to submissive adversaries. . . . The deed can never be forgotten."[76]

Chaplain McCabe also recorded his thoughts at the time of the president's death, noting as he wrote the grief of the former slaves. To the chaplain, it seemed that God had destined Lincoln for the task he had performed so well, and the hand of God was evident in the president's mental, moral, and political training: "Oh, he has lifted from the nation the awful burden of slavery. . . . Nothing is more sad than the silent, undemonstrative sorrow of that long-suffering race whose best friend he was."[77]

Chaplain Adams, who had been so favorably impressed with the "moral tone" of Lincoln's Second Inaugural, reacted in disbelief when told of the president's murder. It was unthinkable to the chaplain that such a man, who acknowledged publicly his dependence on God for wisdom and guidance and was so widely upheld by the prayers of the people, should be taken at such a crucial time. It was, as he described it, "one of the fruits of secession."[78]

Chaplain Pepper related his profound grief upon hearing of the assassination, a grief shared by the entire army. And yet, the chaplain was certain that though Lincoln had died his principles would not. "By the hand of the accursed assassin, all that was perishable of ABRAHAM LINCOLN has passed away—but his principles, like the words of the holy man, shall endure forever."[79]

Chaplain Humphreys, in his sorrow over the loss of the president, shared the confident belief of Chaplain Pepper that Lincoln's principles would endure. He had once met the president and had fond and lasting memories of that occasion: "I rejoice to have held in mine the *firm* hand that kept true the rudder of the Ship of State through all the storms of war, the *kindly* hand that heartened the soldiers in the field and in the hospital, wrote letters for the sick, and smoothed the pillow of the dying; the *tender* hand that wrote the Gettysburg Address and the Second Inaugural with its 'malice toward none' and its 'charity for all.'"[80] Even more than for all these, however, the chaplain was proud "to have clasped the *strong* hand that struck the fetters from millions of slaves and laid firm and forever in freedom the foundations of our nationality."[81]

Reactions to the tragedy of Lincoln's death were found, in some instances, in the official monthly reports of the chaplains to the adjutant general. Chaplain R. L. Chittenden of the Forty-third Ohio Infantry reported: "The grief manifested by our soldiers upon hearing of the murder of our late beloved President was more honorable to his memory than any public resolutions or funeral ceremonies could have been."[82] Chaplain Thomas Calahan of the Forty-eighth U.S. Colored Troops reported that his men were shocked when told of the president's death but that even in their deep grief their faith in God was unshaken.[83] One other chaplain referred to the assassination in an official report. Chaplain G. T. Carruthers, Fifty-first U.S. Colored Troops, stated: "Amid our joy over our recent victories, the fall of Mobile and Richmond, and the surrender of Gen. Lee with his army, we were struck dumb with astonishment and grief at the news of the assassination of our much loved President."[84]

It is difficult to estimate the influence chaplains had on the men they served. In all probability the degree of influence varied with the personality and character of the individual chaplain. It may be concluded quite reasonably, however, that in many cases the chaplain's influence was profound. As the men listened to the chaplain at the weekly Sunday service, or informally during the week, or perhaps even while recovering from a wound or on a deathbed, there was every opportunity to assimilate much of the chaplain's attitudes about the war. Private Wilbur Fisk of the Second Vermont Infantry was an eloquent example of this phenomenon when he wrote: "Slavery is a relic of the darkest ages, and the poorest government on earth is better in principle than that. If we are going to have a free government at all, let us have it all free, or else we had better give up the name. Slavery has fostered an aristocracy of the rankest kind, and this aristocracy is the bitterest foe that a really free government can have. Slavery and despotism have challenged war with us, and by it she must abide. Slavery was jealous of the comelier strength that Freedom possessed; and maliciously envied her irresistible march onward to a higher destiny." Fisk continued, "Slavery drew the sword, and would have stabbed Freedom to the heart, had not God denied her the strength. She could not bear that her more righteous neighbor should be prospered, while she herself was accursed, and in her foolish madness she has tried to rend the Union in twain. With that institution it is success or death. Compromise with Slavery, and restore the Union with Slavery in it still! As well might Jehovah compromise with Satan and give him back part of Heaven."[85] Few wrote more eloquently than did Fisk.

Chaplain Denison believed that he spoke for the men with whom he had served when he stated: "The seceding States fought for the dismemberment of the Union, and the permanent, legal establishment of slavery. The loyal States fought for the unity of the Nation, and the brotherhood of all men within its boundaries." He continued: "We of the North and West fought not for a man, not for a party, not for a name, not for spoils; but for great political and moral principles. We battled for the great rights of the Union, and the freedom and equality of men."[86]

Once more the words of Private Fisk (Second Vermont) reflect the sentiments of the chaplains. "The Almighty, who made mankind in the first place," said the private, "knows how to classify them, and we have no certain account that he ever made but two distinctions, the righteous and unrighteous. Will it not be ill then with that man who shall unwittingly despise whom God delights to honor?"[87]

Despite the rather cynical tendency today to dismiss moral principles as motivation for men's actions, it now seems evident that the chaplains of the Union armies and many of the thousands of soldiers they influenced fought not for the economic subjugation of the South, nor the political supremacy of the North, but for the end of human bondage as well as for the preservation of the Union.

It is interesting to compare the views Union chaplains expressed about the causes of the Civil War with the conflicting interpretations offered by revisionist and counterrevisionist historians over the years. None of the chaplains spoke of divergent economic development, conflicting social structures, or states' rights. Their views of the South and of the war have proved to be largely correct and have stood the test of time, Southern apologists and some historians to the contrary notwithstanding. The chaplains believed that the Founding Fathers had acted to create a nation, not a confederation, that the "contract" binding the states together could not be broken unilaterally by ordinances of secession. They took Confederate leaders at their word when they proclaimed boldly that the Confederacy's "foundations are laid, its cornerstone rests, upon the great truth that the negro is not equal to the white man; that slavery, subordination to the superior race, is his natural and moral condition. This, our new Government, is the first, in the history of the world, based upon this great physical, philosophical, and moral truth."[88]

It is understandable that after slavery was destroyed by four years of bloody civil war, by presidential proclamation, and by constitutional amendment, apologists for the Confederate cause would seek alternative explanations for secession, but the words of those who created the Confederacy cannot be discounted. They were acting to protect slavery. "The South's insecurity [had been] heightened by having to defend against constant attack an institution it knew to be discredited throughout the civilized world and of which Southerners had once been among the severest critics. Its reaction was to withdraw increasingly from contact with the offending world, to retreat into an isolationism of spirit, and to attempt by curtailing freedom of speech to avoid criticism."[89] Union chaplains knew this and said so.

Secession, then, was the ultimate act to protect the future of slavery. A careful reading of the several ordinances of secession and the accompanying statements of causes makes this abundantly clear to any thoughtful reader. Perhaps the statement of causes adopted by the South Carolina secession convention offers the clearest enunciation of the fear that slavery was threatened in the Southern mind. To wit: "A geographical line has been drawn across the Union, and all the States north of that line have united in the election of a man to the high office of President of the United States whose opinions and purposes are hostile to Slavery. He is to be intrusted with the administration of the common Government, because he has declared that 'Government cannot endure permanently half slave, half free,' and that the public mind must rest in the belief that Slavery is in the course of ultimate extinction."[90]

Public policy in the South was not formed by "poor whites," the yeoman farmers, the artisans and craftsmen, nor even by the small planters to any great extent. It was created by the great planters, men of great wealth and social/political prominence, and those policies clearly served their ends. That the substantial majority of Southerners who had no real stake in slavery supported these public policies is a tribute to the political skills of the Southern politicians who had formed them, but it cannot be argued persuasively that those policies were based on broad democratic participation in the elective process. In his excellent book, *The South and the Politics of Slavery*, William Cooper clearly and convincingly documents this. "The politics of slavery built a politics of unity that blunted class differences and helped prevent any political clash between slaveowners and non-slaveowners which could threaten the security of the slave system. . . . In the political arena southern politicians did not speak simply for the few who actually owned a slave. In its political form slavery became the visible symbol of independence, honor, and equality precisely because it embraced the most fundamental values of southern white society held in common by slaveholders and non-slaveholders alike." Cooper discusses at length the attempts of the competing political parties' leaders to convince Southern voters that their party was the better defender of slavery. They were particularly concerned about convincing the yeoman who desired to preserve the institution of slavery either because he hoped at some point to become a slaveholder or simply because it assured white supremacy and, hence, his standing in Southern society.[91]

It may be true that the average Confederate soldier, in his own mind, was fighting for home and hearth more than he was to sustain an institution in which he had only an indirect interest. Yet while it is undoubtedly true that the personal valor and bravery of the Confederate American soldier was exemplary, it remains undeniable that by implication the Southern soldier *did* fight to maintain Confederate public policy, which was to secure slavery for all time, the clear and unmistakable intent of the Confederate constitution. And the Confederate soldier understood that he fought to maintain Southern institutions. A recent study of Civil War soldiers' letters to their friends and loved ones is quite revealing in this regard. To wit: A young Kentucky Confederate wrote in April of 1861, "We are fighting for our liberty against tyrants of the North . . . who are determined to destroy slavery."[92] And again: "a stand must be made for African slavery or it is forever lost."[93] Yet further: "I never want to see the day when a negro is put on an equality with a white person. There is too many free niggers . . . now to suit me, let alone having four million."[94] Though only about one in five Southern soldiers evinced explicit proslavery opinion in his letters or diary, many more spoke indirectly of their "institutions" and their "property," and *none* spoke in opposition to slavery. "They took slavery for granted as one of the Southern 'rights' and institutions for which they fought and did not feel compelled to discuss it."[95]

Again, the chaplains knew that these attitudes dominated Southern thinking and action and that the Southern soldier's view of blacks simply reflected the prevailing view of the typical Confederate citizen. That view was probably stated most cogently by Chief Justice Roger B. Taney in the Dred Scott decision (1857), a decision hailed throughout the South as the definitive legal statement concerning the rights of blacks even as prevailing public opinion in the free states found the decision to be morally reprehensible. Blacks were, said Taney, "beings of an inferior order; and altogether unfit to associate with the white race, either in social or political relations." They were "so far inferior that they had no rights which the white man was bound to respect, and . . . the negro might justly and lawfully be reduced to slavery for his benefit."[96] By 1860, then, citizens of the North and South recognized that chattel slavery had become a chasm that could no longer be bridged by the spirit of compromise prevailing in the United States prior to Lincoln's election, and the war came.

The sounds of gunfire had hardly ceased at Appomattox when the "lost cause" argument denying that slavery was the primary cause of the war began to emerge. Latter-day arguments that the average Confederate was not really fighting in defense of slavery continue to this

day, but they are unconvincing, even though they may be understandable. Yet the denial is ever present.

As recently as 1996, a noted Civil War historian offered what appears
to be a logical contradiction with regard to the role played by slavery in
the hearts and minds of Confederate soldiers. He said:

> It is impossible to point to any other local issue but slavery and
> say that Southerners would have seceded and *fought over it* [em-
> phasis added]. However, if slavery is the reason secession came, that
> does not mean it is the reason 1 million Southern men subsequently
> fought. In fact, study reveals that the two had absolutely nothing
> in common. Probably 90 percent of the men who wore the gray had
> never owned a slave and had no personal interest at all either in
> slavery or of the shadow issue of state rights. The widespread North-
> ern myth that the Confederates went to the battlefield to perpetu-
> ate slavery is just that, a myth. Their letters and diaries, in the tens
> of thousands, reveal again and again that they fought and died be-
> cause their Southern homeland was invaded and their natural in-
> stinct was to protect home and hearth.[97]

His first premise is compelling—*what but slavery prompted secession?*
To argue, then, that those who fought to sustain secession were not
fighting for slavery seems logically contradictory. And to assert that they
(slavery and secession) had nothing in common without offering any
documentation of that bold assertion—not one of the "tens of thousands" of letters or diaries is cited—is unconvincing to say the least.
That is the *Southern myth*, that they did not fight for slavery, but for
the abstract right of secession. It is time now to address that great myth
of the "lost cause," that Confederates fought not to preserve and perpetuate chattel slavery but only for home and hearth. *Of course they
fought for home and hearth, but they also fought to preserve and extend slavery.*

Racism, the motive force that had sustained slavery from the earliest
days of British colonization in North America, was also behind secession. It was also the cause of the massacre at Fort Pillow, the slaughter
at the Crater, and the butchery at Battery Wagner. Racism was with the
Army of Northern Virginia—R. E. Lee commanding—when it seized
blacks encountered during the Pennsylvania campaign and sent them
south under guard to be sold into slavery. And racism sustained rigid
segregation, Jim Crow laws, the lynch mob, and the Ku Klux Klan for

another century after Appomattox. Racism was, and is, endemic in the North as well as in the South—it *is* a national phenomenon—but until it is acknowledged for what it was and is, and addressed directly, it will not be overcome in American society.

Perhaps General Grant, reflecting years later upon his thoughts at Appomattox when he received Lee's surrender of the Army of Northern Virginia, best expressed the conflicting feelings many Americans experience when pondering the valor of the Confederate soldier: "I felt like anything rather than rejoicing at the downfall of a foe who had fought so long and valiantly, and had suffered so much for a cause, though that cause was, I believe, one of the worst for which a people ever fought, and one for which there was the least excuse."[98]

In the final analysis, the words of the men who took their states from the Union and who founded the Confederate States of America are unambiguous, inescapable, and compelling: the Confederacy was founded to preserve slavery and to extend its influence. That enduring fact remains regardless of the artful legal and constitutional arguments constructed, after the defeat of the Confederacy, by Jefferson Davis, Alexander Stephens, and others who had created and served the Confederate government. This is truly "the burden of Southern history," to use the haunting and tragic phrase made so familiar to students of the Civil War by the distinguished C. Vann Woodward.

It is clear that the chaplains understood these basic issues, that they saw the political leadership of the South and Southern attitudes about race for what they truly were. Although their understanding of the true nature of the war of which they were an important and integral part may have been intuitive at the time, it was unerringly accurate. As chaplains ministered to the men they served, they sought to influence their attitudes toward the former slaves through moral suasion, the best tool available to clergy save only the example of a consistent, godly life. And they succeeded in helping to create a sense of mission, as it were, among those men, an understanding that they fought not just to preserve the Union but also to free those held in the bondage of chattel slavery. The chaplains had quite rightly identified slavery as the cause of it all.

6

THE MEASURE OF A MAN

In assessing the contributions to the Union effort made by those who served as army chaplains, it seems appropriate to recall the words of Saint Paul, addressed to the early Christians as he described his own ministry: "I am made all things to all men, that I might by all means save some" (1 Corinthians 9:22). Service as a chaplain was certainly no easy task. The men whose names filled the regimental muster rolls of the Union army (many of whom spent long hours and days in army hospitals) came from widely diverse backgrounds—social, political, religious, economic, and ethnic. It would be unreasonable to expect that any one man, however saintly, could be completely satisfactory to everyone in a regiment. Different individuals desired and expected different things of a chaplain. Some men wanted only friendship, some a financial agent. Others wanted a spiritual adviser or an evangelist or a teacher. Still others wanted an example of courage—moral and physical—a model after whom they could pattern their own deportment.

If there was a moment in the soldier's life in which a universal need was felt, however, it probably occurred with the realization that death, that unknown quantity, was imminent. This moment of dread and uncertainty, heightened perhaps by a sense of guilt, often prompted men to an interest in matters spiritual that had long been scorned, or ignored, or simply forgotten.

When weighing the value of religious counsel given to dying men or to men facing probable death, it is important to remember that religion in America at the time of the Civil War had not yet felt the full impact of Darwin's *The Origin of Species* or of modern scientific discovery. Even the Unitarians and their offspring, the Transcendentalists, were considered radical and rather dangerous by the orthodoxy of the day; and although there were doubtless many who were irreligious, the belief in a life beyond this one with accompanying punishment or reward was more common and much stronger than is the case today.

Certainly the memoirs of the chaplains indicate their belief that their spiritual contributions were their greatest. On page after page they relate with poignancy the occasions on which they knelt beside dying men to hear their confessions, to administer Extreme Unction, or to pray with them a simple prayer of faith. In report after report they wrote down—if only for the eyes of a clerk in the office of the adjutant general or the surgeon general—the number of men with whom they had prayed and counseled and who subsequently died with confidence and faith. In his final report, after serving nearly three and a half years as chaplain at Douglas Hospital in Washington, Chaplain Brown wrote:

> I have endeavored honestly, faithfully, and conscientiously, to do my duty, first to *the Souls of Soldiers*; then, to mitigate their physical sufferings, and make them as comfortable as the circumstances of the case would allow, and to relieve the anxieties of their families while they were living, and to comfort the bereaved relatives when death has called the Soldier from the conflict of earth to the realities of another world. . . . Dying men have thrown their arms around my neck as we joined in prayer, and others seemed to struggle for language adequately to express their overflowing gratitude for being led to Jesus, through whome [*sic*] they have obtained a good hope, by faith, of eternal life beyond the grave.[1]

It is impossible to quantify the value of such service. How can we establish the worth of a bereaved family's comfort in the knowledge that a son, husband, father, or brother had been comforted at death and accorded a Christian or religious burial? Can we measure the good to the individual, to the community in which he subsequently lived, and to the nation of a "conversion experience" in an army chapel that changed a soldier's life and made him a better person? We simply cannot measure such intangible service, yet only the most cynical among us would deny the contribution.

But spiritual labors did not constitute the full contribution of the chaplains. They were in a very real sense the morale officers of the army. If anyone in the regiment was in a position to raise the spirits of the men, it was the chaplain. The writing of letters, the distribution of mail, the transmission of funds to loved ones at home—all of these things and countless others—clearly boosted the morale of the men. These tasks were undertaken by the chaplains and were a substantial contribution to a larger total military effort.

There are no statistics revealing the number of lives that were saved through the aid rendered by a chaplain on the field of battle. It cannot be determined how often frightened men remained to fight because a chaplain encouraged them to do their duty and by setting an example of personal courage prevented their flight to the rear. But instances of courage and determination were commonplace. Remember, for example, Chaplain Ouellet, under fire at Malvern Hill during the Peninsular campaign; Chaplain Trumbull, whose fortitude and selflessness on behalf of the men imprisoned with him for six months at Castle Pinckney in Charleston bolstered their spirits; and Chaplain Fuller who volunteered to help drive Confederate sharpshooters from Fredericksburg and lost his life protecting army engineers from hostile fire. And consider the personal bravery of Chaplain Springer of the Third Wisconsin, whose willingness to fill a gap in the line at Resaca cost him his life when he, too, fell from multiple wounds. Each acted in the face of gravest personal danger and in doing so made a significant personal contribution to the Union cause.

Again, what yardstick can measure the value of Chaplain McCabe's buoyancy of spirit when men about him were fast losing the will to live, confined together in Libby Prison for months on end? We simply cannot know how many Union soldiers took renewed hope from the examples of faith and courage exhibited in similar trying circumstances, but many must have lived because of the example of a chaplain who did not stop caring, and no one can place a dollar-and-cents value on service such as that.

Still further, how can we evaluate with precision either the immediate or the more enduring effects of the chaplains' labor among former slaves? Those desperately needy people were aided by men of God in uniform, when their history of bondage left them without protection from the uncertainties of the future. They were fed, clothed, employed, and housed, and, above all, educated to help them take their rightful place as citizens of this great republic.

Chaplains also molded and influenced opinion among the men they served, just as they had as clergy in the communities in which they served as priests, pastors, rabbis, and rectors before their military service. They helped men to understand the nobility of fighting to free a race from bondage. The men they served looked to them as examples, and when the words they spoke were validated by the conduct of their lives, when they "walked their talk"—to use today's idiom—their impact on the men of the regiment or in the hospital was substantial and

Reverend Andrew Hartsock (From Soldiers of the Cross
by James Duram and Eleanor Duram, eds.)

positive. They did their utmost to prepare Union soldiers for courageous fighting and confident dying.

These are contributions that defy measurement by all usual standards, yet few would deny that they added substantially to the whole. Not every chaplain contributed equally. There were poor chaplains, some because they lacked ability, others because they were poor in heart and spirit. There were average chaplains, and good chaplains, and a few who were outstanding chaplains; but together they added something to the army that almost defies description. Perhaps it was sacrifice, a willingness to serve when service was not really demanded, and perhaps this spirit of sacrifice is the gauge by which their contribution can be pondered. No chaplain was ever *required* to carry ammunition, to swab the bore of a brass Napoleon, to shoulder a musket and lead a charge. No chaplain *had* to baptize converts, or teach illiterate backward farm boys to read, or remain behind with the wounded and risk capture by the enemy. There were no laws *requiring* chaplains to aid wounded men to the rear during the heat of battle, thereby risking life and limb. But chaplains did these and other things that went far beyond duty as prescribed by law or the War Department.

It is true that individual chaplains were the subject of sharp criticism from time to time during the war and that the chaplaincy as an institution became the target of more generalized criticisms as well on occasion. But a balanced view of the work they did reveals that they actually helped to establish the chaplaincy as a permanent and continuing institution in the American military tradition.

The clergymen who volunteered as chaplains responded to a variety of motives, some conscious and others unconscious, and in this respect were not unlike their fellow countrymen who also served in the ranks of the military during the Union's greatest crisis. They were constrained by both love of country and a concern for the souls of those whose lives were at risk when they decided, individually, to serve as chaplains. Because they identified the cause of their nation with the cause of God, they entered military service with clear consciences, not deserting their parishes at home but discovering greater usefulness and a higher calling in a national emergency. At a time that united nearly all citizens in a common cause, the duties of patriot and minister seemed to merge into a single identity. Chaplains believed that they were uniquely situated to inspire the men they served to fight the good fight, to shield them from the vice of camp life, "and to bring their souls spotless to Christ in the world to come."[2]

This obviously is not to imply that the chaplains alone gave of themselves sacrificially, for thousands of officers and men of the Union armies gave valorous service to their country. But these men, ministers of God, apostles of peace and love, left behind the safety, respect, and responsibility of the parish, the comfort of home and joy of loved ones, and journeyed to the seat of war, there to serve their God, their country, and their fellow men.

What was the measure of the man who served as a chaplain? It was many things—moral courage, quiet example, moral suasion, a consistent life, kindness, self-sacrifice—among yet other qualities. Not every chaplain was equally gifted or prepared for effective service, and some fell short, even far short, of the expectations of their men, for there were chaplains who hid from danger. And there were those who sought the company only of the officers and the emoluments of office. But the service records demonstrate quite convincingly that most of those who served as chaplains were fully devoted to their duties as men of God in the ranks. And a good number gave that "last full measure of devotion" of which Lincoln spoke so eloquently at Gettysburg in November of 1863, for sixty-six Union chaplains died in the service of their country during the war.[3]

Reviewing his service as a chaplain nearly fifty years after it ended, Chaplain William Eastman summarized it in these words:

> In one word, the significance of the chaplaincy was this: that the government offered to each regiment one man to be a friend to every man. While other officers might be good friends, this man was to make a business of kindliness. Not a commander, not a fighter, not hemmed in by any rules or any rank; left to himself to reach men by their hearts if he touched them at all, and by their hearts to make them better soldiers; to stand for truth, purity, and all righteousness; for honorable living and hopeful dying; and having done all to stand by, in the spirit of service, according to the pattern of the Master. Many regiments did not understand and did not care; many commanders found it impossible to secure the man they would gladly have welcomed to such a post; many men who undertook the service fell short, perhaps far short of their opportunities; but many also gained for themselves much love and a good name and a share in the final triumph.[4]

The service rendered by chaplains in the Union armies between 1861 and 1865 deserves the nation's gratitude. The examples of self-sacrifice, courage, and honor abound, and men of every represented religious persuasion contributed immeasurably to the ultimate success of the war effort primarily through the positive impact, on the attitudes and conduct of the men they served, not only of their words but also of the example of their lives. The chaplaincy as a military tradition has continued through the years since Appomattox, building on the record of those who served in this unique capacity during the gravest threat to the life of the nation, the American Civil War. Such service was, in a word, an act of love—love of God, love of country, and, most assuredly, love of fellow men.

NOTES

CHAPTER ONE: DEFINING THE CHARGE

1. Roy P. Basler (ed.), *The Collected Works of Abraham Lincoln* (New Brunswick, NJ, 1953), IV, 271. Hereafter cited as Basler, *Lincoln: Collected Works.*

2. Ibid., 331–32.

3. The figures vary slightly: Kenneth P. Williams, *Lincoln Finds a General* (New York, 1957), I, 62, gives 17,113 officers and men as the total strength of the regular army on April 15, 1861. R. Ernest Dupuy and Trevor N. Dupuy, *The Compact History of the Civil War* (New York, 1962), 27, give the strength of the regular army at that time as 16,367 officers and men.

4. *Congressional Globe,* 30 Cong., 2 Sess., 644–56 (1849).

5. Roy J. Honeywell, *Chaplains of the United States Army* (Lakewood, CO, 1958), 30–34, 78–87. Hereafter cited as Honeywell, *Chaplains.*

6. Basler, *Lincoln: Collected Works,* IV, 353–54.

7. *The War of the Rebellion: A Compilation of the Official Records of the Union and Confederate Armies* (Washington, 1880–1901), Series III, Vol. I, 151–57. Hereafter cited as *Official Records.*

8. Basler, *Lincoln: Collected Works,* IV, 354.

9. *Official Records,* Series III, Vol. I, 368, 375.

10. The act stated: "That there shall be allowed to each regiment one chaplain, who shall be appointed by the regimental commander on the vote of the field officers and company commanders on duty with the regiment at the time the appointments shall be made. The chaplain so appointed must be a regular[ly] ordained minister of a Christian denomination, and shall receive the pay and allowance of a captain of cavalry." *Revised United States Army Regulations of 1861* (Washington, 1863), 507. Hereafter referred to as *Revised Regulations.*

11. Ibid., 526.

12. The text of the form letter is as follows: "Sir: Having been solicited by Christian ministers and other pious people, to appoint suitable persons to act as chaplains at the hospitals for our sick and wounded soldiers, and feeling the intrinsic propriety of having such persons to so act, and yet believing there is no law conferring the power upon me to appoint them I think it fit to say that if you will voluntarily enter upon and perform the appropriate duties of such position, I will recommend that Congress make compensation therefor at the same rate as chaplains in the army are compensated." Rev. William Young Brown, *The Army Chaplain: His Office, Duties, and Responsibilities, and the Means of Aiding Him* (Philadelphia, 1863), 22. Hereafter cited as Brown,

The Army Chaplain; Basler, Lincoln: Collected Works, V, 53; Official Records, Series III, Vol. I, 721.

13. The president stated:

By mere omission, I presume, Congress has failed to provide chaplains for hospitals occupied by volunteers. This subject was brought to my notice, and I was induced to draw up the form of a letter, one copy of which, properly addressed, has been delivered to each of the persons, and at the dates respectively named and stated, in a schedule, containing also the form of the letter, marked A and herewith transmitted.

These gentlemen, I understand, entered upon the duties designated, at the times respectively stated in the schedule, and have labored faithfully therein ever since. I therefore recommend that they be compensated at the same rate as chaplains in the army. I further suggest that general provision be made for chaplains to serve at hospitals, as well as with regiments.

Basler, Lincoln: Collected Works, V, 40. Schedule A named the following ministers as recipients of the form letter and included the dates when such letters were sent: Rev. G. G. Goss; Rev. John G. Butler; Rev. Henry Hopkins; Rev. F. M. Magrath; Rev. F. E. Boyle; Rev. John C. Smith; Rev. Wm. Y. Brown.

14. This statute was enacted on May 20, 1862. Raphael P. Thian (ed.), Legislative History of the General Staff of the Army of the United States (Its Organization, Duties, Pay, and Allowances) from 1775 to 1901 (Washington, 1901), 418. Hereafter cited as Thian, Legislative History.

15. Philip M. Fragasso, "Wanted: Army Chaplains. Christians Only Need Apply," Liberty 74, no. 1 (1979): 2–5.

16. Congressional Globe, 37 Cong., 1 Sess., 100 (1861).

17. Lee M. Friedman, Jewish Pioneers and Patriots (Philadelphia, 1942), 45–49.

18. Basler, Lincoln: Collected Works, V, 69.

19. The law stated: "That no person shall be appointed a chaplain in the United States army who is not a regularly ordained minister of some religious denomination, and who does not present testimonials of his good standing as such minister with a recommendation for his appointment as an army chaplain from some authorized ecclesiastical body, or not less than five accredited ministers belonging to said denomination." Revised Regulations, 536–37.

20. Official Records, Series III, Vol. II, 519.

21. Frank Milton Bristol, The Life of Chaplain McCabe (New York, 1908), 137. Hereafter cited as Bristol, Chaplain McCabe.

22. Revised Regulations, 36–37.

23. Basler, Lincoln: Collected Works, VIII, 102–3.

24. Service Record, Files of the Adjutant General's Office, National Archives, Record Group 94. The chaplain's file contains an affidavit from the Prussian ambassador to the United States that certified Sarner's theological training at and graduation from the Royal University. The degree he had been awarded was "Doctor of Divinity." The certification of the chaplains' board also contained herein stated that he was "a graduate of two of the German Universities, a regularly ordained minister of the Lutheran Church, and we therefore cordially recommend him to the office of Chaplain in the 54th Regt. of N.Y. Vols. in which regiment he has received an appointment." Bertram Korn, American Jewry and the Civil War (Philadelphia, 1951), 265, note 94, states that Sarner had served as a rabbi both previous to and subsequent to his service as a chaplain and that he was in contact with Jewish periodicals during

his service. He concludes that the chaplaincy board was in error, probably due to a misunderstanding of Sarner's educational background.

25. *Revised Regulations,* Appendix A, 507.

26. *Congressional Globe,* 37 Cong., 2 Sess., 1079–82 (1862).

27. *Revised Regulations,* Appendix A, 526.

28. Thian, *Legislative History,* 418.

29. This is evident from the vast number of reports from chaplains assigned to this type of temporary duty. The reports contain statements as to both the regimental affiliation and the specific type of detached service. Chaplain L. D. Ames of the Twenty-ninth Ohio is a representative case. On October 31, 1864, he reported to the Office of the Surgeon General that as regimental chaplain of the Twenty-ninth Ohio Volunteers, he was on detached service at the Second Division Field Hospital of the Twentieth Army Corps, at Atlanta, Georgia. Letters Received, Files of the Surgeon General's Office, National Archives, Record Group 679.

30. Basler, *Lincoln: Collected Works,* VI, 313–14.

31. *Congressional Globe,* 30 Cong., 2 Sess., 644–56 (1849).

32. *Revised Regulations,* 36–37.

33. Brown, *The Army Chaplain,* 120–25.

34. *Official Records,* Series III, Vol. 1, 154; *Congressional Globe,* 37 Cong., 1 Sess., 50–54, 100 (1861).

35. *Revised Regulations,* Appendix A, 507.

36. *Congressional Globe,* 37 Cong., 2 Sess., 1079–82 (1862); Thian, *Legislative History,* 418.

37. *Congressional Globe,* 37 Cong., 2 Sess., 1085–88 (1862). Senator James Grimes of Iowa was the author of the amendment to provide rations.

38. *Revised Regulations,* 87.

39. Ibid.

40. *Congressional Globe,* 38 Cong., 1 Sess., 1163 (1864).

41. Ibid.

42. *Official Records,* Series III, Vol. III, 728.

43. *Congressional Globe,* 38 Cong., 1 Sess., 1165 (1864). This information was supplied by Senator Lafayette Foster of Connecticut, who charged that chaplains were constantly subjected to petty discrimination.

44. *Congressional Globe,* 38 Cong., 1 Sess., 1165 (1865); *Official Records,* Series III, Vol. IV, 728.

45. M. C. Meigs to Lorenzo Thomas, February 11, 1864, Letters Received, Files of the Adjutant General's Office, National Archives, Record Group 94.

46. *Official Records,* Series III, Vol. IV, 227–28; *Revised Regulations,* 160.

47. *Congressional Globe,* 37 Cong., 2 Sess., 1078–88 (1862).

48. Basler, *Lincoln: Collected Works,* VII, 280n. The letter of Governor Andrew, dated March 24, 1864, was endorsed by Lincoln and sent to Bates on April 4, 1864. The opinion of the attorney general was returned to the president on April 23, 1864, and was in turn transmitted to the Senate on May 7, 1864.

49. Basler, *Lincoln: Collected Works,* VII, 332; *Congressional Globe,* 38 Cong., 1 Sess., 1164 (1864).

50. Basler, *Lincoln: Collected Works,* VII, 332; *Congressional Globe,* 38 Cong., 1 Sess., 1164 (1864). Some fourteen black clergymen served black regiments during the war. Most black regiments, however, were served by white clergy, and almost all the officers in black units were white. Edwin S. Redkey, "Black Chaplains in the Union Army," *Civil War History* 33, no. 4 (1987): 331–50.

51. *Revised Regulations,* Appendix BB, 524; Brown, *The Army Chaplain,* 26, quoting General Order Number 102 of November 25, 1861. The term *chapeau de bras* refers to a three-cornered hat that could be folded and carried under the arm. Common in the eighteenth century, it was, apparently, still used by some for religious ceremonies.

52. Brown, *The Army Chaplain,* 27.

53. Printed copy of General Order Number 247, dated August 25, 1864, found in the records of the Adjutant General's Office, National Archives, Record Group 94.

54. The Chaplains Council was an informal association of the chaplains in the department. It was not an official body and did not imply that it was speaking for all chaplains in the department, as relatively few could attend its meetings.

55. The petition read as follows:

We would most respectfully ask that in addition to the uniform already prescribed in General Order 247, published August 15 [*sic*], 1864, a suitable ensignia [*sic*] be adopted distinctly denoting the rank of chaplain; and we would further respectfully suggest that it be the same as the shoulder strap adopted for the Surgeons, omitting the leaf at the ends of the strap.

We believe that the addition of a suitable device to the uniform of Chaplains would relieve them from many inconveniences arising from the fact that their rank and position is not known and recognized as is the case of every other Officer—by the shoulder strap. And we also believe that it would promote their usefulness by securing to them the respect and courtesy due to their rank and position in the army.

N. B. Critchfield to Lorenzo Thomas, October 24, 1864, Letters Received, Files of the Adjutant General's Office, National Archives, Record Group 94. This letter carried the endorsement of Chaplain Springer pertaining to the proceedings of the Chaplains Council.

56. Ezra Sprague to Lorenzo Thomas, October 28, 1864, Letters Received, Files of the Adjutant General's Office, National Archives, Record Group 94.

57. *Revised Regulations,* Appendix A, 527.

58. Thian, *Legislative History,* 418.

59. Brown, *The Army Chaplain,* 24–25.

60. Ibid., 90–91.

61. *Congressional Globe,* 38 Cong., 1 Sess., 1163 (1864).

62. Henry Clay Trumbull, *War Memories of a Chaplain* (Philadelphia, 1898), 3. Hereafter cited as Trumbull, *War Memories.*

63. *Official Records,* Series III, Vol. IV, 807–9.

CHAPTER TWO: WHAT TO DO
AND HOW TO DO IT

1. Brown, *The Army Chaplain,* 3.

2. Ibid., 15–16.

3. Ibid.

4. Ibid., 16–18.

5. Ibid., 18–20.

6. James H. Bradford, *The Chaplains in the Volunteer Army,* War Papers No. 11, Military Order of the Loyal Legion of the United States, D.C. Commandery (Washington, 1892), 8–9.

7. The legislation that provided for the position of post chaplain has been discussed earlier (Chapter 1). Chaplain Brown included in his chaplain's handbook a brief chapter outlining the duties of the post chaplain with suggestions concerning the proper approach to the assignment. No memoirs written by men who served in this capacity have been located. Brown, *The Army Chaplain*, 120–23. In the examination of the hundreds of reports in the files of the adjutant and surgeon general's offices, only one item relating to post chaplains was found. This was a manuscript copy of a special order assigning to Rev. N. L. Brakeman, the post chaplain at Baton Rouge, Louisiana, the task of providing supplies for the families of destitute soldiers, citizens, and refugees, in accordance with his judgment, from the post commissary. Special Order Number 261, dated July 29, 1864, Files of the Surgeon General's Office, National Archives, Record Group 679. It might also be mentioned here that Father Germain, in his work on Catholic chaplains, indicated that the hospital chaplains of wartime had the same status as post chaplains of the Regular Army in time of peace. Dom Aidan Henry Germain, *Catholic Military and Naval Chaplains, 1776–1917* (Washington, 1929), 52. Although the legislation providing for the appointment of hospital chaplains did not explicitly state this, the similarity of the two positions was great. Hereafter cited as Germain, *Catholic Chaplains.*

8. Brown, *The Army Chaplain*, 120–23.

9. Ibid., 123–25.

10. Honeywell, *Chaplains*, 120.

11. *Official Records*, Series III, Vol. I, 151–57.

12. "The chaplain so appointed shall be a regular[ly] ordained minister . . . and shall be required to report to the colonel commanding the regiment to which he is attached, at the end of each quarter, the moral and religious condition of the regiment, and such suggestions as may conduce to the social happiness and moral improvement of the troops." *Revised Regulations*, Appendix A, 507.

13. Brown, *The Army Chaplain*, 117. The regret of the chaplain is seconded. Very few regimental chaplain's reports dated prior to April 1864 are extant.

14. *Official Records*, Series III, Vol. IV, 227–28; *Congressional Globe*, 38 Cong., 1 Sess., 1164 (1864). The monthly reports submitted to the adjutant general, beginning in April 1864, are not filed separately in the National Archives but are distributed throughout Record Group 94 (Letters Received, Files of the Adjutant General's Office) as they were received.

15. This is a personal impression, formed through the reading of many such reports, in manuscript form, filed in Record Group 94 (Letters Received, Files of the Adjutant General's Office), at the National Archives. These reports provide invaluable insight into how the chaplains viewed their duties.

16. This requirement did not actually have the force of law until April 9, 1864, when Congress passed a bill with an amendment requiring religious services at all burials and on each Sunday. *Congressional Globe*, 38 Cong., 1 Sess., 1164 (1864). Yet the reports and memoirs of the chaplains indicate an almost universal understanding that this duty was their first responsibility from the outset.

17. Richard F. Fuller, *Chaplain Fuller: Being a Life Sketch of a New England Clergyman and Army Chaplain* (Boston, 1864), 175, 179, 181–83. Hereafter cited as Fuller, *Life Sketch.*

18. Trumbull, *War Memories*, 29, 70–104.

19. Service Record, Files of the Adjutant General's Office, National Archives, Record Group 94.

20. Trumbull, *War Memories*, 286.

21. Ibid., 297.

22. Letter to wife dated July 5, 1861, quoted in *Memorial and Letters of Rev. John R. Adams, D.D.* (1890), 22. Hereafter cited as Adams, *Memorial and Letters*.

23. Charles A. Humphreys, *Field, Camp, Hospital, and Prison in the Civil War, 1863–1865* (Boston, 1918), 12–14. Hereafter cited as Humphreys, *Field, Camp, Hospital, and Prison*.

24. Humphreys, *Field, Camp, Hospital, and Prison*, 14–17.

25. The Very Reverend William Corby, *Memoirs of Chaplain Life* (Notre Dame, IN, 1894), 27. Hereafter cited as Corby, *Memoirs*.

26. Ibid., 37–38, 42–44, 87.

27. Ibid., 140–44, 265–66.

28. Ibid., 99–101.

29. Rev. William W. Lyle, *Light and Shadows of Army Life: Or, Pen Pictures from the Battlefield, the Camp, and the Hospital* (Cincinnati, 1865), 117–18. Hereafter cited as Lyle, *Light and Shadows*.

30. Ibid., 177. This was on the battlefield, September 22, 1861, just five days after the battle.

31. Ibid., 289–91. Lyle here quotes an unnamed correspondent who had described the chaplain's performance for the press.

32. Ibid., 199–200.

33. Fuller, *Life Sketch*, 181–84, 193.

34. Report dated May 31, 1864, Letters Received, Files of the Adjutant General's Office, National Archives, Record Group 94.

35. James J. Marks, *The Peninsular Campaign in Virginia or Incidents and Scenes on the Battlefield and in Richmond* (Philadelphia, 1864), 55–64. Hereafter cited as Marks, *The Peninsular Campaign*.

36. Brown, *The Army Chaplain*, 8.

37. Fuller, *Life Sketch*, 208–09.

38. Adams, *Memorial and Letters*, 52.

39. Rev. J. Pinkney Hammond, *The Army Chaplain's Manual* (Philadelphia, 1863), 103–42. Hereafter cited as Hammond, *Chaplain's Manual*.

40. Published in the *Alleghanian*, January 22, 1863. James C. Duram and Eleanor A. Duram, eds., *Soldier of the Cross: The Civil War Diary and Correspondence of Rev. Andrew Jackson Hartsock* (Manhattan, KS, 1979), 169.

41. Fuller, *Life Sketch*, 191.

42. James B. Rogers, *War Pictures: Experiences and Observations of a Chaplain in the U.S. Army in the War of the Southern Rebellion* (Chicago, 1863), 80–81. Hereafter cited as Rogers, *War Pictures*.

43. Trumbull, *War Memories*, 117.

44. Adams, *Memorial and Letters*, 187.

45. Humphreys, *Field, Camp, Hospital, and Prison*, 5.

46. Ibid., 303.

47. Hammond, *Chaplain's Manual*, 71–86.

48. Marks, *The Peninsular Campaign*, 49.

49. Ibid., 44–54.

50. Report dated June 1, 1864, Letters Received, Files of the Adjutant General's Office, National Archives, Record Group 94.

51. Lyle, *Light and Shadows*, 199–200. The former chaplain to whom Lyle referred was the Reverend George W. Dubois.

52. Corby, *Memoirs*, 146–51.

53. Service Record, Files of the Adjutant General's Office, National Archives, Record Group 94.

54. Service Record, Files of the Adjutant General's Office, National Archives, Record Group 94. This file contains numerous similar requests, each having been approved with no apparent difficulty. Evidently these requests were considered normal and legitimate.

55. Hammond, *Chaplain's Manual*, 71–86.

56. Brown, *The Army Chaplain*, 82.

57. Humphreys, *Field, Camp, Hospital, and Prison*, 6, 7.

58. Corby, *Memoirs*, 27, 291–92.

59. Lyle, *Light and Shadows*, 200–201.

60. Humphreys, *Field, Camp, Hospital, and Prison*, 385–89. The chaplain here quotes from a quarterly report to his regimental commander, dated January 8, 1864.

61. Adams, *Memorial and Letters*, 141–43.

62. Fuller, *Life Sketch*, 193–94.

63. Report dated May 31, 1864, Letters Received, Files of the Adjutant General's Office, National Archives, Record Group 94.

64. Report dated June 1, 1864, Letters Received, Files of the Adjutant General's Office, National Archives, Record Group 94.

65. Corby, *Memoirs*, 291–94.

66. Trumbull, *War Memories*, 134–39.

67. Hammond, *Chaplain's Manual*, 71–86; Brown, *The Army Chaplain*, 48–49.

68. Humphreys, *Field, Camp, Hospital, and Prison*, 7.

69. Rev. George S. Bradley, *The Star Corps: Or Notes of an Army Chaplain, during Sherman's Famous "March to the Sea"* (Milwaukee, 1865), 86–87. Hereafter cited as Bradley, *The Star Corps*.

70. Hammond, *Chaplain's Manual*, 87–102.

71. Ibid.

72. Lyle, *Light and Shadows*, 199–200.

73. Fuller, *Life Sketch*, 197.

74. Bristol, *Chaplain McCabe*, 103.

75. Service Record, Files of the Adjutant General's Office, National Archives, Record Group 94; Trumbull, *War Memories*, 296–98.

76. Corby, *Memoirs*, 111–13.

77. David Powers Conyngham, *The Irish Brigade and Its Campaigns: With Some Account of the Corcoran Legion, and Sketches of the Principal Officers* (New York, 1867), 415. Corby, *Memoirs*, 181–84. Corby quotes Colonel St. Clair Mulholland, who described the scene after the war.

78. Rogers, *War Pictures*, 32–43.

79. George Whitfield Pepper, *Personal Recollections of Sherman's Campaigns in Georgia and the Carolinas* (Zanesville, OH, 1866), 185–98. Hereafter cited as Pepper, *Personal Recollections*.

80. Trumbull, *War Memories*, 265–67.

81. Ibid.

82. Humphreys, *Field, Camp, Hospital, and Prison*, 248–50.

83. Lyle, *Light and Shadows*, 49–61, 82–83, 165.

84. Service Record, Files of the Adjutant General's Office, National Archives, Record Group 94. The chaplain was captured on June 30, 1862, and exchanged on July 19, 1862; Marks, *The Peninsular Campaign*, 239–40.

85. Service Record, Files of the Adjutant General's Office, National Archives,

Record Group 94. McCabe was captured on June 15, 1863, and exchanged on October 17, 1863; Bristol, *Chaplain McCabe*, 125.

86. Service Record, Files of the Adjutant General's Office, National Archives, Record Group 94; Humphreys, *Field, Camp, Hospital, and Prison*, 109–13.

87. Both Union and Confederate chaplains believed that the most difficult task they faced was providing religious counsel for men sentenced to death for the military crime of desertion. See Gorrell Prim, Jr., "Born Again in the Trenches: Revivalism in the Confederate Army," Ph.D. diss., Florida State University, 1982, and Frank L. Hieronymus, "For Now and Forever: The Chaplains of the Confederate States Army," Ph.D. diss., University of California, Los Angeles, 1964.

88. William R. Eastman, *The Army Chaplain of 1863* (New York, 1912), 343–44. Hereafter cited as Eastman, *The Army Chaplain.*

89. Thian, *Legislative History*, 418.

90. This is a personal impression, formed through the reading of many such reports, in manuscript form, filed in Record Group 679 (Files of the Surgeon General's Office), at the National Archives. These reports are the only substantial source of information concerning the hospital chaplains and their work. They provide an invaluable insight into how the chaplains so engaged viewed and fulfilled their duties.

91. The act of May 20, 1862, which gave legislative authority to the appointment of chaplains at all "permanent" army hospitals, required the chaplains to hold such services. Thian, *Legislative History*, 418.

92. Service Record, Files of the Adjutant General's Office, National Archives, Record Group 94. Brown received a letter from Lincoln dated November 7, 1861, in which the president requested his voluntary service as a hospital chaplain until Congress could pass appropriate legislation. He served voluntarily until his official appointment on May 31, 1862, based on the law of May 20, 1862. He was mustered out on September 18, 1865, having served at Douglas Hospital (Washington, D.C.) throughout the war.

93. The chaplain, as explained earlier, had written a compact handbook for chaplains, explaining their functions as he viewed them.

94. Brown, *The Army Chaplain*, 30–37.

95. Report dated October 31, 1864, Files of the Surgeon General's Office, National Archives, Record Group 679.

96. Report dated March 31, 1864, Files of the Surgeon General's Office, National Archives, Record Group 679. The chaplain's post was Hospital No. 8 at Nashville, Tennessee.

97. Report dated November 21, 1863, Files of the Surgeon General's Office, National Archives, Record Group 679. The chaplain was stationed at the Third Division General Hospital in Alexandria, Virginia.

98. Brown, *The Army Chaplain*, 62–67. A circular from the office of the assistant medical director of the Department of the Cumberland in Nashville, Tennessee, dated April 18, 1864, stated that "it shall be the duty of the Chaplain . . . to notify the friends on the death of any patient, giving them such information as may have been communicated to him by the man previous to his death." Manuscript copy, Files of the Surgeon General's Office, National Archives, Record Group 679.

99. Abbott reported from the Third Division General Hospital in Alexandria, Virginia; Ames reported from the Second Division General Hospital, Twentieth Corps, at Atlanta, Georgia; Anderson was stationed at the Barrack

Hospital in Detroit, Michigan. Reports found in the Files of the Surgeon General's Office, National Archives, Record Group 679.

100. Brown, *The Army Chaplain*, 40–46.

101. Hammond, *Chaplain's Manual*, 135–42.

102. The special order dated April 7, 1864, carried this endorsement by Dr. John Campbell, the medical director for the department: "Hospt. Chaplain Jacob Frankel, USA, having reported at this office in compliance with instructions from the Act. Surgeon General, USA, is hereby assigned to duty as visiting Chaplain to the hospitals in this City and vicinity and will be respected accordingly." Printed copy of Special Order No. 139, Department of the Susquehanna, Files of the Surgeon General's Office, National Archives, Record Group 679.

103. Brown, *The Army Chaplain*, 46–51, 82–84.

104. Hammond, *Chaplain's Manual*, 71–86.

105. Manuscript copy of a circular, dated April 18, 1864, from the office of the assistant medical director of the Department of the Cumberland in Nashville, Tennessee, found in the Files of the Surgeon General's Office, National Archives, Record Group 679.

106. Brown, *The Army Chaplain*, 87–102.

107. Report from Satterlee Hospital, West Philadelphia, dated October 31, 1864, Files of the Surgeon General's Office, National Archives, Record Group 679.

108. Reports from the Third Division General Hospital, Alexandria, Virginia, dated May 16 and May 30, 1863, Files of the Surgeon General's Office, National Archives, Record Group 679.

109. Allington was the chaplain of the Ninety-fourth Ohio Infantry, temporarily on detached service at Hospital No. 14, Nashville, Tennessee. Report dated October 31, 1864, Files of the Surgeon General's Office, National Archives, Record Group 679.

110. Brown, *The Army Chaplain*, 72–76, 127–41; Hammond, *Chaplain's Manual*, 83–86.

111. Report dated October 31, 1864, Files of the Surgeon General's Office, National Archives, Record Group 679.

112. Report from Fort Williams, Baton Rouge, Louisiana, dated June 30, 1864, Files of the Surgeon General's Office, National Archives, Record Group 679.

113. Report dated November 30, 1864, Files of the Surgeon General's Office, National Archives, Record Group 679.

CHAPTER THREE: THE SHEPHERD
AND HIS FLOCK

1. The regimental histories are another source of information regarding the relationships that prevailed between the chaplain and his men. They must, however, be used with caution for two reasons. First, most of them are basically military histories; consequently such other information as they included is given peripheral treatment. Second, they were written after the fact, some long afterward, when harsher memories were somewhat softened; hence there is rarely a derogatory comment about anyone who served in the "old regiment."

2. Marks, *The Peninsular Campaign*, 46–47.

3. Reverend P. V. Ferree, *The Heroes of the War for the Union and Their Achievements* (Cincinnati, 1864), 475–77.

4. Bradley, *The Star Corps,* 286.

5. Reid Mitchell, *Civil War Soldiers* (New York, 1988), 120.

6. Letter to Dr. Campbell, dated November 23, 1863. Manuscript copy of the letter found with the monthly reports of Chaplain Alfred Nevin, Letters Received, Files of the Surgeon General's Office, National Archives, Record Group 679.

7. Reports dated October 31, 1864, and January 21, 1865, Letters Received, Files of the Surgeon General's Office, National Archives, Record Group 679.

8. Honeywell, *Chaplains,* 114–15.

9. Henry Norman Hudson, *A Chaplain's Campaign with General Butler* (New York, 1865), 35–50.

10. Ibid.; Honeywell, *Chaplains,* 115.

11. George A. Leakin to Abraham Lincoln, November 5, 1863, with endorsements by Major B. M. Etting and Major B. N. Brice, who were members of the board that reviewed the case. The note from Acting Surgeon General Joseph K. Barnes was attached to the chaplain's letter. Letters Received, Files of the Surgeon General's Office, National Archives, Record Group 679.

12. Bristol, *Chaplain McCabe,* 77–78.

13. Corby, *Memoirs,* 140–42, 265–66; see also Bristol, *Chaplain McCabe,* 51.

14. Humphreys had no experience as a pastor prior to his service as a chaplain. Service Record, Files of the Adjutant General's Office, National Archives, Record Group 94; Humphreys, *Field, Camp, Hospital, and Prison,* 3, 15–19.

15. Adams, *Memorial and Letters,* 172.

16. Report dated May 31, 1864, Letters Received, Files of the Adjutant General's Office, National Archives, Record Group 94.

17. Report dated January 1, 1865, Letters Received, Files of the Adjutant General's Office, National Archives, Record Group 94.

18. Hammond, *Chaplain's Manual,* 34–35.

19. Basler, *Lincoln: Collected Works,* II, 254.

20. Report dated May 31, 1865, Letters Received, Files of the Adjutant General's Office, National Archives, Record Group 94.

21. Quarterly report dated January 8, 1864, quoted in Humphreys, *Field, Camp, Hospital, and Prison,* 385–89.

22. Rogers, *War Pictures,* 229–31.

23. Ibid., 87.

24. Report dated January 1, 1865, Letters Received, Files of the Adjutant General's Office, National Archives, Record Group 94; Trumbull, *War Memories,* 106.

25. Report dated August 31, 1864, Letters Received, Files of the Surgeon General's Office, National Archives, Record Group 679.

26. Reports dated May 16 and December 17, 1863, and November 1, 1864, Letters Received, Files of the Surgeon General's Office, National Archives, Record Group 679.

27. Anderson stated in part: "Profanity is the glaring vice of our army, and meets you everywhere. It would do much good were some restrictive rules for the discouragement of it put in operation. Our hospitals are by no means free of it. I wish I could report otherwise." Report dated October 31, 1864, Letters Received, Files of the Surgeon General's Office, National Archives, Record Group 679.

28. Report dated June 1, 1864, Letters Received, Files of the Adjutant General's Office, National Archives, Record Group 94. This report of Chap-

lain Hamilton contained the most thorough statement of a chaplain's analysis in regard to the moral condition of his regiment in any of the reports examined by this author.

29. Reports dated February 28 and March 31, 1865, Letters Received, Files of the Adjutant General's Office, National Archives, Record Group 94.

30. Marks, *The Peninsular Campaign*, 59–60.

31. Report dated January 23, 1863, Letters Received, Files of the Adjutant General's Office, National Archives, Record Group 94.

32. Emil Rosenblatt and Ruth Rosenblatt, eds., *Hard Marching Every Day: The Civil War Letters of Private Wilbur Fisk, 1861–1865* (Lawrence, KS, 1992), 212. Hereafter cited as Rosenblatt and Rosenblatt, *Hard Marching*.

33. Reports dated throughout 1863 and 1864, Letters Received, Files of the Surgeon General's Office, National Archives, Record Group 679. The report quoted is dated December 26, 1863.

34. Report dated December 1, 1864, Letters Received, Files of the Surgeon General's Office, National Archives, Record Group 679.

35. Report dated June 30, 1864, Letters Received, Files of the Surgeon General's Office, National Archives, Record Group 679.

36. Honeywell, *Chaplains*, 132–33; Clifton E. Olmstead, *History of Religion in the United States*, (Englewood Cliffs, NJ, 1960), 323–28, hereafter referred to as Olmstead, *History of Religion*; Marcus Lee Hansen, *The Immigrant in American History* (Cambridge, MA, 1940), 97–125.

37. Corby, *Memoirs*, 314, 345–47.

38. Trumbull, *War Memories*, 23–24.

39. Lyle, *Light and Shadows*, 32–38.

40. Fuller, *Life Sketch*, 179–83.

41. Adams, *Memorial and Letters*, 46–47, 163–65, 176–77.

42. Rogers, *War Pictures*, 78–79.

43. David Power Conyngham, *Soldiers of the Cross: Heroism of the Cross or Nuns and Priests on the Battlefield*, manuscript in Notre Dame Archives, 81, 212.

44. Corby, *Memoirs*, 57–58, 185–86.

45. Eastman, *The Army Chaplain*, 346–48.

46. Rollin W. Quimby, "The Chaplain's Predicament," *Civil War History* 8 (March 1962): 25. Professor Quimby has made limited use of the *Official Records*, and apparently none of the service records and reports of the chaplains filed in the National Archives. His sources include a double handful (nine) of chaplains' memoirs, plus a few (twelve) regimental histories written by chaplains or containing references to chaplains. It is doubtful that such sweeping conclusions are warranted by such limited research.

47. Ibid., 20–21. The debate in the Senate was indicative of the extent of this criticism; see also Pepper, *Personal Recollections*, 197.

48. Pepper, *Personal Recollections*, 197–98.

49. Ibid.

50. Ibid., 4.

51. Olmstead, *History of Religion*, 248–69; William Warren Sweet, *The Methodist Episcopal Church and the Civil War* (Cincinnati, 1912), 134–35. Hereafter cited as Sweet, *The Methodist Episcopal Church*.

52. Sweet, *The Methodist Episcopal Church*, 134–35.

53. Ibid., 9–11.

54. Ibid., 11–12.

55. Gerald F. Linderman, *Embattled Courage* (New York, 1987), 253–54.

56. S. K. Berridge to William A. Hammond, May 31, 1864, Letters Received, Files of the Surgeon General's Office, National Archives, Record Group 679.

57. Brown, *The Army Chaplain*, 142–43.

58. Lyle, *Light and Shadows*, 273–75.

59. Benjamin F. Taylor, *Pictures of Life in Camp and Field* (Chicago, 1875), 120–22.

60. Louis P. Masur, ed. *The Real War Will Never Get in the Book: Selections from Writers During the Civil War* (New York, 1993), 88.

61. Sprague served the regiment as acting chaplain from March 18 to June 27, 1863. At that time he was appointed as regular chaplain. The alleged offenses had occurred on or about October 6, 1863, and the charges were brought on January 11, 1864. There is no reason given for the delay in filing charges. Service Record, Files of the Adjutant General's Office, National Archives, Record Group 94.

62. Service Record, Files of the Surgeon General's Office, National Archives, Record Group 679.

63. Reports and Service Record, Letters Received, Files of the Surgeon General's Office, National Archives, Record Group 679.

64. Service Record, Files of the Adjutant General's Office, National Archives, Record Group 94.

65. Reports and Service Records, Files of the Adjutant and Surgeon General's Offices, National Archives, Record Groups 94 and 679.

66. Biographical sketch appended by the publisher to an address by Rev. George W. Pepper, *Ireland . . . Liberty Springs from Her Martyr's Blood: An Address* (Boston, 1868); Service Record, Files of the Adjutant General's Office, National Archives, Record Group 94.

67. Pepper, *Personal Recollections*, 198–200.

68. Ibid., 201.

69. Ibid., 201–2.

70. Ibid., 202–3.

71. Ibid., 203–5.

72. Ibid.

73. The heavy fighting at Resaca took place on May 13, 1864. Isaac Springer volunteered for the position of chaplain and was appointed to that office on July 15, 1864. Service Record, Files of the Adjutant General's Office, National Archives, Record Group 94. The temptation to assume that the younger chaplain was the son of the elder Springer is indeed tantalizing, but such a relationship cannot be verified from the service records.

74. Pepper, *Personal Recollections*, 204; letter dated January 12, 1863, from the battlefield near Murfreesboro, Tennessee, in "The War Letters of Father Peter Paul Cooney," *Records of the American Catholic Historical Society* 44 (June 1933): 152.

75. Service Record, Files of the Adjutant General's Office, National Archives, Record Group 94.

76. *History of the Fifth Maine Regiment*, quoted in Adams, *Memorial and Letters*, 87, 241.

77. J. D. Cox to Edwin M. Stanton, December 3, 1862, Letters Received, Files of the Adjutant General's Office, National Archives, Record Group 94.

78. Charles M. Blake to William A. Hammond, January 3, 1863, Letters Received, Files of the Adjutant General's Office, National Archives, Record Group 94.

79. The monthly report quoted is dated March 14, 1863. Letters Received, Files of the Surgeon General's Office, National Archives, Record Group 679.

80. Basler, *Lincoln: Collected Works*, VIII, 526.

81. The resolution adopted by the officers of the First Indiana Heavy Artillery, dated June 28, 1864, at Baton Rouge, Louisiana. Printed copy filed with the reports of Chaplain Nelson L. Brakeman, Letters Received, Files of the Surgeon General's Office, National Archives, Record Group 679.

82. John G. B. Adams, *Reminiscences of the Nineteenth Massachusetts Regiment* (Boston, 1899), 118.

83. Bristol, *Chaplain McCabe*, 136–37, 191–203.

84. William Sumner Dodge, *History of the Old Second Division, Army of the Cumberland* (Chicago, 1864), 447.

85. Corby, *Memoirs*, 297–306.

86. *Official Records*, Series I, Vol. XV, 329.

87. *Official Records*, Series I, Vol. XLII, Part I, 732.

88. Service Record, Files of the Adjutant General's Office, National Archives, Record Group 94; Fuller, *Life Sketch*, 290–304.

89. Quoted in Fuller, *Life Sketch*, 333; a copy of Richard Fuller's letter on behalf of the chaplain's widow is filed with Fuller's Service Record, Files of the Adjutant General's Office, National Archives, Record Group 94; see also Honeywell, *Chaplains*, 122–23.

90. Robert Garth Scott, ed., *Fallen Leaves* (Kent, OH, 1991), 142.

91. *Congressional Globe*, 37 Cong., 2 Sess., 1082 (1862).

92. Trumbull, *War Memories*, 105–7.

93. Report dated October 31, 1864, Letters Received, Files of the Surgeon General's Office, National Archives, Record Group 679.

94. Rogers, *War Pictures*, 79–80.

95. Bradley, *The Star Corps*, 286.

CHAPTER FOUR: A FUTURE
FOR THE FREEDMEN

1. Fuller, *Life Sketch*, 198–206.

2. Rogers, *War Pictures*, 218–19.

3. Ibid., 157–58, 218–19, 220–26.

4. Ibid., 122–24.

5. Ibid., 131–35.

6. Pepper, *Personal Recollections*, 236–37, 250.

7. Ibid., 250–59.

8. Marks, *The Peninsular Campaign*, 90–97.

9. George H. Hepworth, *The Whip, Hoe, and Sword: Or the Gulf-Department in '63* (Boston, 1864), 139–40. Hereafter cited as *The Whip, Hoe, and Sword*.

10. Chaplain Baldwin was stationed at an army hospital in Beverly, Virginia. His request for a transfer was stated in an eight-page letter to President Lincoln dated August 23, 1862. He had, he stated in the letter, supported the colonization movement for more than twenty years. He did not believe that blacks and whites could live together harmoniously once the institution of slavery had been abolished. He failed to indicate in his epistle, however, how colonization could be of benefit to the blacks. No action was taken to grant his re-

quest for a post in the Washington area. Letter in manuscript form found in the Files of the Surgeon General's Office, National Archives, Record Group 679.

11. Of all the chaplains whose reports or memoirs have been examined by this author, Baldwin alone spoke favorably of colonization as a solution to the problems of the former slaves.

12. Stephen A. Hodgman, *The Nation's Sin and Punishment: Or the Hand of God Visible in the Overthrow of Slavery* (New York, 1864), 208–16. Hereafter cited as Hodgman, *The Nation's Sin.*

13. Trumbull, *War Memories*, 375–82.

14. Adams, *Memorial and Letters*, 30–40; Rev. S. L. Gracey, *Annals of the Sixth Pennsylvania Cavalry* (Philadelphia, 1868), 228–30; John Eaton, *Grant, Lincoln, and the Freedmen* (New York, 1907), 1–3.

15. Bristol, *Chaplain McCabe*, 157, quoting an entry in McCabe's journal from October 1864. The mention of Fort Pillow refers to a still controversial incident that took place on April 12, 1864, in Tennessee. Confederate General Nathan Bedford Forrest was alleged to have refused quarter to the surrendering black troops of the garrison, and Confederate troops reportedly massacred several hundred of them rather than taking them prisoners. The facts of the case are still disputed.

16. Hodgman, *The Nation's Sin*, 228–41; Hepworth, *The Whip, Hoe, and Sword*, 187–91.

17. Report dated April 30, 1865, Letters Received, Files of the Adjutant General's Office, National Archives, Record Group 94.

18. Report dated May 1, 1865, Letters Received, Files of the Adjutant General's Office, National Archives, Record Group 94.

19. The general to whom the chaplain referred was probably Major General Edward R. S. Canby, who was the field commander in the department under the overall direction of Major General George Thomas.

20. Reports dated April 30 and May 1, 1865, Letters Received, Files of the Adjutant General's Office, National Archives, Record Group 94.

21. Quoted in Chester Forrester Dunham, *The Attitude of the Northern Clergy Toward the South, 1860–1865* (Toledo, OH, 1942), 207. Hereafter cited as Dunham, *The Attitude of the Northern Clergy.*

22. Badger was stationed first at the "Joe Holt" General Hospital, Jeffersonville, Indiana, and then in Louisville, Kentucky, as a post chaplain when that city was designated as a military post by the War Department in August 1865. In his report of August 28, 1865, he indicated that if there was no further work for him in the army he intended to offer his services to the Freedmen's Bureau in order to continue his work of educating the former slaves. Reports dated between October 31, 1864, and August 28, 1865, Files of the Surgeon General's Office, National Archives, Record Group 679.

23. Fuller, *Life Sketch*, 193, 198–99.

24. Report dated September 30, 1864, Letters Received, Files of the Surgeon General's Office, National Archives, Record Group 679. The report stated in part: "I am enabled to spend two or three hours [daily] teaching the Colored convalesents [sic] of figures, all of whom are learning to read."

25. Reports dated October 31, 1864, and February 28, 1865, Letters Received, Files of the Adjutant General's Office, National Archives, Record Group 94.

26. Olmstead, *History of Religion*, 396.

27. Reverend Frederick Denison, *Shot and Shell: The Third Rhode Island Heavy Artillery Regiment in the Rebellion, 1861–1865* (Providence, RI, 1879),

131–32. Hereafter cited as Denison, *Shot and Shell.* There were probably other and earlier incidents of this sort. This particular instance, however, is the earliest (the winter of 1862–1863) about which *specific* details have been located.

28. Lincoln's endorsement, directed to Stanton and dated September 29, 1862, is as follows: "It seems by the within that there is danger of the different religious denominations having some collision in their ministering among the colored people about Port-Royal, and perhaps elsewhere. I should think each church should minister according to it's [sic] own rules, without interference by others differing from them; and if there still be difficulties about *places* of worship, a real christian charity, and forbearance on the part of all might obviate it. With these views, I submit the subject to the Secretary of War." No reply from Stanton to either Peck or the president has been found. Lincoln's endorsement and portions of Peck's letter, on which it was written, are quoted in Basler, *Lincoln: Collected Works,* V, 445, 446n.

29. Olmstead, *History of Religion,* 396–97; Denison, *Shot and Shell,* 132–35.

30. Lincoln's letter, dated August 21, 1863, was also published in the Washington *Morning Chronicle,* August 26, 1863. Basler, *Lincoln: Collected Works,* VI, 401.

31. Printed copy of a circular dated January 14, 1864, Files of the Adjutant General's Office, National Archives, Record Group 94.

32. The resolutions were presented to Lincoln on May 28, 1864. His written response was dated May 30, 1864. Basler, *Lincoln: Collected Works,* VII, 365n, 368.

33. Olmstead, *History of Religion,* 396–97; the circular, dated November 30, 1863, reads as follows:

> To the Generals commanding the Departments of the Missouri, the Tennessee, and the Gulf, and all Generals and officers commanding armies, detachments, and posts, and all officers in the service of the United States in the above mentioned Departments:
>
> You are hereby directed to place at the disposal of Rev. Bishop Ames all houses of worship belonging to the Methodist Episcopal Church South in which a loyal minister, who has been appointed by a loyal Bishop of said church, does not now officiate.
>
> It is a matter of great importance to the Government, in its efforts to restore tranquility to the community and peace to the nation, that Christian ministers should, by example and precept, support and foster the loyal sentiment of the people.
>
> Bishop Ames enjoys the entire confidence of this Department, and no doubt is entertained that all ministers who may be appointed by him will be entirely loyal. You are expected to give him all the aid, countenance, and support practicable in the execution of his important duties.
>
> You are also authorized and directed to furnish Bishop Ames and his clerk with transportation and subsistence when it can be done without prejudice to the service, and will afford them courtesy, assistance and protection.

Printed copy found in the Files of the Adjutant General's Office, National Archives, Record Group 94.

34. Olmstead, *History of Religion,* 396.

35. The petition, dated March 15, 1864, stated in part: "In consequence of our Discipline excluding slaveholders from membership, we have no Societies in the South, excepting a few in the border States; but the way being now

open, we desire to do what we can for the elevation of the Freedmen." Stanton's permission in a circular of March 23, 1864, did not take into consideration the point made by the Brethren, i.e., that they had no churches in the South due to their antislavery position. Letters Received, Files of the Adjutant General's Office, National Archives, Record Group 94.

36. See note 28.

37. Flickinger's letters to Stanton were dated April 28, May 2, and June 3, 1864. Letters Received, Files of the Adjutant General's Office, National Archives, Record Group 94.

38. Pressly's letter, dated February 6, 1864, pointed out the schism over slavery and urged that the Southern counterpart of his church be specifically designated in the circular. Letters Received, Files of the Adjutant General's Office, National Archives, Record Group 94; Lewis G. Vander Velde, *The Presbyterian Churches and the Federal Union, 1861–1869* (Cambridge, MA, 1932), 458–62. Hereafter cited as Vander Velde, *The Presbyterian Churches.*

39. Vander Velde, *The Presbyterian Churches,* 440.

40. Ibid.; Olmstead, *History of Religion,* 394–97.

41. Germain, *Catholic Chaplains,* 88–89. Service Record, Files of the Adjutant General's Office, National Archives, Record Group 94. *The War of the Rebellion: A Compilation of the Official Records of the Union and Confederate Armies* (Washington, 1880–1901), Series II, Vol. XLVIII, 1293.

42. Anson Phelps Stokes, *Church and State in the United States* (New York, 1950), II, 216–17.

43. See note 33.

44. The situation was brought to Lincoln's attention by the Reverend John Hogan, who had pastored the congregation of dispossessed Methodists. Hogan wrote to Lincoln in February 1864, protesting his loyalty and that of his people and pointing out that the state of Missouri had *not* seceded from the Union. The president instructed Stanton to modify his order so as to exclude Missouri and sent a copy of the modified circular to Hogan with this endorsement: "As you see within, the Secretary of War modifies his order so as to exempt Missouri from it. Kentucky never was within it. Nor, as I learn from the Secretary, was it ever intended any more than a means of rallying the Methodist people in favor of the Union in localities where the rebellion had disorganized and scattered them. Even in that view I fear it is liable to some abuses, but it is not quite easy to withdraw it entirely and at once." This endorsement, dated February 13, 1864, was attached to a copy of the circular and filed with the correspondence from Hogan. Letters Received, Files of the Adjutant General's Office, National Archives, Record Group 94; for a slightly different version of the same incident, see Basler, *Lincoln: Collected Works,* VII, 182–83.

45. This is the author's personal impression formed through the reading of the chaplains' monthly reports filed in the Records of the Adjutant General's Office, National Archives, Record Group 94.

46. See Chapter 2, note 13.

47. This author has discovered but a single exception to the practice of resignation from the chaplaincy to accept a commission. This was the Reverend Edward O'Brien (Seventeenth Illinois Cavalry), who as a Roman Catholic priest was not at liberty to accept military rank with command.

48. W. E. Burghardt DuBois, *The Souls of Black Folk,* 16th ed. (Chicago, 1928), 15. The blacks who first prompted this action were three slaves owned by a Confederate colonel. They told the Union officer in command of the Union pickets that they were to be sent to North Carolina to build fortifications for

the Confederate army. When Butler heard of this he is reported to have re-marked, "These men are contraband of war; set them at work." Quoted in George W. Williams, *A History of the Negro Troops in the War of the Rebellion, 1861–1865* (New York, 1888), 70. Hereafter cited as Williams, *A History of the Negro Troops.*

49. For a more detailed view of Butler's policy see his public statement and correspondence with the War Department in *Official Records,* Series I, Vol. II, 52, 649. It is not possible to establish whether chaplains were involved in this system from the *Official Records.*

50. Eaton, *Grant, Lincoln, and the Freedmen,* 46–47; DuBois, *The Souls of Black Folk,* 15–18.

51. *Official Records,* Series I, Vol. VI, 185–86; Eaton, *Grant, Lincoln, and the Freedmen,* 47; DuBois, *The Souls of Black Folk,* 17–18; Williams, *A History of the Negro Troops,* 86–87. A more detailed study of a specific application of antislavery principles is found in Willie Lee Rose's *Rehearsal for Reconstruction: The Port Royal Experiment* (New York, 1964).

52. Saxton had served in the department under General Sherman as a captain in the capacity of assistant quartermaster. It was in this capacity that he encountered the extreme need of the contrabands for clothing, adequate housing, and rations. In November 1861, he had addressed a letter to the Adjutant General's Office requesting permission to distribute such supplies to the blacks at Port Royal. He was later promoted and made commander of the department. *Official Records,* Series I, Vol. VI, 186.

53. *Official Records,* Series I, Vol. XIV, 192, 377–78; Eaton, *Grant, Lincoln, and the Freedmen,* 52; DuBois, *The Souls of Black Folk,* 18–20.

54. Eaton, *Grant, Lincoln, and the Freedmen,* 2–3.

55. Ibid.

56. This is true because of the fact that Chaplain Eaton wrote a lengthy account of his activities among the blacks of the Mississippi Valley, and because in his capacity as superintendent of freedmen for the Department of the Tennessee he corresponded with the War Department, that correspondence being partially preserved in the Files of the Adjutant General's Office at the National Archives. Two other chaplains who wrote memoirs of their service in the army, George H. Hepworth (Fourth Louisiana Native Guards) and James B. Rogers (Fourteenth Wisconsin Infantry, later a captain in the Sixty-fourth U.S. Colored Troops), mentioned work of this nature to which they had been assigned. No specific details of the assignments were mentioned by either chaplain, however, and their Service Records at the National Archives do not provide sufficient additional information to give a clear picture of their service with the former slaves. Hepworth, *The Whip, Hoe, and Sword,* 25; Rogers, *War Pictures,* 109–10.

57. Halleck, who on November 9, 1861, was made commander of the Department of the Missouri, which then included western Tennessee and Kentucky, had issued on November 20 an order excluding fugitives from his lines. On February 23, 1862, the order was modified slightly to exclude fugitives except for instances in which he would grant a special order. *Official Records,* Series I, Vol. III, 370.

58. The order, dated February 26, 1862, at Fort Donelson, reads as follows (quoted in Williams, *A History of Negro Troops,* 75):

I. General Order No. 3, series 1861 [Halleck's order of November 20, 1861], from headquarters Department of Missouri, is still in force and must be observed. The necessity of its strict enforcement is made apparent by the numerous applications from citizens for permission to pass through the camps to look for fugitive slaves. In no case whatever will permission be granted to citizens for this purpose.

II. All slaves at Fort Donelson at the time of its capture, and all slaves within the line of military occupation that have been used by the enemy in building fortifications, or in any manner hostile to the Government, will be employed by the quartermaster's department for the benefit of the Government, and will under no circumstances be permitted to return to their masters.

III. It is made the duty of all officers of this command to see that all slaves above indicated are promptly delivered to the chief quartermaster of the district.

59. Eaton, *Grant, Lincoln, and the Freedmen*, 3.
60. The order, designated Special Order Number 16, read as follows:

Captain [*sic*] John Eaton, Jr., Chaplain 27th O.V.I. is hereby detailed under Special Field Order No. 127 from the Head Quarters of the Department of the Mississippi as Brigade Inspector.

He will thoroughly inspect the camps of this command and on Monday of each week will make reports to these Head Quarters concerning their police, the cleanliness of the men, and the character of the cooking.

Manuscript copy filed with Eaton's Service Record, Files of the Adjutant General's Office, National Archives, Record Group 94. In the book relating his experiences with the former slaves, Eaton expressed mystification over his selection as superintendent by Grant. The preceding order is not mentioned in the book. It probably never occurred to him that this was the logical reason for his appointment.

61. Special Order Number 15, dated November 11, 1862, reads as follows:

Chaplain Eaton of the 27th Ohio Infantry Vols. is hereby appointed to take charge of the Contrabands that come into camp in the vicinity of this Post [LaGrange, Tennessee], organizing them into suitable Companies for working, see that they are properly cared for, and set them to work picking, ginning, and Baleing [*sic*] all cotton now out and ungathered in fields.

Suitable Guards will be detailed by commanding officers nearest where the parties are at work to protect them from molestation.

For further instructions the Officer in charge of these Laborers will call at these Hd. Qrs.

Manuscript copy filed with Eaton's Service Record, Files of the Adjutant General's Office, National Archives, Record Group 94.

62. Eaton, *Grant, Lincoln, and the Freedmen*, 13–15.
63. Ibid., 21–22.
64. Ibid., 18–19.
65. Martha Mitchell Bigelow, "Freedmen of the Mississippi Valley, 1862–1865," *Civil War History* 8 (March 1962): 39.
66. Special Field Order Number 4, dated November 14, 1862, read in part as follows:

One Regiment of Infantry from Brigadier-General McArthur's Division will be temporarily detailed as guard, in charge of such contrabands, and the Surgeons of said Regiment will be charged with the c₃re of the sick. Commissaries of Subsistence will issue on the requisitions of Chaplain J. Eaton, jr., omitting the coffee rations and substituting rye.

Manuscript copy filed with Eaton's Service Record, Files of the Adjutant General's Office, National Archives, Record Group 94; Special Order Number 21, dated November 17, 1862, read as follows (quoted in Eaton, *Grant, Lincoln, and the Freedmen,* 21–22):

> Lieut.-Col. Charles A. Reynolds, Chief Quartermaster of the Department, will furnish Chaplain J. Eaton, jr., in charge of Contrabands at Grand Junction, Tenn., on his requisition, such tools and other implements as he may require; also materials for baling cotton, and clothing for contraband men, women, and children. Unsalable soldier's clothing will also be issued to him.

67. General Order Number 13, dated December 17, 1862, at Oxford, Mississippi, read as follows:

> Chaplain John Eaton, jr., of the Twenty-seventh Regiment Ohio Volunteers, is hereby appointed General Superintendent of Contrabands for the Department.
> He will designate such Assistant Superintendents as may be necessary for the proper care of these people, who will be detailed for their duty by the Post or District Commander.
> All Assistant Superintendents will be subject to the orders of the Superintendent.
> It will be the duty of the Superintendent of Contrabands to organize them into working parties in saving cotton, as pioneers on railroads and steamboats, and in any way where their service can be made available.
> Where labor is performed for private individuals, they will be charged in accordance with the tariff fixed in previous orders.
> When abandoned crops of cotton are saved for the benefit of Government, the officer selling the same will turn over to the Superintendent of Contrabands the same amount charged individuals.
> The negroes will be clothed, and in every way provided for, out of their earnings so far as practicable, the account being kept of all earnings and expenditures, and subject to the inspection of the Inspector General of the Department when called for.
> Such detail of men as may be necessary for the care and superintendence of the contrabands will be made by Post or Division Commander on application of the Superintendent; as far as practicable such men as are not fit for active field duty will be detailed.
> The Superintendent will take charge of all contributions of clothing, etc., for the benefit of negroes and distribute the same.
> All applications for the service of contrabands will be made on the General Superintendent, who will furnish such labor from negroes who voluntarily come within the lines of the army.
> In no case will negroes be forced into the service of the Government, or be enticed away from their homes except when it becomes a military necessity.

Official Records, Series I, Vol. VXII, Part 2, 395–96; Eaton, *Grant, Lincoln, and the Freedmen,* 26–27.

68. In a preliminary draft of the final proclamation, dated December 30, 1862, Lincoln stated in part: "And I further declare, and make known, that such persons of suitable condition, will be received into the armed service of the United States to garrison and defend forts, positions, stations, and other places, and to man vessels of all sorts in said service." Basler, *Lincoln: Collected Works*, VI, 24.

69. For a more detailed description of this program see Eaton, *Grant, Lincoln, and the Freedmen*, Chapters 11 and 12.

70. Eaton, *Grant, Lincoln, and the Freedmen*, 59–61, 144–46; Bigelow, "Freedmen of the Mississippi Valley," 44–45.

71. The joint plan was agreed upon in March 1864. Eaton, *Grant, Lincoln, and the Freedmen*, 152–55.

72. Ibid., 167–72.

73. Bruce Catton, *Grant Moves South* (Boston, 1960), 360–64; Bigelow, "Freedmen of the Mississippi Valley," 43–45.

74. Father James J. Pillar, *The Catholic Church in Mississippi, 1837–1865* (New Orleans, 1964), 270–73.

75. Ibid. Concerning Hewit's proposal Elder wrote: "I told him I should put no obstacle to it, but from the very nature of the case, it was necessary that it be conducted entirely by the people of the North, & connected with the army, without any positive cooperation on my part."

76. Ibid., 174–75. Father Pillar states further: "That Elder was unable to secure their services or those of any other religious community does not come as a surprise to modern historians of the Catholic Church in the United States. It fit into the pattern of circumstances which caused the church to lose an opportunity for large scale conversion of the Negroes to Catholicism [during and] after the Civil War."

77. Ibid., 99–100.

78. Many of these churches and their missions agencies have been discussed in a previous section of this chapter. For that reason their contributions will not be discussed here. The number of agencies that participated in this activity is too great to permit a detailed discussion within the framework of this study. For example, William Warren Sweet lists sixteen separate agencies with which the Methodist Episcopal Church cooperated, in addition to its own church organizations. *The Methodist Episcopal Church*, 168–76. See also Vander Velde, *The Presbyterian Churches*, 433–75, for an extended discussion of Presbyterian efforts. Chester Forrester Dunham also discusses various church activities among the blacks, although the main emphasis is religious rather than educational. *The Attitude of the Northern Clergy*, 204–12, 219–29. The black historian W. E. Burghardt DuBois also discusses, rather generally, the contributions to black education of the churches and aid societies. *Black Reconstruction* (New York, 1935), 78–80, 190–91, 348–49.

79. Eaton, *Grant, Lincoln, and the Freedmen*, 192–93.

80. Ibid., 193–96.

81. Special Order Number 63 from the War Department, dated September 29, 1863, read in part as follows (quoted in Eaton, *Grant, Lincoln, and the Freedmen*, 194):

VI. Transportation will be furnished for persons and goods, for the benefit of these people [blacks] on Government Transports and Military Railroads within the Department on the order of the General Superintendent [Eaton].

VII. Citizens voluntarily laboring for the benefit of these people, saving as they do to the Government, cost of labor in providing for their care, will, when properly accredited by the General Superintendent, be entitled to rations, quarters, and transportation on Government Transports and Military Railroads within the Department.

82. Order Number 26, dated September 26, 1864, read in part as follows: "To prevent confusion and embarrassment, the General Superintendent of Freedmen will designate officers, subject to his orders as Superintendent of Colored Schools, through whom he will arrange the location of all schools, teachers, and the occupation of houses and other details pertaining to the education of Freedmen. All officers commanding, and others, will render the necessary aid." Printed copy filed with Eaton's Service Record, Files of the Adjutant General's Office, National Archives, Record Group 94.

83. These were the Reverend L. H. Cobb, superintendent of the Colored Schools in the Memphis District; the Reverend James A. Hawley and a Reverend Mr. Buckley, both superintendents in the large Vicksburg district; C. S. Crossman, a former teacher of the Toledo public schools, superintendent in Natchez; Reverend Joel Grant, superintendent of the Arkansas district; W. F. Allen, superintendent of the Helena district, and J. L. Roberts, superintendent at Columbus, Kentucky. Eaton, *Grant, Lincoln, and the Freedmen*, 196.

84. Ibid., 197.

85. Ibid., 197–201.

86. Printed copy filed with Eaton's Service Record, Files of the Adjutant General's Office, National Archives, Record Group 94.

87. Eaton, *Grant, Lincoln, and the Freedmen*, 215–16.

88. He was appointed colonel of the Ninth Louisiana on October 10, 1863. Service Record, Files of the Adjutant General's Office, Record Group 94.

89. Dudley Taylor Cornish, *The Sable Arm: Negro Troops in the Union Army, 1861–1865* (New York, 1966), 49.

90. John Eaton to Edwin Stanton, October 20, 1864. Copy filed with Eaton's Service Record, Files of the Adjutant General's Office, National Archives, Record Group 94; much of the substance of this chapter appeared earlier in an article by the author published in *The Journal of Negro History* in April 1967.

CHAPTER FIVE: THE CAUSE OF IT ALL

1. Reverend Joseph Cross, D.D., *Camp and Field: Papers from the Portfolio of an Army Chaplain* (Columbia, SC, 1864), Books Third and Fourth, 7–8. Courtesy of the Library of Congress, Rare Book Collection.

2. Ibid., 376.

3. Rogers, *War Pictures*, 22.

4. Ibid., 25. He urged this theme while preaching at the courthouse in Savannah, Tennessee, to a mixed congregation including Union troops, residents of the community, and blacks.

5. Ibid., 35–36.

6. Ibid., 118.

7. Ibid., 157–58.

8. Ibid., 249–52. Quoting Senator Orville H. Browning of Illinois, the chaplain agreed on this manner of pursuing a total victory.

9. Fuller, *Life Sketch*, 87, quoting the chaplain's diary.

10. Ibid., 162–63.

11. Ibid., 173, quoting a letter dated August 19, 1861. He evidently referred to the measures taken by Lincoln to prevent a recurrence of the violence that had occurred in Baltimore on April 19, 1861, and for several days following, when mobs attacked Northern troops passing through the city on the way to Washington.

12. Ibid., 254.

13. Eastman, *The Army Chaplain*, 445.

14. Ibid., 236–37.

15. Ibid., 250–51.

16. Ibid., 260–63, 298, 329–30.

17. This is Hepworth's statement. It was not possible to verify this by his service record in the National Archives. It is possible that his service as a chaplain was unofficial or that he served on an interim basis while awaiting confirmation by the War Department and accepted his commission in the Fourth Louisiana before such confirmation became official.

18. Hepworth, *The Whip, Hoe, and Sword*, 39–84.

19. Ibid., 91–92.

20. Ibid., 127–39.

21. Trumbull, the founder and for years editor of the *Sunday School Times*, became convinced that the North could no longer compromise with slavery when first the Kansas-Nebraska Act (1854) and then the Dred Scott decision (1857) set aside the Missouri Compromise. He became a Republican in 1856 because of the antislavery nature of the new party. Philip E. Howard, *The Life Story of Henry Clay Trumbull* (Philadelphia, 1905).

22. Trumbull, *War Memories*, 65.

23. Ibid., 372–73.

24. Ibid., 375.

25. Bradley, *The Star Corps*, 62–65. Bradley quotes the colonel's written response, dated October 18, 1862, to the order that had demanded the surrender of the fugitives.

26. Ibid., 62–65. The act of Congress referred to is no doubt the act of March 13, 1862, which prevented the use of military power for returning fugitive slaves who had found their way within Union lines.

27. Ibid.

28. Ibid., 65–80.

29. Ibid., 59–60.

30. Ibid., 75. Bradley here quotes a letter from the former chaplain of the regiment, Reverend Caleb Pillsbury, dated February 2, 1863.

31. Ibid., 59–60.

32. Copperhead was a derogatory term used in the North to describe Northerners with Southern sympathies.

33. Bradley, *The Star Corps*, 88–89.

34. Ibid., 157–59, 224–25.

35. Ibid., 194.

36. Ibid.

37. Ibid., 151, quoting a letter by the chaplain to his family dated September 12, 1864, at the camp of the Twenty-second Wisconsin Infantry outside Atlanta, Georgia.

38. Ibid., 151.

39. Service Record, Files of the Adjutant General's Office, National Archives, Record Group 94.

40. Adams, *Memorial and Letters*, 95. Adams here refers, apparently, to a speech delivered by Vice President Stephens at Savannah, Georgia, shortly after the adoption of the Confederate constitution.

41. Ibid., 38, 49.

42. Ibid., 93. Chaplain Adams went on to state his belief that 80 percent of the men in the ranks supported the president in the proclamation. This was also true in the election of 1864.

43. Ibid., 121, 159.

44. Ibid., 126, 175, 222.

45. Service Record, Files of the Adjutant General's Office, National Archives, Record Group 94.

46. Humphreys, *Field, Camp, Hospital, and Prison*, 131. The chaplain had stated to his captors, when accused of being an abolitionist minister (and as such the cause of the war), that he was not an abolitionist. He did, however, acknowledge his hatred of human bondage.

47. Ibid., 132–35. Obviously, the chaplain was unaware of the marginal conditions in POW camps in the North. Although they were better than POW camps/prisons in the South by a substantial margin, they were far from ideal, and many Confederates died of disease while in captivity.

48. Service Record, Files of the Adjutant General's Office, National Archives, Record Group 94; Marks, *The Peninsular Campaign*, 239–40.

49. Marks, *The Peninsular Campaign*, 434.

50. Ibid.

51. Ibid., 434–36.

52. Ibid., 389.

53. Ibid., 90–95.

54. Corby, *Memoirs*, 320–21.

55. Denison, *Shot and Shell*, 328.

56. Ibid., 54–55.

57. Ibid., 208–9.

58. Ibid., 319.

59. Ibid., 330.

60. Alice Katherine Fallows, *Everybody's Bishop: Being the Life and Times of the Right Reverend Samuel Fallows, D.D.* (New York, 1927), 183, 194–97.

61. Ibid., 185.

62. Lyle, *Light and Shadows*, 24–31. Although condemning the American Tract Society, the chaplain had words of praise for the American Reform Tract and Book Society, which, he said, had never hesitated in issuing antislavery literature.

63. Ibid., 139, 141.

64. Ibid., 320–21. The slaveholders with whom he had spoken on this occasion were women, a fact that appalled the chaplain as he sensed their callousness toward human suffering.

65. Ibid., 223–24.

66. Ibid., 345–47.

67. Ibid., 343.

68. Ibid., 344.

69. Ibid., 226–35. The two papers named in this charge by the chaplain were the Cincinnati *Enquirer* and the Dayton *Empire*.

70. Service Record, Files of the Adjutant General's Office, National Archives, Record Group 94. Since he was a member of the Brazos Presbytery of Texas, the chaplain's file contains a letter attesting to that fact, and to his loyalty, signed by the ministers of his acquaintance in the North. This was the basis for his appointment to the chaplaincy.

71. Hodgman, *The Nation's Sin*, 242–43.

72. Ibid., 112, 245–48.

73. Ibid., 68.

74. Ibid., 198–201.

75. Ibid., 53.

76. Denison, *Shot and Shell*, 304.

77. Bristol, *Chaplain McCabe*, 208–9. The author here quotes from the diary of Chaplain McCabe an entry dated April 17, 1865.

78. Adams, *Memorial and Letters*, 210, 217–18.

79. Pepper, *Personal Recollections*, 396–98.

80. Humphreys, *Field, Camp, Hospital, and Prison*, 295–96.

81. Ibid.

82. Report dated May 4, 1865, Letters Received, Files of the Adjutant General's Office, National Archives, Record Group 94.

83. Report dated April 30, 1865, Letters Received, Files of the Adjutant General's Office, National Archives, Record Group 94.

84. Ibid.

85. Rosenblatt and Rosenblatt, *Hard Marching*, 206–7.

86. Denison, *Shot and Shell*, 328.

87. Rosenblatt and Rosenblatt, *Hard Marching*, 309.

88. Alexander H. Stephens, "The Chief Stone of the Corner in Our New Edifice," quoted in Edwin C. Rozwenc, ed., *Slavery as a Cause of the Civil War* (Boston, 1963), 45.

89. C. Vann Woodward, *The Burden of Southern History* (New York, 1960), 62.

90. Henry Steele Commager, ed., "199. South Carolina Declaration of Causes of Secession, December 24, 1860," *Documents of American History* (New York, 1949), 374. Hereafter cited as Commager, *Documents*.

91. William J. Cooper, Jr., *The South and the Politics of Slavery, 1828–1856* (Baton Rouge, LA, 1978), xiii, xiv. See also Chapter 3.

92. Lunsford Yandell, Jr., to Sally Yandell, April 22, 1861, quoted in James M. McPherson, *For Cause and Comrades: Why Men Fought in the Civil War* (New York, 1997), 106. Hereafter cited as McPherson, *For Cause*. Veteran Civil War historian James M. McPherson's latest book samples both Confederate and Union diaries and collections of letters and gives a very clear picture of the thoughts and beliefs of the men who fought that greatest of American wars.

93. William Grimball to Elizabeth Grimball, November 20, 1860, quoted in McPherson, *For Cause*, 20.

94. George Hamill Diary, probably in March 1862. Quoted in McPherson, *For Cause*, 109.

95. McPherson, *For Cause*, 110.

96. *Dred Scott v Sandford*, 19 Howard, 393, 1857. Quoted in Commager, *Documents*, 342.

97. William C. Davis, *The Cause Lost* (Lawrence, KS, 1996), 182–83.

98. U. S. Grant, *Personal Memoirs of U. S. Grant* (New York, 1894), 629–30.

CHAPTER SIX: THE MEASURE OF A MAN

1. Report dated September 16, 1865, Letters Received, Files of the Surgeon General's Office, National Archives, Record Group 679.
2. Gardiner H. Shattuck, Jr., *A Shield and Hiding Place: The Religious Life of the Civil War Armies* (Macon, GA, 1987), 58.
3. Honeywell, *Chaplains*, 122.
4. Eastman, *The Army Chaplain*, 349–50.

BIBLIOGRAPHY

MANUSCRIPTS

By far the most important source of information in the preparation of this study has been the records of the War Department filed at the National Archives in Washington, D.C. Two record groups were used extensively. They are Record Group 94, which contains the files of the Adjutant General's Office including both Service Records and Reports, and Record Group 679, containing the files of the Surgeon General's Office including the reports of the hospital chaplains. Limited used was also made of Record Group 105, the Records of the Freedmen's Bureau.

The Soldiers of the Cross: Heroism of the Cross or Nuns and Priests on the Battlefield, a lengthy manuscript compiled about 1870 by David P. Conyngham, and filed in the Archives, Notre Dame University, was of especial value in clarifying the role of the Roman Catholic Church in connection with the chaplaincy.

GOVERNMENT PUBLICATIONS

Congressional Globe, Containing the Debates and Proceedings, 1833–1873. 109 vols. Washington: Blair and Rives, 1834–1873.

Indiana in the War of the Rebellion: Official Report of W. H. H. Terrell, Adjutant General. Indianapolis: Douglas & Conner, Journal Office, Printers, 1869.

Michigan in the War. Rev. ed. Compiled by John Robertson. Lansing: W. S. George & Co., State Printers and Binders, 1882.

New York in the War of the Rebellion, 1861–1865. 3d ed. Compiled by Frederick Phisterer. 6 vols. Albany: J. B. Lyon Company, State Printers, 1912.

Report of the Adjutant General of the State of Illinois. Revised by Brigadier General J. N. Reece. 9 vols. Springfield, IL: Phillips Bros., State Printers, 1900.

Report of the Adjutant General of the State of Indiana. 8 vols. Indianapolis, IN: Alexander H. Conner, State Printer, 1869.

Report of the Adjutant General of the State of Kansas, 1861–1865. Leavenworth, KS: Bulletin Cooperative Printing Company, 1867.

Roll of Honor: Names of Soldiers Who Died in Defense of the American Union,

Interred in the National Cemeteries at Washington, D.C., from August 3, 1861, to June 30, 1865. 27 vols. Washington: Government Printing Office, 1869.

United States War Department. *Index of General Orders, Adjutant General's Office, 1866.* Washington: Government Printing Office, 1867.

————. *Legislative History of the General Staff of the Army of the United States (Its Organization, Duties, Pay, and Allowances) from 1775 to 1901.* Compiled and annotated under the direction of Major-General Henry C. Corbin, Adjutant General of the Army, by Raphael P. Thian, Chief Clerk, Adjutant General's Office. Washington: Government Printing Office, 1901.

————. *Official Army Register of the Volunteer Force of the United States Army for the Years 1861, '62, '63, '64, '65.* 8 vols. Published by order of the secretary of war, Adjutant General's Office. Washington: Government Printing Office, 1865.

————. *Revised Regulations for the Army of the United States, 1861.* Published by the authority of the War Department. Philadelphia: G. W. Childs, 1862.

————. *Revised United States Army Regulations of 1861, with an Appendix Containing the Changes and Laws Affecting Army Regulations and Articles of War to June 25, 1863.* Washington: Government Printing Office, 1863.

————. *Subject Index of the General Orders of the War Department from January 1, 1861, to December 31, 1880.* Compiled under the direction of Brigadier General Richard C. Drum, Adjutant General, United States Army, by Jeremiah C. Allen, Adjutant General's Office. Washington: Government Printing Office, 1882.

————. *The War of the Rebellion: A Compilation of the Official Records of the Union and Confederate Armies.* 4 series, 70 vols. in 128. Published under the direction of the Hon. Russell A. Alger, Secretary of War, by Brigadier General Fred C. Ainsworth, Chief of the Record and Pension Office, War Department, and Mr. Joseph W. Kirkley. Washington: Government Printing Office, 1880–1901.

COLLECTIONS OF PRIMARY MATERIALS

Adams, Rev. John R., D.D. *Memorial and Letters of Rev. John R. Adams, D.D.* Privately printed by friends, 1890.

Basler, Roy P., ed. *The Collected Works of Abraham Lincoln.* 8 vols. New Brunswick, NJ: Rutgers University Press, 1953.

Benjamin, Marcus, ed. *Washington During War Time: A Series of Papers Showing the Military, Political, and Social Phases During 1861 to 1865.* Washington City: N.p., published in connection with the Thirty-sixth Annual Encampment of the Grand Army of the Republic, 1902.

Bradford, James H. *The Chaplains in the Volunteer Army.* War Papers, no. 11. Washington: Military Order of the Loyal Legion of the United States, Commandery of the District of Columbia, 1892.

Callan, John F. *The Military Laws of the United States, Relating to the Army, Volunteers, Militia, and to Bounty Lands and Pensions, from the Foundation of the Government to 4 July, 1864.* Philadelphia: G. W. Childs, 1864.

Cross, Rev. Joseph. *Camp and Field: Papers from the Portfolio of an Army Chaplain.* Columbia, SC: Evans and Cogswell, 1864.

Currie, George E. *Warfare Along the Mississippi.* Edited by Norman E. Clark, Sr. Mount Pleasant, MI: Clark Historical Collection, Central Michigan University, Edwards Brothers, Ann Arbor, MI 1961.

Denison, Rev. Frederic. *A Chaplain's Experience in the Union Army.* Personal Narratives, 4th series. Providence, RI: Soldiers and Sailors Historical Society of Rhode Island, 1891–1893.

Downing, Alexander G. *Downing's Civil War Diary.* Edited by Olynthis B. Clark. Des Moines: Historical Department of Iowa, Homestead Printing Company, 1916.

Dyer, Frederick H. *A Compendium of the War of the Rebellion, Compiled and Arranged from Official Records of the Federal and Confederate Armies, Reports of the Adjutant Generals of the Several States, the Army Registers, and Other Reliable Documents and Sources.* Des Moines, IA: Dyer Publishing Company, 1908.

Eastman, William R. *The Army Chaplain of 1863.* Personal Recollections of the War of the Rebellion, 4th series. Edited by A. Noel Blakeman. New York: G. P. Putnam's Sons, 1912.

Fox, William F. *Regimental Losses in the American Civil War, 1861–1865.* Albany, NY: Albany Publishing Company, 1889.

Hartwig, Robert Norman. "A Recollection of Chaplain Thomas Scott Johnson of the 127th United States Colored Troops and 36th United States Colored Troops During and After the Civil War." Seminar Paper, Wisconsin State University at La Crosse, May 1970.

Hedrick, David T., and Gordon Barry Davis, Jr., eds. *I'm Surrounded by Methodists.* Diary of John H. W. Stuckenberg, Chaplain of the 145th Pennsylvania Volunteer Infantry. Gettysburg, PA: Thomas Publications, 1995.

Heg, Hans Christian. *The Civil War Letters of Col. Hans Christian Heg.* Edited by Theodore C. Blegen. Northfield, MN: Norwegian-American Historical Association, 1936.

Nicolay, John G., and John Hay, eds. *Abraham Lincoln: Complete Works.* 2 vols. New York: Century, 1894.

Phisterer, Frederick. *Statistical Record of the Armies of the United States.* New York: Charles Scribner's Sons, 1886.

Stockwell, Elisha. *Private Elisha Stockwell, Jr., Sees the Civil War.* Edited by Byron R. Abernathy. Norman: University of Oklahoma Press, 1958.

Stokes, Anson Phelps. *Church and State in the United States.* 3 vols. New York: Harper and Brothers, 1950.

Sweet, William Warren. *Religion on the American Frontier: A Collection of Source Material.* 4 vols. I: *The Baptists, 1783–1830.* New York: Henry Holt and Company, c. 1931. II: *The Presbyterians.* New York: Harper and Brothers, 1936. III: *The Congregationalists.* Chicago: University of Chicago Press, 1939. IV: *The Methodists.* Chicago: University of Chicago Press, 1946.

Watson, William. *Letters of a Civil War Surgeon.* Purdue University Studies, Humanities Series. Edited by Paul Fatout. West Lafayette, IN: Purdue University Press, 1961.

OTHER PRIMARY MATERIALS

Abbott, Rev. Stephen G. *The First Regiment New Hampshire Volunteers in the Great Rebellion.* Keene, NH: Sentinal Printing Company, 1890.

Adams, John G. B. *Reminiscences of the Nineteenth Massachusetts Regiment.* Boston: Wright & Potter Printing, 1899.

B[ickham], W[m]. D. *Rosecrans' Campaign with the Fourteenth Army Corps,* or the Army of the Cumberland. Cincinnati, OH: Moore, Wilstach, Keys & Co., 1863.

Bishop, Judson W. The Story of a Regiment: Being a Narrative of the Service of the Second Regiment Minnesota Veteran Volunteer Infantry. St. Paul, MN: by the regiment, 1890.

Boies, Andrew J. Record of the Thirty-third Massachusetts Volunteer Infantry. Fitchburg, MA: Sentinel Printing Company, 1880.

Bowen, James L. Massachusetts in the War, 1861–1865. Springfield, MA: Clark W. Bryan & Co., 1889.

Bradley, Rev. George S. The Star Corps; Or Notes of an Army Chaplain, During Sherman's Famous "March to the Sea." Milwaukee: Jermain and Brightman, 1865.

Brown, Rev. William Young. The Army Chaplain: His Office, Duties, and Responsibilities, and the Means of Aiding Him. Philadelphia: William S. and Alfred Martien, 1863.

Castleman, Alfred L. The Army of the Potomac. Milwaukee: Strickland & Co., 1863.

Chamberlin, Thomas. History of the One Hundred and Fiftieth Regiment Pennsylvania Volunteers. Philadelphia: F. McManus, Jr., & Co., 1905.

Conyngham, David Powers. The Irish Brigade and Its Campaigns: With Some Account of the Corcoran Legion, and Sketches of the Principal Officers. New York: Wm. McSorley & Co., 1867.

Corby, Very Rev. W[illiam]. Memoirs of Chaplain Life. Notre Dame, IN: Scholastic Press, 1894.

Cox, Samuel S. Three Decades of Federal Legislation, 1855 to 1885. Providence, RI: J. A. and R. A. Reid, 1888.

Curtis, Newton Martin. From Bull Run to Chancellorsville: The Story of the Sixteenth New York Infantry Together with Personal Reminiscences. New York: G. P. Putnam's Sons, 1906.

Curtis O[rson] B. History of the Twenty-fourth Michigan of the Iron Brigade. Detroit: Winn & Hammond, 1891.

Day, L[ewis] W. History of the Twenty-fourth Michigan of the Iron Brigade. Cleveland: W. N. Bayne Printing Co., 1894.

Denison, Rev. Frederic. Sabers and Spurs: The First Regiment Rhode Island Cavalry in the Civil War, 1861–1865. Central Falls, RI: First Rhode Island Cavalry Veteran Association, Press of E. L. Freeman & Co., 1876.

———. Shot and Shell: The Third Rhode Island Heavy Artillery Regiment in the Rebellion, 1861–1865. Providence, RI: J. A. and R. A. Reid, 1879.

Dodge, William Sumner. History of the Old Second Division, Army of the Cumberland. Chicago: Church and Goodman, 1864.

———. A Waif of the War: Or the History of the Seventy-fifth Illinois Infantry. Chicago: Church and Goodman, 1866.

Duram, James C., and Eleanor A. Duram, eds. Soldier of the Cross: The Civil War Diary and Correspondence of Rev. Andrew Jackson Hartsock. Manhattan, KS: Military Affairs/Aerospace Historian Publishing, 1979.

Eastman, William R. The Army Chaplain of 1863, Read Before the New York Commandery, December 13, 1911. New York: Knickerbocker Press, 1912.

Eaton, John. Grant, Lincoln, and the Freedmen. New York: Longmans, Green and Co., 1907.

Eddy, T[homas] M[ears], D.D. The Patriotism of Illinois. 2 vols. Chicago: Clarke & Co., 1866.

Ferree, Rev. P. V. *The Heroes of the War for the Union and Their Achievements.* Cincinnati: R. W. Carroll & Co., 1864.

Fiske, John. *The Mississippi Valley in the Civil War.* Boston and New York: Houghton, Mifflin and Company, 1900.

[Fitch, John]. *Annals of the Army of the Cumberland.* Philadelphia: J. B. Lippincott & Co., 1863.

Floyd, Rev. David Bittle. *History of the Seventy-fifth Regiment of Indiana Infantry Volunteers, Its Organization, Campaign, and Battles (1862–1865).* Philadelphia: Lutheran Publication Society, 1893.

French, Samuel L. *The Army of the Potomac from 1861 to 1863.* New York: Publishing Society of New York, 1906.

Gracey, Rev. S. L. *Annals of the Sixth Pennsylvania Cavalry.* Philadelphia: E. H. Butler & Co., 1868.

Grant, U. S. *Personal Memoirs of U. S. Grant.* 2 vols. in one. New York: Charles L. Webster & Company, 1894.

Gregg, J[ohn] Chandler. *Life in the Army, in the Departments of Virginia, and the Gulf.* 2d ed. Philadelphia: Perkinpine & Higgins, 1868.

Hammond, Rev. J[onathan] Pinkney. *The Army Chaplain's Manual.* Philadelphia: J. B. Lippincott & Co., 1863.

Hepworth, George H. *The Whip, Hoe, and Sword: Or, the Gulf-Department in '63.* Boston: Walker, Wise and Company, 1864.

Higginson, Thomas Wentworth. *Army Life in a Black Regiment.* Boston: Houghton, Mifflin and Company, 1900.

[Hodgman, Stephen A.] *The Nation's Sin and Punishment: Or the Hand of God Visible in the Overthrow of Slavery.* New York: R. Craighead, Printer, 1864.

Hudson, Henry Norman. *A Chaplain's Campaign with General Butler.* New York: N.p., 1865.

Humphreys, Andrew A. *From Gettysburg to the Rapidan.* New York: Charles Scribner's Sons, 1883.

———. *The Virginia Campaign of '64 and '65. Campaigns of the Civil War.* New York: Charles Scribner's Sons, 1883.

Humphreys, Charles A. *Field, Camp, Hospital, and Prison in the Civil War, 1863–1865.* Boston: George H. Ellis Co., 1918.

Irvin, Richard B. *History of the Nineteenth Army Corps.* New York: G. P. Putnam's Sons, 1893.

Knox, Thomas W. *Camp-fire and Cotton-field.* New York: Blelock and Company, 1865.

Logan, John A. *The Great Conspiracy: Its Origin and History.* New York: A. R. Hart & Co., 1886.

Love, Wm. DeLoss. *Wisconsin in the War of the Rebellion: A History of All the Regiments and Batteries.* Chicago: Church and Goodman, 1866.

Lyle, Rev. William W. *Light and Shadows of Army Life: Or, Pen Pictures from the Battlefield, the Camp, and the Hospital.* Cincinnati, OH: R. W. Carroll & Co., 1865.

Marks, James J. The *Peninsular Campaign in Virginia or Incidents and Scenes on the Battlefield and in Richmond.* 5th ed. Philadelphia: J. B. Lippincott & Co., 1864.

McClellan, George B[rinton]. *Report on the Organization and Campaigns of the Army of the Potomac.* New York: Sheldon & Company, 1864.

Moore, Frank. *The Civil War in Song and Story.* New York: P. F. Collier, 1889.

Newton, James K. *A Wisconsin Boy in Dixie.* Edited by Stephen E. Ambrose. Madison: University of Wisconsin Press, 1961.

Parker, John L. *Henry Wilson's Regiment.* Boston: Rand Avery Company, 1887.

Parton, James. *General Butler in New Orleans.* 5th ed. New York: Mason Brothers, 1864.

Pepper, George Whitfield. *Ireland . . . Liberty Springs from Her Martyr's Blood: An Address.* Boston: Patrick Donahoe, 1868.

———. *Personal Recollections of Sherman's Campaigns in Georgia and the Carolinas.* Zanesville, OH: Hugh Dunne, 1866.

Perry, Henry Fales. *History of the Thirty-eighth Regiment Indiana Volunteer Infantry.* Palo Alto, CA: F. A. Stuart, 1906.

Petroff, Peter. *Ante-Mortem Depositions of Peter Petroff.* San Francisco: Press of Thos. J. Davis, 1895.

Pickerill, W. N. *History of the Third Indiana Cavalry.* Indianapolis: Aetna Printing, 1906.

Powell, William H. *The Fifth Army Corps (Army of the Potomac).* New York: G. P. Putnam's Sons, Knickerbocker Press, 1896.

Regimental Committee. *History of the One Hundred and Twenty-fifth Regiment Pennsylvania Volunteers, 1862–1863.* Philadelphia: J. B. Lippincott & Co., 1906.

Rogers, Rev. James B. *War Pictures: Experiences and Observations of a Chaplain in the U.S. Army in the War of the Southern Rebellion.* Chicago: Church and Goodman, 1863.

Rosenblatt, Emil, and Ruth Rosenblatt, eds. *Hard Marching Every Day: The Civil War Letters of Private Wilbur Fisk, 1861–1865.* Lawrence: University Press of Kansas, 1992.

Royse, Isaac Henry Clay. *History of the 115th Regiment Illinois Volunteer Infantry.* Terre Haute, IN: Published by the author, 1900.

Scott, Robert Garth, ed. *Fallen Leaves: The Civil War Letters of Major Henry Livermore Abbott.* Kent, OH: Kent State University Press, 1991.

Sheldon, Winthrop D. *The "Twenty-Seventh" [Connecticut], A Regimental History.* New Haven, CT: Morris & Benham, 1866.

Sprague, Homer B. *History of the 13th Infantry Regiment of Connecticut Volunteers, During the Great Rebellion.* Hartford, CT: Case, Lockwood & Co., 1867.

Stevens, George T. *Three Years in the Sixth Corps.* Albany, NY: S. R. Gray, 1866.

Stine, J[ames] H[enry]. *History of the Army of the Potomac.* 2d ed. Washington: Gibson Brothers, 1893.

Taylor, Benjamin F. *Pictures of Life in Camp and Field.* Chicago: S. C. Griggs & Company, 1875.

Truesdale, John. *The Blue Coats.* Philadelphia: Jones Brothers & Co., 1867.

Trumbull, Henry Clay. *War Memories of a Chaplain.* Philadelphia: J. D. Wattles & Co., 1898.

Vaill, Dudley Landon. *The County Regiment: A Sketch of the Second Regiment of Connecticut Volunteer Heavy Artillery, Originally the Nineteenth Volunteer Infantry, in the Civil War.* Litchfield, CT: County University Club, 1908.

Walker, Aldace F[reeman]. *The Vermont Brigade in the Shenandoah Valley, 1864.* Burlington, VT: Free Press Association, 1869.

Walker, Francis A. *History of the Second Army Corps in the Army of the Potomac.* 2d ed. New York: Charles Scribner's Sons, 1893.

Way, Virgil G. *History of the Thirty-third Regiment Illinois Veteran Volunteer Infantry in the Civil War.* Gibson City, IL: Press of the Gibson Courier, 1902.

Williams, George W. *A History of the Negro Troops in the War of the Rebellion, 1861–1865.* New York: Harper and Brothers, 1888.
Woodbury, Augustus. *Major General Ambrose E. Burnside and the Ninth Army Corps: A Narrative of Campaigns in North Carolina, Maryland, Virginia, Ohio, Kentucky, Mississippi, and Tennessee, During the War for the Preservation of the Republic.* Providence, RI: Sidney S. Rider & Brother, 1867.
Wright, Henry H. *A History of the Sixth Iowa Infantry.* Iowa City: State Historical Society of Iowa, 1923.

BIOGRAPHIES

Alexander, Philip. *John Eaton, Jr., Preacher, Soldier, and Educator.* New York: Macmillan, 1940.
Bristol, Frank Milton. *The Life of Chaplain McCabe.* New York: Fleming H. Revell, 1908.
Church, William Conant. *Ulysses S. Grant and the Period of National Preservation and Reconstruction.* Garden City, NY: Garden City Publishing Company, 1926.
Fallows, Alice Katherine. *Everybody's Bishop: Being the Life and Times of the Right Reverend Samuel Fallows, D.D.* New York: J. H. Sears and Company, 1927.
Fuller, Richard F. *Chaplain Fuller: Being a Lifesketch of a New England Clergyman and Army Chaplain.* Boston: Walker, Wise, and Company, 1864.
Howard, Philip E. *The Life Story of Henry Clay Trumbull.* Philadelphia: Sunday School Times, 1905.
Sandburg, Carl. *Abraham Lincoln: The War Years.* 4 vols. New York: Harcourt, Brace & Company, 1939.

SECONDARY MATERIAL

Books and Special Studies

American Army Chaplaincy. Prepared in the Office of the Chief of Chaplains. Washington: Government Printing Office, 1946.
Aptheker, Herbert. *The Negro in the Civil War.* New York: International Publishers Co., 1938.
Blied, Rev. Benjamin J. *Catholics and the Civil War.* Milwaukee, WI: Np., 1945.
Borritt, Gabor, ed. *Lincoln: The War President.* New York: Oxford University Press, 1992.
Budd, Richard M. "Serving Two Masters: The Professionalization and Bureaucratization of American Military Chaplaincy, 1860–1920." Ph.D. diss., Loyola University, Chicago, 1995.
Castel, Albert. *A Frontier State at War: Kansas, 1861–1865.* Ithaca, NY: Cornell University Press, 1958.
Catton, Bruce. *Grant Moves South.* Boston: Little, Brown and Company, 1960.
Cole, Arthur Charles. *The Irrepressible Conflict, 1850–1865.* New York: Macmillan, 1934.
Commager, Henry Steele, ed. *Documents of American History.* New York: Appleton-Century-Crofts, 1949.
Cooper, William J., Jr., *The South and the Politics of Slavery, 1828–1856.* Baton Rouge: Louisiana State University Press, 1978.

Cornish, Dudley Taylor. *The Sable Arm: Negro Troops in the Union Army, 1861–1865.* New York: W. W. Norton & Company, 1966.

Davis, William C. *The Cause Lost.* Lawrence: University Press of Kansas, 1996.

DuBois, W. E. Burghardt. *Black Reconstruction.* New York: Harcourt, Brace & Company, 1935.

———. *The Souls of Black Folk.* 16th ed. Chicago: A. C. McClurg & Co., 1928.

Dunham, Chester Forrester. *The Attitude of the Northern Clergy Toward the South, 1860–1865.* Toledo, OH: Gray, 1942.

Dupuy, R. Ernest, and Trevor N. Dupuy. *The Compact History of the Civil War.* New York: Collier Books, 1962.

Ellis, John Tracy. *American Catholicism.* Chicago: University of Chicago Press, 1956.

Elson, Henry W. *The Civil War Through the Camera.* New York: McKinlay, Stone & Mackenzie, 1912.

Fite, Emerson David. *Social and Industrial Conditions in the North During the Civil War.* New York: Macmillan, 1910.

Fogarty, Walter P. "The Preaching of the Chaplaincy During the Civil War." B.D. thesis, Lutheran Theological Seminary, Gettysburg, PA, 1964.

Frank, Emma L., comp. *The Chaplaincy in the Armed Services: A Preliminary Bibliography.* Oberlin, OH: The Library, Oberlin Graduate School of Theology, 1945.

Franklin, John Hope. *From Slavery to Freedom.* New York: Alfred A. Knopf, 1956.

Fredrickson, George M. *The Inner Civil War.* New York: Harper & Row, 1965.

Friedman, Lee M. "Abraham Lincoln and Jewish Army Chaplains." In *Jewish Pioneers and Patriots.* Philadelphia: Jewish Publication Society of America, 1942.

Germain, Aidan Henry. *Catholic Military and Naval Chaplains, 1776–1917.* Washington: Catholic University of America, 1929.

Glover, Edwin A. *Bucktailed Wildcats.* New York: Thomas Yoseloff, 1960.

Grimsley, Mark. *The Hard Hand of War.* New York: Cambridge University Press, 1995.

Handlin, Oscar, ed. *Immigration as a Factor in American History.* Englewood Cliffs, NJ: Prentice-Hall, 1959.

Hansen, Marcus Lee. *The Immigrant in American History.* Cambridge, MA: Harvard University Press, 1940.

Hess, Earl J. *The Union Soldier in Battle.* Lawrence: University Press of Kansas, 1997.

Hieronymus, Frank L. "For Now and Forever: The Chaplains of the Confederate States Army." Ph.D. diss., University of California, Los Angeles, 1964.

Hollister, Ovando J. *Boldly They Rode: A History of the First Colorado Regiment of Volunteers.* Lakewood, CO: Golden Press, 1949.

Honeywell, Roy J. *Chaplains of the United States Army.* Washington: Office of the Chief of Chaplains, Department of the Army, 1958.

Klement, Frank L. *Wisconsin and the Civil War.* Madison: State Historical Society of Wisconsin, 1963.

Korn, Bertram Wallace. *American Jewry and the Civil War.* Philadelphia: Jewish Publication Society of America, 1951.

———. *Eventful Years and Experiences.* Studies in Nineteenth Century American Jewish History. Cincinnati, OH: American Jewish Archives, 1954.

Leech, Margaret. *Reveille in Washington, 1860–1865.* New York: Harper and Brothers, 1941.

Linderman, Gerald F. *Embattled Courage*. New York: Free Press, 1987.

Masur, Louis P., ed. *The Real War Will Never Get in the Books: Selections from Writers During the Civil War*. New York: Oxford University Press, 1993.

McConnell, S. D. *History of the American Episcopal Church, from the Planting of the Colonies to the End of the Civil War*. 3d ed. New York: Thomas Whittaker, 1891.

McPherson, James M. *The Negro's Civil War: How American Negroes Felt and Acted During the War for the Union*. New York: Pantheon Books, 1965.

———. *For Cause and Comrades: Why Men Fought in the Civil War*. New York: Oxford University Press, 1997.

Mitchell, Reid. *Civil War Soldiers: Their Expectations and Their Experiences*. New York: Touchstone, 1988.

———. *The Vacant Chair*. New York: Oxford University Press, 1993.

Monaghan, Jay. *Civil War on the Western Border, 1854–1865*. Boston: Little, Brown and Company, 1955.

Nolan, Alan T. *The Iron Brigade: A Military History*. New York: Macmillan, 1961.

Norton, Herman. "The Organization and Function of the Confederate Chaplaincy, 1861–1865." M.A. thesis, Vanderbilt University, 1956.

Olmstead, Clifton E. *History of Religion in the United States*. Englewood Cliffs, NJ: Prentice-Hall, 1960.

Pillar, James J. *The Catholic Church in Mississippi, 1837–1865*. New Orleans: Hauser Press, 1964.

Pitts, Charles F. *Chaplains in Gray*. Nashville, TN: Broadman, 1957.

President's Committee on Religion and Welfare in the Armed Forces. *The Military Chaplaincy: A Report to the President by the President's Committee on Religion and Welfare in the Armed Forces*. Washington: Government Printing Office, 1950.

Prim, Gorrell, Jr., "Born Again in the Trenches: Revivalism in the Confederate Army." Ph.D. diss., Florida State University, 1982.

Pullen, John J. *The Twentieth Maine, a Volunteer Regiment in the Civil War*. Philadelphia and New York: J. B. Lippincott & Co., 1957.

Pyne, Henry R. *Ride to War: The History of the First New Jersey Cavalry*. New Brunswick, NJ: Rutgers University Press, 1961.

Qualben, Lars D. *A History of the Christian Church*. 4th ed. New York: Thomas Nelson and Sons, 1942.

Quarles, Benjamin. *The Negro in the Civil War*. Boston: Little, Brown and Company, 1953.

Robertson, James I., Jr. *Soldiers Blue and Gray*. Columbia: University of South Carolina Press, 1988.

Rose, Willie Lee. *Rehearsal for Reconstruction: The Port Royal Experiment*. New York: Vintage Books, 1964.

Rothensteiner, Rev. John. *History of the Archdiocese of St. Louis*. 2 vols. St. Louis: Blackwell Wielandy, 1928.

Rozwenc, Edwin C., ed. *Slavery as a Cause of the Civil War*. Rev. ed. Boston: D. C. Heath and Company, 1963.

Schaff, Rev. Philip, et al. *The American Church History Series*. 13 vols. New York: Christian Literature Co., 1893–1897.

Schlesinger, Arthur Meier. *Political and Social Growth of the United States, 1852–1933*. Rev. ed. New York: Macmillan, 1936.

Shannon, Fred Albert. *The Organization and Administration of the Union Army, 1861–1865*. 2 vols. Cleveland: Arthur H. Clark Company, 1928.

Shattuck, Gardiner H., Jr. *A Shield and Hiding Place: The Religious Life of the Civil War Armies.* Macon, GA: Mercer University Press, 1987.
Slomovitz, Albert Isaac. "The Fighting Rabbis: A History of Jewish Military Chaplains, 1860–1945." Ph.D. diss., Loyola University, Chicago, 1995.
Smith, Charles Edward. "The Work of the Civil War Chaplains." M.A. thesis, University of Arizona, 1965.
Sweet, William Warren. *The Methodist Episcopal Church and the Civil War.* Cincinnati, OH: Methodist Book Concern Press, 1912.
———. *The Story of Religion in America.* 2d ed. New York: Harper and Brothers, 1950.
Vander Velde, Lewis G. *The Presbyterian Churches and the Federal Union, 1861–1869.* Cambridge, MA: Harvard University Press, 1932.
Vedder, Henry C. *A Short History of the Baptists.* Philadelphia: American Baptist Publication Society, 1907.
Vickers, Robert C. "The Military Chaplaincy: A Study in Role Conflict." Ph.D. diss., Vanderbilt University, 1984.
Weatherford, Willis Duke. *American Churches and the Negro.* Boston: Christopher Publishing House, 1957.
Wiley, Bell Irwin. *The Life of Billy Yank.* Indianapolis, IN: Bobbs-Merrill, 1952.
Williams, Kenneth P. *Lincoln Finds a General.* 5 vols. New York: Macmillan, 1957.
Winn, Robert Howard. "The Diary of Thomas Harwood: A Personal Perspective of the Northern Chaplaincy During the Civil War." M.T. thesis, Dallas Theological Seminary, 1981.
Woodward, C. Vann. *The Burden of Southern History.* New York: Vintage Books, 1960.

ARTICLES IN PERIODICALS

Bigelow, Martha Mitchell. "Freedmen of the Mississippi Valley, 1862–1865." *Civil War History* 8:38–47 (March 1962).
Brown, Kenneth O. "Milton L. Haney: Pastor, Chaplain, Evangelist, Seventy-six Years a Methodist Minister." *Methodist History* 31, no. 2:113–17 (1993).
Budd, Richard M. "Ohio Army Chaplains and the Professionalization of Military Chaplaincy in the Civil War." *Ohio History* 102:5–19 (winter/spring 1993).
Connor, Charles P. "The Northern Catholic Position on Slavery and the Civil War: Archbishop Hughes as a Test Case." *American Catholic Historical Society of Philadelphia* 96, no. 1–4:35–48 (1986).
Cooney, Father Peter Paul. "The War Letters of Father Peter Paul Cooney." *Records of the American Catholic Historical Society* 44:145–77 (June 1933).
Fragasso, Philip M. "Wanted: Army Chaplains. Christians Only Need Apply." *Liberty* 74, no. 1:2–5 (1979).
Jervey, Edward D. "Prison Life Among the Rebels: Recollections of a Union Chaplain." *Civil War History* 34, no. 1:22–45 (1988).
———, ed. "Notes and Documents. Ten Weeks in a Macon Prison, 1864: A New England Chaplain's Account." *Georgia Historical Quarterly* 70, no. 4:669–702 (1986).
Korn, Bertram W. "Jewish Chaplains During the Civil War." *American Jewish Archives* 1:7–19 (summer 1948).
Larson, C. Kay. "Bonny Yank and Ginny Reb." *Minerva* 8, no. 1:33–48 (1990).

Myers, James E. "Lincoln and the Jews." *Midstream* 27, no. 2:26–29 (1981).

Potts, Gregg, and Kevin Hardy, Jr. "Letters of a Union Chaplain at Mansfield, 1864." *North Louisiana State Historical Association* 16, no. 2–3,:69–77 (1985).

Quimby, Rollin W. "The Chaplain's Predicament." *Civil War History* 8:25–37 (March 1962).

Redkey, Edwin S. "Black Chaplains in the Union Army." *Civil War History* 33, no. 4:331–50 (1987).

———. "They Are Invincible." *Civil War Times Illustrated* 28, no. 2:32–37 (1989).

Riforgiato, Leonard R. "Bishop Timon, Buffalo, and the Civil War." *Catholic Historical Review* 73, no. 1:62–80 (1987).

Simpson, Robert Drew. "A Forgotten Chaplain of the Civil War: Commander John L. Lenhart." *Methodist History* 29, no. 3:131–39 (1991).

Stewart, Miller J. "A Touch of Civilization: Culture and Education in the Frontier Army." *Nebraska History* 65, no. 2:257–82 (1984).

Stratton, David H. "The Army and the Gospel in the West." *Western Humanities Review* 8:247–62 (summer 1954).

Washburn, Henry Bradford. "The Army Chaplain." *Papers of the American Society of Church History*, series 2, 7:1–23 (March 1923).

Westwood, Howard C. "Ben Butler Takes on a Chaplain." *Civil War History* 35, no. 3:225–38 (1989).

INDEX